T0355210

Sentencing and Artificial Intelligence

Sentencing and Artificial Intelligence

Edited by

JESPER RYBERG AND JULIAN V. ROBERTS

OXFORD
UNIVERSITY PRESS

OXFORD
UNIVERSITY PRESS

Oxford University Press is a department of the University of Oxford. It furthers
the University's objective of excellence in research, scholarship, and education
by publishing worldwide. Oxford is a registered trade mark of Oxford University
Press in the UK and certain other countries.

Published in the United States of America by Oxford University Press
198 Madison Avenue, New York, NY 10016, United States of America.

© Oxford University Press 2022

Library of Congress Control Number: 2021917982
ISBN 978-0-19-753953-8

DOI: 10.1093/oso/9780197539538.001.0001

Contents

Acknowledgments

We are very grateful to the authors for contributing to this volume. In addition, we would like to thank Meredith Keffer, Macey Fairchild, and their colleagues at the Oxford University Press for assistance in publishing this book.

Jesper Ryberg and Julian V. Roberts
Copenhagen and Oxford
1 December, 2020

Contributors

Mirko Bagaric is Dean of Law at Swinburne University.

Shmuel Baron is an S. J. D. candidate at the University of Toronto Faculty of Law.

Vincent Chiao is Associate Professor of Law at the University of Toronto.

Netanel Dagan is Lecturer of Law at the Institute of Criminology, Hebrew University of Jerusalem.

Benjamin Davies is a Research Fellow at the University of Oxford.

Thomas Douglas is Professor of Applied Philosophy at the University of Oxford.

Dan Hunter is Professor of Law and Executive Dean, Faculty of Law, Queensland University of Technology.

Kasper Lippert-Rasmussen is Professor of Political Theory at University of Aarhus.

Richard L. Lippke is Professor of Criminal Justice at Indiana University.

Thomas S. Petersen is Professor of Ethics at Roskilde University.

Mojca M. Plesničar is a Research Associate at the Institute of Criminology Ljubljana and Assistant Professor of Criminology and Criminal Law at the University of Ljubljana.

Julian V. Roberts is Professor of Criminology at the University of Oxford.

Jesper Ryberg is Professor of Ethics and Philosophy of Law at Roskilde University.

Mathis Schwarze is a Researcher at Freie Universität Berlin.

Frej Klem Thomsen is Associate Professor of Political Theory at the University of Aarhus.

Sigrid G. C. van Wingerden is Associate Professor of Criminology at Leiden University.

John Zerilli is a Leverhulme Trust Fellow at the University of Oxford.

1

Sentencing and Artificial Intelligence

Setting the Stage

Jesper Ryberg and Julian V. Roberts

Artificial intelligence (AI) is everywhere. The term "AI" retains a futuristic aura, but is no longer restricted to science fiction. Some of the objectives formulated by scientists and entrepreneurs in the 1950s (when the term "AI" was first introduced) addressed the future and, to some extent, continue to do so today. Many of the possible applications of AI that attract popular attention—such as the replacement of humans across all levels of contemporary life—are not imminent. However, if by AI one means technology capable of tasks that until now have required human intelligence to perform, then AI has already become an integral part of society. This does not mean that we share a clear understanding of the extent to which AI influences our daily lives. John McCarthy (the computer scientist who coined the term "artificial intelligence") noted a tendency to underestimate the accomplishments of AI when we cease to think of a new technology as AI as soon as it works properly (Vardi 2012). Today, AI is deeply embedded in many aspects of society. It is no longer hyperbolic to assert that if every computer algorithm that qualifies as AI suddenly ceased to function, it would end civilization as we know it (Domingo 2018).

It is no surprise therefore that AI technology has also permeated several stages of the criminal justice system including policing. It is employed to solve crimes (e.g., by analyzing photos from crime scenes or other types of evidence); to identify suspects (e.g., by the use of various types of surveillance technology); and to prevent crime (e.g., by identifying crime "hot spots" and to permit intervention before crimes are committed). Many of these applications are controversial and have prompted much discussion. Beyond policing, AI is also employed to assist bail courts in deciding which prisoners to release on bail. AI-based programs employ a wide range of factors in an attempt to predict the defendant's flight risk or likelihood of offending while

Jesper Ryberg and Julian V. Roberts, *Sentencing and Artificial Intelligence* In: *Sentencing and Artificial Intelligence*.
Edited by: Jesper Ryberg and Julian V. Roberts, Oxford University Press. © Oxford University Press 2022.
DOI: 10.1093/oso/9780197539538.003.0001

on bail. This book focuses on the other end of the criminal process, namely, sentencing. This book is the first collective work devoted to the ethical and penal theoretical considerations of the use of AI at sentencing. In light of this, some preliminary comments are appropriate. Subsequently, we will briefly outline some of the ways AI can be used at sentencing and, finally, provide an overview of various themes and issues addressed in the ensuing chapters.

1.1 Why Consider the Use of AI at Sentencing?

Why devote a whole volume to penal theoretical and ethical aspects of AI at sentencing? First, the criminal court is a critical societal institution and sentencing requires thorough consideration. At sentencing, the state's power over the lives of citizens is at its height. A legal punishment entails acts that, in other contexts, would constitute the quintessential example of wrongful treatment: namely, the imposition of death, penal confinement, or various deprivations of property and liberty. These consequences require a persuasive justification. It is precisely this need for justification that has given rise to the ethics of punishment as an academic discipline. However, the importance of determining why (and how) punishment should be inflicted also requires us to consider how sentencing decisions are reached. If AI enhances the quality of sentencing decisions, this may constitute a significant ethical improvement. There is, after all, much room to improve the sentencing process (for discussion of the current state of sentencing in Western nations, see Tonry 2020; Spohn and Brennan 2019). However, if AI has undesirable side effects, this may be very serious in such an important context as the state's infliction of sentences. Thus, the reasons that render the ethics of punishment an important academic field also make it crucial to consider whether (and how) AI should be used at sentencing. Furthermore, this connection also explains why it is impossible to provide an adequate analysis of the use of AI at sentencing without considering the ethics of punishment and current sentencing practices.

The second and closely related justification for this book is that it makes little sense to consider AI independent of the context. Given the proliferation of AI in all aspects of our lives, it is unsurprising that AI attracts great attention. Advisory boards aid governments in the use of AI, and many books and articles are accumulating on the ethics of artificial intelligence. However, consideration of a technology on a purely abstract level, independent of the specific purpose which this technology might serve, makes little sense.

Consider a simple analogy. Imagine that a new micro-camera has been invented. To discuss the ethics of micro-cameras in the abstract seems pointless. Obviously, it makes all the difference whether this device is used to make covert recordings in peoples' homes, to monitor the production of chocolate bars on an assembly line, or to investigate the behavior of mammals in the rainforest. Technologies can be used in many ways, and for good or evil. The ethical assessment of a technology cannot be separated from its specific application. Thus, irrespective of the more comprehensive discussions of the ethics of AI, questioning how AI should be used *at sentencing* is justified in its own right.

The third reason why this book is timely and important is that AI technology, which computer assisted sentencing, has already infiltrated the courtroom—in the form of informational sentencing aids to assist judges at sentencing. The academic study of AI has experienced many fluctuations over time, ranging from the rapid progress and optimism of research in the early era, to periods of resignation and disillusionment—such as the so-called AI winter of the 1970s and subsequent setbacks of the late 1980s and early 1990s, when several trial projects were launched.

The first concrete and relatively detailed proposal for a computer-assisted sentencing was made in 1971 by John Hogarth, paradoxically, in his book entitled *Sentencing as a Human Process*. Hogarth envisioned an algorithm based on an accumulating database of sentencing decisions and subsequent outcomes in terms of reoffending (Hogarth 1971, 391–393). The computer would then provide a court with a range of information to guide sentencing decisions, including sentences imposed in similar cases by previous courts; reconviction statistics for specific sentences; a risk score for the offender currently being sentenced; a sentence recommendation which matched offender profiles with specific dispositions. The database would grow over time and would incorporate "new methods of correctional treatment" (1971, 392). The outputs would then be employed by all courts in the jurisdiction. Hogarth's proposal ensured that the program would remain a tool for judges. He noted that "Judicial decision-making is, therefore, in no way threatened by scientific sentencing aids" (393). The proposal was oriented toward preventive sentencing, at the expense of retribution, restoration, or other approaches. It therefore suffered from what Michael Donohue describes as "philosophy anchoring" (2019, 659); judges would be anchored within this approach. Since sentencing statutes generally specify multiple goals and competing sentencing philosophies, such a scheme would likely not appeal to legislatures or courts.

A different approach was adopted by several computer-based information systems that emerged in the 1980s. For example, Anthony Doob and Norm Park (1987) created and launched a computer-based information system in Canada. This project enabled judges to access previous decisions by courts for cases comparable to the one being sentenced. In addition to trial court decisions, the database also included summaries of court of appeal judgments. The model was representative of what Hutton termed "a database approach"—it provided the information that would "form the basis for the application of sentencing skills and knowledge of judges" (558). It was ultimately discontinued, as were other schemes in Canada, Scotland, Australia, and elsewhere (see Hogarth 1988; Chan 1991; Bainbridge 1991; Hutton 1995). These systems failed to take root for a number of reasons. Judges appeared less interested in information than in the likelihood of appellate intervention, and there was some resistance to employing technology to assist in determining sentence. Whatever the reason, it is surprising that half a century after Hogarth's proposal, judges sentence offenders without the benefit of a sophisticated and computer-based sentencing information scheme.

Today, research in this field is experiencing a boom, characterized by impressive progress in areas such as machine learning. AI has become a million-dollar industry. Many of the techniques that might be relevant if AI were to become more prominent at sentencing are already in use. The most obvious example is risk assessment algorithms, which are currently (and controversially) employed in many US states (e.g., Freeman 2016; Garrett and Monahan 2019; Hamilton 2019; Wisser 2019). Thus, one does not need to resort to science fiction to consider how AI may improve the sentencing process. There is an urgent need to consider the potential use of AI in order to avoid being overwhelmed by existing technological possibilities. Cases where new technologies have been prematurely implemented due to narrow considerations of efficiency or economy, and where it has been very difficult to modify or redraw the technology when it has turned out to have undesirable side effects, exist. However, as noted, in the case of sentencing, the consequences of a technological *glitch* are serious.

1.2 Using Algorithms at Sentencing

Discussion of AI at sentencing is complicated by the fact that it is not always clear what this application of technology is referring to. The question seems open to several interpretations, depending on what we mean by "AI," "use," and "at sentencing."

First, the term "AI" itself is ambiguous. There is much discussion of how AI should be defined and numerous definitions have been proposed. Some refer to AI as technology capable of accurately reproducing human intelligence. A standard philosophical question associated with this "strong" conception of AI concerns the possibility of creating systems that can think in the same way as humans, and which may be deemed to possess consciousness. Conversely, references to AI in a "weak" sense refer to systems that can execute tasks without attempting to mimic human reasoning. Computer-driven algorithms that qualify as AI in this sense vary a great deal. For instance, machine learning algorithms can take many forms, from relatively simple algorithms to highly complex systems.

Second, if we talk about "using" AI at sentencing, this includes many different applications. For instance, AI can be used simply as an aid for judges at sentencing (as in the examples cited earlier), or it may fully replace human decision-making. It is also possible to imagine various types of division of labor between the human judge and an algorithm. For instance, an algorithmic system could be used to make decisions in minor crimes while the judge would determine sentence in more serious or complex cases.

Third, whether we are considering AI as a supplement or substitute for human decision-making, there is also the question of the purpose underlying the technology. A sentencing decision involves balancing multiple objectives and many factors. The most limited way of applying AI would be in relation to the determination of a single factor among the many considerations that lead to the ultimate sentencing decision. This is how AI is currently employed when it estimates an offender's risk profile. Offenders are not sentenced exclusively on the grounds of such a profile; on the contrary, whether an individual is considered high or low risk is simply one among many factors that a judge takes into account. A more extensive application would include AI directly in the determination of the sentence, such as the decision of whether an offender should spend two or three years in prison. Thus, within the sentencing process AI may be used in different ways.

The use of AI at sentencing is therefore open to different interpretations and applications. At one extreme, the use of AI at sentencing may refer to the application of a simple algorithm implemented to inform a judge in the determination of a single factor that should be included in the sentencing decision. At the other extreme, it may refer to a fully automated "Robo judge" that specifies sentences without any human involvement. As these extremes indicate, it is important to clarify which one has in mind when engaging in ethical and penal theoretical considerations of the use of AI at sentencing. As will become clear, several of these applications of AI are considered in the following chapters.

1.3 Overview of the Volume

Ethical scrutiny of AI should not proceed in the abstract, without considering the specific domain within which AI technology is being applied. However, some challenges arise across different applications. In relation to different algorithm-based services, particular attention has been directed to topics such as Fairness, Accountability, and Transparency. In fact, it has become conventional to simply refer to the "FAT" of algorithms. However, given our focus on the use of AI at sentencing, the three topics do not merit equal concern. While accountability is important in many contexts, such as when AI replaces decision-making by private parties who own the systems (e.g., whether the owner should be held accountable if a self-driving vehicle causes an accident), it is of less concern in relation to sentencing where the state is the responsible authority. In contrast, fairness and transparency have repeatedly been held to be of significance in the context of sentencing. These topics constitute the subjects of the first group of chapters in this volume.

In Chapter 2 Jesper Ryberg begins by underlining that even though increasing attention has been directed to the significance of transparency when algorithms are used at sentencing—such as in relation to the much-debated Loomis v. Wisconsin case—there is still considerable opacity with regard to the two related questions of for whom is transparency important and with regard to what. Ryberg addresses these issues by drawing on the traditional discussion of the importance of judicial reason-giving. A number of reasons for reason-giving—concerning the quality of sentencing decisions, defendants' experience of the court process as fair, and the impact on confidence and perceived legitimacy on the part of the general public—are considered in relation to algorithmic transparency. It is argued that several of these arguments are not directly applicable to the question of algorithmic transparency, and also that even though there are some reasons against algorithmic opacity, there is little empirical evidence with regard to the potential effects of a lack of transparency when algorithms are used for sentencing purposes.

Transparency is also the focus of the chapter by Vincent Chiao, who stresses that the ethical concerns about algorithmic opacity also arise in human decision-making (including sentencing). His argument then proceeds on the assumption that adopting algorithmic sentencing methods should be evaluated by comparing them to the status quo ante. In short, are algorithms more or less transparent than the decisions of human judges? As Chiao argues, this point is important because human decision-making often suffers from significant shortcomings.

Whereas the first two chapters deal with the extent to which algorithmic opacity constitutes an ethical problem when AI is involved in sentencing decisions, the perspective changes in the subsequent chapter by Jesper Ryberg and Thomas S. Petersen. As previously noted, algorithmic instruments can take various forms. Some instruments consist of relatively simple algorithms (e.g., decision trees), while others are highly complicated (e.g., deep learning). However, as noted by computer scientists, there is often a negative relationship between the transparency of an algorithm and its accuracy. This may give rise to an ethical dilemma. Suppose that one is interested in applying an algorithmic tool to assess the risk that an offender will recidivate. Suppose, further, that one can either choose between an algorithm which produces more accurate predictions of future criminality, but is highly complicated and also opaque; or an algorithm which is more transparent, but which produces less accurate predictions. Which is preferable? This chapter reflects on the nature of this dilemma. The authors argue that even if there is a conflict between transparency and accuracy, this need not constitute an *ethical* conflict. Acknowledging this, the authors suggest, carries a range of theoretical and practical implications.

While the contributors who discuss the importance of transparency when algorithmic tools are used at sentencing agree that this is not a simple issue, the complexity of this discussion is certainly no less if one turns to the question of algorithmic fairness. The idea of *fair* decision-making can assume many different interpretations. A crucial aspect of fairness is the question of whether algorithmic predictions are discriminatory. It might be hoped that, in contrast to human decision-making, which is known to be vulnerable to various biases, a prediction by an algorithm would be basically unbiased. If this were the case, it would constitute a strong reason in favor of permitting algorithmic predictions to play a more prominent role at sentencing. However, matters are more complicated. For instance, if a machine learning algorithm makes predictions based on a dataset containing biased decisions, these biases may be absorbed by the algorithm and will affect the predictions. Algorithmic decisions may end up reproducing historical patterns of discrimination. More specifically, one of the important discussions that have accompanied the use of algorithmic risk assessment instruments—such as the Compas algorithm, which is widely used in US jurisdictions—has focused on the fact that this algorithm does not treat Afro American and white offenders equally.

In a much-cited study, the Compas algorithm was criticized for wrongfully predicting recidivism much more often for Black Americans than White Americans, even though race was not a factor input into the algorithm (Angwin et al. 2016). Should such differences in predictions be regarded as directly discriminatory or are they indirectly discriminatory? Or should one hold, as does the company that produced the algorithm, that this result is not discriminatory at all? These questions are considered by Kasper Lippert-Rasmussen who suggests that algorithms that produce such predictions are indirectly discriminatory against Black defendants and may also be *perceived* by Black Americans as directly discriminatory. The author also considers and rebuts objections such as the contention that the fact that most crimes are intra-racial leaves Black Americans as the main beneficiaries of algorithm-based sentencing.

Benjamin Davies and Tom Douglas also explore discriminatory risk assessment algorithms. More precisely, the authors consider whether the fact that risk assessment tools can be designed to avoid direct racial discrimination is sufficient to ensure that they avoid the *wrongness* of direct racial discrimination. This question leads the authors to considerations of various accounts of the wrongness of racial discrimination.

Other chapters focus either on the use of AI for specific purposes at sentencing or the implications of using AI in different sentencing contexts. For instance, one widespread application is algorithmic crime prediction. This is the subject of the chapter by Mirko Bagaric and Dan Hunter. In the same way that Vincent Chiao compares the relative limitations of humans and algorithms in relation to transparency in decision-making, these authors compare the capabilities of making crime predictions in humans and algorithmic systems. They argue that much of the criticism that has been directed against algorithmic crime prediction is unpersuasive and that predictive algorithms have the potential to make more effective and fair decisions than human judges.

Another example of how AI may be used for specific purposes at sentencing is provided by Netanel Dagan and Shmuel Baron. They question whether it is possible to integrate mercy within algorithmic sentencing. This topic is interesting because the use of algorithms has often been accused of leading to a dehumanization of sentencing decisions. And, as the two authors note, there seems to be a blatant contradiction between, on the one hand, mechanical automated algorithmic sentencing decisions and; on the other, the compassionate, *human* nature of mercy. However, by considering different accounts of mercy (and different types of algorithmic decision-making), they conclude that this apparent contradiction can be resolved. As the authors note, if a policymaker accepts the plausibility of algorithmic sentencing in all other respects, and the need for the exercise of mercy in sentencing, the mere need to exercise mercy, by itself, should not be a reason to reject algorithmic sentencing.

While the idea of implementing AI at sentencing requires considerations of the technological capabilities of algorithmic systems, there is another aspect that calls for scrutiny if algorithms are to be increasingly introduced in the process, namely, how will this influence the judge? John Zerilli notes that researchers in the field of "human factors" have long been aware that when humans devolve certain of their functions to technology, the transfer from human to machine can restructure more than the division of labor between them. Humans' perceptions of themselves and their abilities may also change. For instance, in relation to the use of AI as a support system at sentencing, some theorists have feared that it may become too easy for judges simply to defer to the wisdom of the algorithm. However, on the grounds of recent human factors research, Zerilli argues that this concern seems unfounded. As he notes, the incentives, objectives and ideologies of sentencing judges appear to disrupt the usual pattern of results seen in many other domains of human factors research. Whereas Zerilli's focus is on the possible effects of AI on human decision-making, another much broader question is how the sentencing system should function in order for it to benefit from algorithm models. As we have seen, discussions of AI at sentencing focus on the question of whether such technology can support or even replace human judges.

However, most decisions in criminal cases in the United States are not made by a judge, but are a result of plea bargaining.

This is the point of departure for Richard Lippke who focuses on what he calls "a robust plea bargaining regime." This is a system which permits prosecutors to engage in charge and sentencing bargaining with accused persons, or more often, their attorneys. Although within such a regime judges might retain the authority to reject the sentences recommended by prosecutors and to substitute ones that they deem fairer or more appropriate, experience shows that judges are averse to doing so. Lippke argues that the promise of AI as a source of more transparent and consistent outcomes is likely to be thwarted in a "robust" plea bargaining regime such as that operating in the United States. This conclusion is important in light of the widespread use of plea bargaining in the United States, and also because charge and sentence bargaining is increasing in other parts of the world.

The remaining chapters all adopt a higher-level perspective on the question of whether AI should be used in sentencing. In order to be able to draw conclusions on whether and to what extent AI should be implemented in sentencing practice, it is obviously insufficient to focus on a single challenge or aspect of sentencing. Rather, one will have to compare the advantages and disadvantages of human and algorithmic capabilities in relation to the many tasks that are involved in the sentencing process. The final three contributions all make comparisons between the pros and cons of human and AI-based sentencing.

Mathis Schwarze and Julian Roberts set out by mapping the possible applications of AI at sentencing. They argue that the most plausible role is one where AI supplements, but does not completely replace, human judges. However, while the authors regard sentencing as a judicial function that should remain with humans, they also argue that AI could still contribute greatly to the sentencing process. Algorithms could be used to limit the influence of human cognitive biases and discrimination and, more generally, improve sentencing consistency. In addition, and more generally, it is held that AI can help identify problematic aspects of guidance provided to the courts and foster a deeper understanding of sentencing practice.

While Schwarze and Roberts are thus explicit in their defense of a sentencing system which leaves the final decisions in the hands of the judge, two final chapters take the discussion further by considering the possibility of replacing human judges with fully AI. The chapters reach very different conclusions. Sigrid Wingerden and Mojca Plesnicar ask whether the reader would prefer to be sentenced by a human or a machine. On the basis of the proposal that a legitimate sentencing regime must be grounded in sound moral principles, be consistent in application, be clear and transparent, the authors compare the respective merits of human judges and algorithms. While acknowledging that the picture is not simple, they end on a skeptical note with regard to the advantages of replacing humans with machines.

In contrast, Frej K. Thomsen maintains a more optimistic view of the potential of replacing human judges by algorithms. In his view, automated decision-making—not based on machine learning, but on algorithms programmed in accordance with our best theory of sentencing—is likely to enjoy several advantages over sentencing by a judge. More specifically, he believes that automated decision-making may do a better job than human sentencing at preserving privacy, providing transparency, and avoiding bias. However, while he concludes that automated sentencing is in principle morally permissible, he also envisions a practical drawback if such procedures are employed within a populist penal system. Within such systems, the use of automated sentencing decisions may become more draconian than if the decisions were made by humans who might exercise a moderating influence on sentences. This concern is interesting in light of the fact that many penal theorists today share the view that penal practice in many countries is dominated by populist punitiveness.

1.4 Conclusion

In its relatively short history, AI has generated many promises and prophecies. An early prediction was made by Nobel laureate Herbert Simon who suggested (in 1965) that "Machines will be capable, within 20 years, of doing any work a man can do" (Vardi 2012). Not quite, not yet. Simon's prediction proved overly optimistic regarding the capabilities of AI. Whether AI will, at some point in the future, replace human judges at sentencing is hard to predict. It seems unlikely, except for minor offenses or administrative penalties involving fines. It is clear, at least, that AI will play an increasingly dominant role at sentencing. This creates a need for an exploration of the ways AI may be used at sentencing and some reflections on the ethical and penal theoretical costs and benefits of different applications. As the brief overview of the book indicates, the subject is complex and still characterized by widespread disagreement. However, this reflects our expectation of this volume, which does not provide definitive conclusions, but rather a starting point that may inspire and provoke future reflections. And sooner rather than later.

References

Angwin, J., J. Larson, S. Mattu, and L. Kirchner. 2016. "Machine Bias." ProPublica May 23, https://www.propublica.org/article/machine-bias-risk-assessments-in-criminal-sentencing.

Bainbridge, D. 1991. "A Computer System to Assist with the Sentencing of Convicted Offenders." International Journal of Public Administration 14 (2): pp. 161–181.

Chan, J. 1991. "A Computerised Sentencing Information System for New South Wales Courts." Computer Law and Practice 7: pp. 137–150.

Domingo, P. 2018. The Master Algorithm. New York: Basic Books.

Doob, A., and N. Park. 1987. "Computerized Sentencing Information for Judges: An Aid to the Sentencing Process." Criminal Law Quarterly 30 (1): pp. 54–72.

Freeman, K. 2016. "Algorithmic Injustice: How the Wisconsin Supreme Court Failed to Protect Due Process Rights in State v. Loomis." North Carolina Journal of Law and Technology 18: pp. 75–106.

Garrett, B., and J. Monahan 2019. Judging the Use of Risk Assessment in Sentencing. Charlottesville: University of Virginia School of Law.

Hamilton, M. 2019. "The Biased Algorithm: Evidence of Disparate Impact on Hispanics." American Criminal Law Review 56: pp. 1553–1577.

Hogarth, J. 1971. Sentencing as a Human Process. Toronto: University of Toronto Press.

Hogarth, J. 1988. Sentencing Database System: User's Guide. Ottawa: Department of Justice Canada.

Hutton, N. 1995. "Sentencing, Rationality, and Computer Technology." Journal of Law and Society 4: pp. 549–570.

Spohn, C., and P. Brennan (eds.). 2019. Handbook on Sentencing Policies and Practices in the 21st Century. Corrections and Sentencing. New York: Routledge.

Tonry, M. 2020. Doing Justice, Preventing Crime. New York: Oxford University Press.

Vardi, M. Y. 2012. "Artificial Intelligence: Past and Future." Communications of the ACM 55: p. 5.

Wisser, L. 2019. "Pandora's Algorithmic Black Bow: The Challenge of Using Algorithmic Risk Assessments in Sentencing." American Criminal Law Review 56: pp. 1811–1832.

2

Sentencing and Algorithmic Transparency

Jesper Ryberg

The use of artificial intelligence at sentencing decisions has in recent years received increasing academic attention. This is not surprising. Computer-run
algorithms have permeated the sentencing process in various ways across
many jurisdictions, and these instruments are likely to play an even more
influential role in the near future. When these facts are perceived in the light
of the generally accepted view that the state's imposition of punishment on its
citizens calls for careful consideration and justification, it is understandable
that the introduction of new technical tools in this work will (and should)
provoke discussion. Algorithmic tools may, on the one hand, carry the potential to improve the work of the criminal court. On the other, however, there
is also the risk that criminal justice practice may be overwhelmed by such
new technologies if they are prematurely introduced without prior thorough
consideration. An understanding of the pros and cons of the implementation
of algorithms in the sentencing process is crucial and is precisely what drives
the current academic discussion.

One of the issues that has repeatedly been highlighted in this debate is
Algorithmic Transparency. In short, the concern is that the introduction or
increased use of algorithms in the sentencing process may challenge the
scrutability of and insight into the decision-making. Theorists have repeatedly stressed transparency as crucial and underlined the potential threat of
algorithmic opacity.[1] However, there is a striking contrast between the repeated emphasis on the alleged challenge of opacity and the lack of elaborate
attempts at answering precisely what this challenge consists in. There is a significant lack of clarity with regard to questions such as these: *What is it that
should be transparent and why does a lack of transparency constitute an ethical
problem*? The answers to these questions are not merely of academic interest.
In order to be able to devise viable solutions, we need to know why and when
a lack of transparency constitutes a problem, and when this is not the case.

Jesper Ryberg, *Sentencing and Algorithmic Transparency* In: *Sentencing and Artificial Intelligence*.
Edited by: Jesper Ryberg and Julian V. Roberts, Oxford University Press. © Oxford University Press 2022.
DOI: 10.1093/oso/9780197539538.003.0002

This chapter examines the reasons why, and with regard to what, transparency in the factors underlying sentencing decisions is important.

2.1 Overview

The chapter proceeds as follows. In section 2.2, the background of the contention that the use of algorithms in sentencing gives rise to a problem of lack of transparency will be presented. Possible answers to the "transparency with regard to what?" question will be distinguished. Section 2.3 outlines the arguments that have traditionally been given for why openness in judicial reason-giving is regarded as valuable. Section 2.4 considers whether any of these general reasons in favor of judicial reason-giving can shed light on whether and why a lack of transparency resulting from the use of algorithms in sentencing constitutes an ethical problem. Finally, section 2.5 summarizes and concludes the chapter.

Before embarking upon these considerations, it should be stressed that the ensuing considerations maintain the framework that is usually set for this discussion; that is, we will be considering algorithms—such as a risk assessment tool—that a (human) judge can draw on at sentencing (see, e.g., Ryberg 2021). The ethical assessment, as will become clear, might change significantly if we were to consider fully automated sentencing decisions. Even though robotic sentencing may well become a reality in the (near?) future, the most urgent concern is still the use of algorithms to support the sentencing process. Therefore, this will be the focus in what follows.

2.2 Transparency with Regard to What?

Transparency and openness have often been emphasized as basic elements of due process. However, the use of algorithms in the decision-making has undoubtedly fueled the traditional requirement of transparency. There are two ways in which algorithmic systems have been held to be at odds with transparent sentencing practice.

The first challenge to transparency pertains to the use of legally protected algorithms. The oft-quoted case which well illustrates this challenge is *State v. Loomis*. This case dealt with a constitutional challenge to the use of the COMPAS risk assessment algorithm at sentencing. Eric Loomis had been accused in a drive-by shooting. As part of the initial sentencing process, the state circuit court ordered an investigation that involved a risk assessment of the defendant. On the grounds of the assessment, the judge stated: "You're identified, through the COMPAS assessment, as an individual who is at high risk to the community. In terms of weighing the various factors, I'm ruling out probation because of the seriousness of the crime and because your history, your history on supervision, and the risk assessment tools that have been utilized, suggest that you're extremely high risk to re-offend" (see Freeman 2016, 90). However, Loomis subsequently filed an appeal on the grounds of the due process argument that he had not had the chance to assess the accuracy of the COMPAS algorithm. The case went to the Wisconsin Supreme Court, which ultimately rejected the argument with direct reference to the fact that the inner workings of the algorithm was a trade secret. The court held that "Northpointe, Inc [the company that sells the COMPAS algorithm] . . . considers COMPAS a proprietary instrument and a trade secret. Accordingly, it does not disclose how the risk scores are determined or how the factors are weighed" (see Carlson 2017, 316). Thus, although the state Supreme Court issued a number of warnings against the use of risk assessment tools, it affirmed the circuit court's use of the COMPAS algorithm. The judgment has spawned a comprehensive academic discussion of the ruling and, more generally, of the use of proprietary algorithms at sentencing. Let us refer to opacity resulting from legal restrictions as "legally caused opacity."

The second source of opacity that has been highlighted concerns the complexity of algorithms. Computer-run algorithms vary significantly in complexity. However, it is generally agreed that when it comes to machine learning algorithms—especially algorithms based on *deep learning*, such algorithms may be highly complex. What this means, firstly, is that for a typical layperson—such as a defendant—it may be very difficult to understand how an algorithm works. This challenge is sometimes captured under the heading of "algorithmic illiteracy" (see, e.g., Lepri et al. 2018). Second, it may also the case, however, that how the output of an algorithm has been determined is not fully comprehensible, even to computer experts. That is, both *ex ante* predictions of outputs and *ex post* explanations of the processing that led to the output will be very difficult, or even impossible, to formulate precisely (see, e.g., Kim and Routledge 2018; Rudin 2019; Springer and Whittaker 2018; Zerilli et al. 2018). Thus, the complexity of an algorithm—even when its formula is not subject to any trade secret protections—has in itself been held to constitute a threat to transparency. Let us refer to this type to opacity as "technically caused opacity."

Having identified the sources of algorithmic opacity, the next question is this: What precisely is concealed in cases where the inner workings of an algorithm are not fully transparent? That is, what is the object of opacity? On this point there is no general agreement among theorists. One possibility is to suggest that the relevant object is the source code of an algorithm.[2] Another possibility is to suggest that what matters is insight into how the input factors have been weighed in order to reach an output.[3] The significance of insight into the weighting process is precisely what several critiques have underlined in relation to the Loomis case. For instance, though both input and output were fully accessible in this case, according to Freeman the problem is that Northpoint "does not explain the value given to each factor, nor does it include a specific breakdown of every factor used in the algorithm" (Freeman 2016, 93). Along the same lines, Leah Wisser contends that the "algorithm's impenetrability is mainly what gives rise to concerns over its use. While we know what information is inputted into the algorithm as well as the score that is outputted, we do not know how the algorithm weighs or processes the different inputs" (Wisser 2019, 1816). Thus, both the lack of access to the source code and the lack of insight into the weighing of input factors have been emphasized as concerns relating to transparency.

It is worth noting that these two objects of transparency may be related in different ways to the two suggested sources of opacity. If an algorithm is protected by trade secret restrictions, then—as with the COMPAS algorithm—it could be the case that both the source code and the weighting of input factors are concealed. However, it could also be the case that users are actually informed of the weight ascribed to input factors while the source code remains closed. Turning instead from legally caused opacity to technically caused opacity, the picture could be the opposite. It may be impossible to understand precisely how a complex algorithm processes and weighs the inputs, even if the source code is open to users. It could of course also be the case that an algorithm is opaque for both legal and technical reasons and, hence, that both the source code and the weighing of input factors remain inaccessible. With these preliminary distinctions in place, we can now proceed to the next step in the discussion of whether and why algorithmic transparency should be regarded as important.

2.3 Reasons for Reason-Giving

Despite the fact that opacity has repeatedly been underlined as a major concern in the discussion of the use of algorithms in sentencing, remarkably few attempts have been made to flesh out in detail the nature of this problem. However, this does not mean that the question of the significance of scrutability and insight into the background of sentencing decisions has *generally* been left untouched. On the contrary, the question has received considerable attention in a closely related context, namely, in the traditional discussion of the significance of *judicial reason-giving* in court decisions. Thus, I will now briefly outline the main reasons that have been advanced as to why it is generally regarded as important that judges provide defendants and other parties with reasons that explain and justify sentencing decisions. On these grounds, we will subsequently return to the question of the challenge of algorithmic opacity. There are three overall traditional categories of reasons for judicial reasons-giving.

2.3.1 Improve the Quality of Decision-Making

Stating reasons for sentencing decisions improves the quality of the decisions. This can occur in several ways. First and foremost, it has been noted that once a judge is forced to provide reasons, the sentencing process will become more reasoned. That is, the judge will be forced to ensure that decisions are based on the actual facts of a case and that he or she draws the right conclusions of law. Moreover, it has been suggested that the giving of reasons suggests that a judge is more attentive to precedent and this will help to ensure parity in sentencing. For instance, Mathilde Cohen contends that the "practice of reason-giving limits the scope of available discretion over time by encouraging judges to treat similarly situated cases alike and to treat differently situated cases differently" (2015, 508). In light of the fact that there is much evidence of sentencing disparity, a procedure that will cause judges to pass sentencing of greater uniformity may be a significant improvement (see Ryberg 2021). Furthermore, and to the same effect, it has also been suggested that a procedure that forces judges to articulate reasons may help reduce the level of biases in decision-making. For instance, Cohen holds that "there is some evidence, drawn from cognitive psychology research, that requiring decision makers to explain may diminish some forms of cognitive bias" (Cohen 2015, 513). Thus, as this indicates, there are several ways in which a requirement of reason-giving has been held to improve the judgment of the individual judge.

In addition to these reasons there are other, closely related arguments in favor of the quality-enhancing effect of reason-giving. For instance, it has been suggested that judicial reason-giving serves the purpose of facilitating appellate review (Cohen 2015, 507; Korbakes 1975). That is, the statement of reasons may enhance accuracy by making it much easier for appellate courts to determine whether a sentence passed by a lower court was "substantially reasonable" (Cohen 2015, 554). Finally, it has been suggested that reason-giving may reduce the risk that judges, who may hold lifetime positions and who enjoy great discretion at sentencing, engage in a deliberate misuse of their power (e.g., Aas 2004).

To summarize the practice of presenting reasons in the courtroom has been held to lead to more thoughtful and consistent sentences by forcing the judge to engage in more careful consideration of the relevant facts and applicable law, by reducing the possible influence of certain cognitive biases, by countering a risk of deliberate unjust decisions, and by facilitating appellate review.

2.3.2 Improving Participants' Confidence in Decision-Making

Another standard justification for the importance of judicial reason-giving pertains to the experience of the court process by defendants (and other court participants). Studies have found that a key determinant of a defendant's reaction to encounters with legal authorities is the degree to which the procedures used in court are perceived as fair (see, e.g., Tyler 1988). What matters with regard to satisfaction and evaluation are not mere outcomes of the work of the criminal court—the sentence—but the perception of procedural fairness in the process that led to the final decision. An important aspect of this experience relates to the participant's ability to express his or her view of the case. This is of course not in itself guaranteed by the fact that a judge provides reasons for the sentencing decision. But the practice of reason-giving may provide the defendant with the impression that his or her reasons have been heard and taken into account; that is, that the party has had some degree of what is often referred to as "process control" (DeMulder and Gubby 1983; Simmons 2018; Tyler 1988). As Cohen notes: "Judges must explain their decisions to show that they are responsive to parties' proofs and arguments. By explaining her determination, a judge indicates to what extent arguments put forward by the parties have been understood and accepted or formed a basis for the decision" (Cohen 2015, 506).

Another factor that has been documented in the literature as a contributor to an individual's perception of procedural fairness is the extent to which a legal authority is perceived as being driven by the motive to be just. As Tyler has documented, judgments about "how hard the authorities tried to be fair emerged as the key overall factor in assessing procedural justice" (Tyler 1988, 129). Insofar as a judge makes an effort to explain and justify a sentencing decision, this may contribute to the impression that he or she is properly motivated and, thereby, promote the experience of procedural fairness. Thus there may be, from the perspective of court participants, several fairness-related reasons in favor of the giving of reasons for the determination of a sentencing.

2.3.3 Enhancing Public Confidence in Judicial Decision-Making

A final standard explanation of the desirability of judicial reason-giving concerns the impact that explanations may have on an audience external to the court, namely, the public at large. Proponents of reason-giving in public administration in general have often referred to the fact that such a practice may be democratically beneficial by generating a more informed citizenry. Along the same lines, it has been underlined that judicial reason-giving does not only address defendants or appellate courts, but the entire citizenry. This has been held to be desirable for several reasons. First, the dissemination of reasons may provide citizens with a more informed background for considering and contesting sentencing practice and thereby for holding the courts accountable. For instance, as Cohen has noted, "reason-giving . . . promotes accountability toward the general public . . . in a variety of ways, ranging from public debate to legislative action. Dissatisfied citizens can elect legislators who can overrule judicial decisions they dislike through statutes or constitutional amendments" (Cohen 2015, 507).

Second, it has been suggested that the giving of reasons may contribute to promote understanding of the law and thereby provide citizens with better legal guidance. As Cohen underlines: "reason-giving is crucial . . . for guidance. . . . Rules that citizens know little about or do not understand are unlikely to provide them with meaningful guidance" (Cohen 2015, 511). Third, and perhaps most importantly, judicial reason-giving may enhance confidence and the perceived legitimacy of the courts. As has been demonstrated, the criminal courts in many countries suffer from severe lack of perceived legitimacy (see, e.g., Roberts and Hough 2005; Roberts and Plesnicar 2015). Thus, reason-giving has been defended as one among several ways in which sentencing courts may try to reach the public and prevent the lack of confidence and perceived legitimacy that follows from being confronted with a system which seems inscrutable and whose decisions are poorly understood. By presenting reasons for sentences, the courts may help the news media—most citizens main (or only) source of information about sentencing practice—to convey a picture of sentencing practice that is more nuanced than the one provided by the notoriously oversimplified standard depiction consisting in nothing beyond an (inadequate) presentation of a (serious) crime and the imposed (incomprehensible) sentence. In short, reasons may promote confidence and perceived legitimacy by contributing to a better public understanding of sentencing.

What this outline of reasons in the traditional discussion of the significance of judicial reason-giving shows is that various arguments have been provided in support of reason-giving, including the quality of sentences, the perceptions of defendants (and other court participants), as well as the public at large. Now, the purpose is not to assess whether these arguments are morally sound or whether they are based on hypotheses rather than empirical findings. Rather, the point here is to examine whether any of these standard reasons concerning clarity and scrutability of sentencing factors can help to shed some light on the nature of the less elaborate challenge of opacity in relation to the use of algorithmic sentencing support systems. This is the question to which we will now turn.

2.4 The Challenge of Algorithmic Opacity

The extent to which opacity constitutes a genuine concern when algorithms are used in the sentencing process is both dependent on the nature of the problem per se and on what it takes to avoid it. Thus, the questions that will now be considered are whether the lack of access either to the source code or to the weighting of input factors—resulting from legal protections or the complexity of an algorithm—can reasonably be expected to have any of the type of undesirable consequences outlined in the previous section and, if so, whether there are ways of avoiding these consequences.

Drawing on the earlier considerations, the first question is whether the lack of insight into the inner workings of an algorithm may affect the quality of sentencing decisions. Obviously, the use of an algorithm may have an impact on the quality of a sentencing decision. For instance, if a risk assessment algorithm provides more accurate risk assessments than physicians and psychologists, then the use of an algorithmic tool may improve the quality of the final decision. Conversely, if the algorithm functions poorly, it may impair the quality of the decision.[4] However, these consequences concern the accuracy of the output of the algorithm. The question here is with regard to the potential quality-enhancing effect of algorithmic *transparency*.

As we have seen, one argument in favor of judicial reason-giving is that such a practice will turn sentencing into a more thoughtful process by forcing the judge to ensure that he or she has paid attention to the relevant facts of a case and has relied on applicable law. However, it is difficult to see that a parallel argument can be given in favor of algorithmic transparency. There is no reason to believe that open access to the source code or to the weighting of input factors will generate a more reflective attitude in judges and thereby lead to more reasoned sentences. Hence, neither are there any reasons to believe that transparency will reduce the possible influence of cognitive biases in a judge. It is hard to see why algorithmic transparency would transform sentencing decisions from being more immediate to being more reflective. Theorists who are skeptical about the use of algorithms in the sentencing process have sometimes underlined that the implementation of such technical tools may deprive this process of some degree of consideration because judges will become more prone to relying heavily on whatever an algorithm prescribes. As noted by Andrea Roth: "Human operators or audiences interacting with machines tend too often to 'defer to the wisdom of algorithms'" (Roth 2016, 1279).[5] If this is the case, then there is of course a risk that the use of algorithms may convert the determination of a sentence into a less thoughtful process. It is worth noting, however, that this is not an implication that follows from the lack of algorithmic *transparency*. The tendency to evade decisional power by simply obeying algorithmic recommendations does not seem to depend upon whether or not the source code or the relative weight of input factors are accessible.

Another aspect of the quality-enhancing effect of judicial reason-giving, as we have seen, pertains to the hypothesis that judges, by being forced to provide reasons, will tend to pay more attention to precedent and will therefore impose more uniform sentences. However, once again it is very difficult to see that a similar reason can be given in support of algorithmic transparency. Surely there is no reason to believe that insight into the inner workings of an algorithm will in itself induce a higher degree of parity in sentencing.[6] Correspondingly, there are no clear grounds for holding that the argument that reason-giving will enhance the quality of decisions in the judicial hierarchical system—by making it easier for appellate courts to scrutinize decisions of lower courts—is applicable with regard to algorithmic transparency. The mere fact that the source code or the weighting of input factors of an algorithm are accessible does not per se seem to contribute anything to the quality of higher court reviews.

While the standard arguments for the quality-enhancing effects of judicial reason-giving do not seem readily applicable to the question of algorithmic transparency, there is, however, one important way in which openness and scrutability can more reasonably be expected to contribute to the quality of sentencing decisions. Simply put, transparency may make it much easier to detect flaws in an algorithmic instrument. This can happen in different ways. Access to the way input factors are balanced against each other may make it easier to determine whether, in a particular case, there are some factors that are given too little or too much weight.[7] Moreover, such access may also help in detecting more general flaws. For instance, it is well-known that the output of a machine learning algorithm reflects the quality of the input. If there are underlying patterns of discrimination, such biases may well be absorbed by the machine learning process. The result may be that the algorithm ends up reproducing historical patterns of prejudice and discrimination. Though the question of whether an algorithm works in a discriminatory manner is basically a question concerning the quality of the output, the fact that there is access to the weighting of the input factors may make it easier to critically scrutinize the workings of an algorithm and thereby detect what may have caused a skewed output. Similarly, if the source code of an algorithm is open, this may make it easier to detect flaws in the way the algorithm has been programmed. Though there is sometimes a tendency—in particular in philosophical discussions—to base ethical considerations on an initial "let's assume it works" assumption, it is a well-known fact that computer-driven systems—such as algorithms used in public administration—are often seriously flawed. The possibility of detecting such flaws constitutes a standard open-source argument among software developers (Kehl et al. 2017).

Therefore, in summary, even though most of the quality-based arguments in favor of judicial reason-giving are not applicable to the question of algorithmic transparency, it seems hard to deny that access to the source code or to the relative weight of input factors may positively affect the quality of decisions by making it possible, or easier, to detect flaws in an algorithm. But if that is the case, is there a way of gaining this type of advantage? If the source of algorithmic opacity is merely legal, then there is, in theory, a simple way of avoiding the quality problem of opaque algorithms: namely, by ensuring open access to the inner workings of algorithms used in sentencing. However, if the source of opacity is technical, that is, if the complexity of an algorithm implies that the relative weight of input factors is opaque (even if the source code is open), then there is no equally simple way of ensuring accessibility. The significance of this is something to which we will return later.

Another traditional argument, as we have seen, in favor of judicial reason-giving in sentencing is that such a practice may contribute to the defendant's experience of being fairly dealt with by the court. Does this argument apply with regard to openness and scrutability of algorithms? Will a lack of access to a source code or to the processing of input factors by an algorithm threaten or even undermine a defendant's perception of procedural fairness?[8]

How people react to decisions made by algorithms has, with the pace at which algorithms of various sorts continue to permeate our daily lives, become a subject of research. Several studies have been conducted in recent years on whether people tend to react differently to a decision depending on whether it is made by a human or by a computerized algorithm.[9] For instance, some studies have shown that people sometimes have an "algorithmic aversion"—they prefer predictions made by humans over those made by algorithms, even when told that the algorithm is more accurate (Dietvorst et al. 2015). However, the results of such studies may be highly context dependent and thus not easily generalizable over different subject matters. More importantly, the question we are considering here is not whether people tend to react differently to human and algorithmic recommendations, but whether the lack of transparency of the inner workings of an algorithm will influence a defendant's perception of procedural justice. As we have seen, this question is complicated by the fact that there are several factors that may have an impact on whether a defendant regards a process as fair.

One important factor in this regard is trust. It is widely agreed that one of the things that may influence the overall experience of procedural fairness is the perceived trustworthiness of the decision makers and their decision-making procedures (see, e.g., Tyler and Lind 1992). Thus, the question is whether a lack of algorithmic transparency may undermine a defendant's trust in the sentencing process. A simple conclusion does not seem warranted on this point either. Even though several studies have been conducted on the effects of algorithmic transparency on trust, the results show a mixed picture. On the one hand, there is a long history of studies showing that trust can be built through transparency (in fact, some studies even show that trust may sometimes be improved to a point of overconfidence (Garcia et al. 2018)). On the other hand, there are also studies showing that trust in an automated system can be undermined by transparency (e.g., Kizilcec 2016; Springer and Whittaker 2018). Part of the explanation of these prima facie contradictory results—which have been confirmed in recent studies (Springer and Whittaker 2018)—may be that the way in which transparency affects trust in an algorithmic system is contingent on the user's initial expectations. As Aaron Springer and Steve Whittaker have recently argued, if a user has low trust in an algorithmic system and little knowledge of how the system works, then transparency can help boost trust in this system. Conversely, if, from the outset, the user possesses a high degree of trust in a system, but has little idea of how it works, then this trust may be undermined if the user gains insight into the workings of the system (and its potential anomalies) (Springer and Whittaker 2018 and 2019). In light of this psychologically plausible explanation, the question as to whether a lack of transparency will have an impact on the perceived trustworthiness of the sentencing process may vary with the initial expectations of the defendant.

However, even if it is assumed for the sake of argument that a defendant will react to algorithmic opacity with a loss of trust, the assessment becomes even more complicated if we turn to the question as to what it takes to remedy this diminished trustworthiness. Once again, it should be kept in mind that the question we are considering here is not how a defendant would react to opacity if he or she were to be confronted with an algorithmic decision rather than one made by a human. As noted, we are not discussing fully automated decision-making such as would be the case in a system of robotic sentencing. Rather, the focus here is on the use of algorithms as a support system in a process where a human judge possesses the decision-making authority. This may be highly important seen from a procedural fairness perspective.

What this means is that even if a defendant's lack of insight into the inner workings of an algorithm would constitute a source of mistrust in its recommendations, this feeling may well also be affected by the way a judge explains the merits of the algorithm and clarifies the role it has played in the final decision-making. It is possible that an explanation by a judge of the information that has been fed into the algorithm, the output recommendations, and of why an algorithm is being used (and how this may be preferable to mere human judgments) may help in alleviating or even removing the lack of confidence which a defendant might have felt toward a purely automated and unexplained decision. And, importantly, this may be the case even if the defendant has not gained insight into the source code of the algorithm or fully comprehends how the algorithm handles input factors. Thus, an assessment of how the use of algorithms may influence the perception of procedural fairness by affecting trust in the sentencing process would also have to take into account how the "human factor" may ultimately affect the defendant's experience.

This is of course also the case if we turn to some of the other factors that have typically been held to influence the perception of procedural fairness. For instance, one aspect that has often been emphasized has been loosely described as a lack of respect or dignity.[10] The view is that an individual may well feel that his or her status or value as a human has been lessened if this individual receives a sentence which has been dictated by an algorithm. The individual in such a case may no longer feel to be a "real, thinking, changing" being (Rainie and Anderson 2017). However, if there is evidence for such an effect, it may also be the case that it can be prevented if the judge who uses the algorithmic tool possesses and exercises the ultimate decision authority. As Simmons observes: "One way to alleviate this potential problem is for . . . judges to explain the reasoning behind their actions to the defendant" (Simmons 2018, 12).[11] But as indicated, it is empirically unclear whether such explanations need to provide a full insight into the inner workings of an algorithm in order to mitigate or prevent a feeling of being treated in a undignified or disrespectful manner. Finally, as we have seen in relation to reasons for reason-giving, another important justification of judicial explanations is that this practice may provide a defendant with a feeling of *process control*. Once again, the feeling that a defendant's views and reasons have been heard and taken into account is not necessarily in any simple way contingent on the transparency of the algorithmic tool that has been applied. It may be the case that a desire for process control can be satisfied if a judge provides an explanation of the sentencing decision and that this is so even if the decision is based partly on recommendations reached by an algorithm whose inner workings remain opaque.

What conclusions are warranted on the grounds of these considerations of the lack of algorithmic transparency and perceived procedural fairness? There is no simple conclusion. Even though many studies have been conducted on various aspects of procedural fairness over the last four decades, when it comes to the specific question as to how the use of algorithmic tools in the sentencing process will affect a defendant's (or other parties') experience of fairness, the views expressed are hypotheses rather than proven conclusions. First, research into the questions of how defendants will react to algorithmic versus human decisions and, in particular, of the significance of transparency of the workings of algorithmic tools is still limited and has shown mixed results. Second, the effects of the use of such tools—even if the inner workings of an algorithm are not fully transparent—in a context in which a judge disseminates the results of an algorithmic assessment, explains some of the reasons for using such instruments in the first place, and—not least— possesses the ultimate decision power seem almost unexplored. This is the case both when it comes to the insight into the source code of an algorithm and the way an algorithm evaluates factors. Therefore, to what extent transparency or opacity of algorithmically informed judicial decision-making will constitute a problem in terms of experienced procedural justice still remains to be shown. No stronger conclusion is warranted.

The final category of reasons for judicial reason-giving seeks to justify this practice by reference to the desirable consequences that follow in relation to an audience external to the court, namely, the wider public. As we have seen, there are two arguments in this category. First, that reason-giving implies accountability in the sense that the public gains a more informed basis for assessing and, if necessary, influencing sentencing practice through democratic channels. Second, that reason-giving may help in informing the public and thereby contributing to a better legal guidance for citizens. Are these arguments applicable when considering algorithmic processes?

With regard to the question as to whether a source code of an algorithm is open or legally protected, it is not obvious that this will have an effect on the extent to which the public will hold courts accountable for sentencing decisions. It seems more likely that the public will react to the decisions themselves and perhaps to the fact that algorithms have been applied, rather than to such detailed matters as how an algorithm has been programmed.

(However, as we have already seen, an open source makes it possible to detect flaws in the programming and does provide some grounds for scrutinizing and opposing the use of algorithms—even though few will possess the requisite technical competence to engage in this work—and the resulting decisions.) It seems more likely, though, that insight into the balancing of input factors may provide some grounds for public evaluation and for holding courts accountable. However, a more thorough assessment of an accountability-based argument will require considerations of questions such as why and, not least, to what extent is it desirable that the public can react to information and hold institutions such as the courts accountable. These are important questions that cannot be addressed within the scope of this chapter. Nevertheless, at the very least it is hard to deny the conclusion that access to information usually provides better grounds for evaluating and holding decision makers accountable. As for the argument that algorithmic transparency will serve an educative function and provides the public with better legal guidance, there is currently little evidence to confirm or reject such an effect. A reasonable guess might be that the illuminating and guiding public effects of having access to the inner workings of an algorithm will, given the very detailed nature of such information, be modest.

The third argument in this category, as we have seen, draws on the importance of public confidence and legitimacy. Applied to our question of algorithmic transparency, the argument is that access to the inner workings of an algorithm is important to ensure public confidence and the perceived legitimacy of the court and its decisions. The argument has some clear parallels to the previous discussion of the impact of algorithms on a defendant's experience of procedural fairness. First, it is basically an empirical question whether the use of algorithms will have an impact on public levels of confidence and perceptions of legitimacy. And, once again, the evidence is rather limited. Second, it should be kept in mind that what we are considering here is not the reaction per se to the use of algorithms, but the potential reactions to the fact that algorithms are not fully transparent. Finally, it also remains an empirically underexplored question how judicial explanations of the fact that an algorithm is being used may influence public perceptions, even if the algorithm is not fully transparent.

The only study, to my knowledge, which has been conducted on such issues involves a survey on how people react to the use of a predictive algorithm as an instrument to advise judges in a bail decision (Simmons 2018). In this experiment, respondents were either given a case in which a judge determined the bail in relation to a hypothetical defendant on the grounds of his or her own judgment, or where the bail was set by a judge who received a recommendation from an algorithm and who then followed this recommendation. The purpose was to compare the satisfaction or dissatisfaction among the respondents to the two processes. There were no differences between the perceived fairness of the processes; respondents were equally satisfied with both scenarios. In fact, the vast majority of respondents who read the scenario in which the judge relied heavily on the predictive algorithm did not even mention the algorithm in their comments (Simmons 2018, 32). The author concludes that this "is consistent with our conclusion that the general population is comfortable with the concept of computers assisting in these decisions, at least as long as a human judge makes the ultimate decisions" (Simmons 2018, 32) To what extent this result can be backed up by research upon other aspects of sentencing still remains to be seen.

2.5 Conclusion

So where does all this lead us? To what extent should a lack of transparency with regard to the source code or the processing of input factors be regarded as a problem? For those who prefer a single clear conclusion, the answer will be disappointing. The discussion cannot justify such a conclusion. Nevertheless, some important conclusions can be drawn.

First, in accordance with the more general move toward requiring reason-giving in government and public administration, the view that the giving of reasons should be regarded as very important in relation to sentencing decisions has also become more widely accepted. Reasoned elaboration has been held to be what distinguishes judicial decision-making from a mere exercise in discretionary fiat (see Liu and Li 2019, 630). As we have seen, many arguments have been advanced to this effect. However, most of these arguments are not directly applicable to the question of legally or technically caused algorithmic opacity. That is, one may well subscribe to the view that openness is very important in the sense that judges should provide statements of which actions, evidence, and other factors and criteria led to the selection of the final penalty, without necessarily being forced to the view that such detailed matters as the lack of transparency into the inner workings of an algorithmic sentencing support system constitute a problem. The direct inference from the importance of judicial openness to the significance of algorithmic transparency may be premature.

Second, even though several of the arguments against judicial reason-giving are not directly applicable in relation to the assessment of potential problems of algorithmic transparency, there are nevertheless arguments that provide reasons in favor of ensuring that there is access to the inner workings of algorithms used in sentencing. As we have seen, the increased possibility of detecting flaws in algorithmic systems does indeed seem to constitute a reason in favor of transparency both with regard to the source code and the weighing of input factors. Furthermore, it is hard to deny that increased access to such information will improve the scrutability of algorithmically informed sentencing decisions. This means that if algorithmic opacity can be prevented by removing trade secret restrictions, then there is reason to do so.

Third, while the fact that it is easier to detect algorithmic flaws and to assess the workings of an algorithm if it is accessible constitute reasons in favor of transparency, the questions as to which other arguments for reason-giving are applicable to the question of algorithmic transparency and, not least, how serious a lack of transparency should be regarded as being do not invite easy answers. On these points, the empirical evidence is still rather limited. Thus, statements which do not only concern the relative desirability of transparency over opacity but also provide nonrelative assessments of algorithmic opacity by underlining this as a very serious problem do not seem well-founded. It may be the case that there are several strong reasons against opaque algorithmic systems. As yet, however, the evidence supporting such assessments seems insufficient. Even though considerations of the possible effects of the lack of algorithmic transparency on audiences internal and external to the court therefore do not warrant as strong conclusions as are sometimes drawn, they may nevertheless serve the important function of helping to clarify on what points evidence is lacking and, therefore, where it would be important to initiate research. For instance, as we have seen, it will be very important to increase our understanding of how defendants will react to algorithmically informed sentencing: that is, more precisely, to the involvement of algorithmic predictions, to a possible lack of insight into the workings of algorithms, and not least, to the extent to which the fact that there is a human judge, who may provide reasons concerning an algorithm, will influence the experience of procedural fairness—even if the inner workings of an algorithm remain opaque. This is also the case with regard to the reactions in the public at large.

Although these conclusions therefore do not leave a very simple picture when it comes to our overall assessment of the significance of algorithmic transparency, it is finally worth remembering the fact that when we turn from the question of possible reasons against algorithmic opacity to the question as to whether we should, at the end of the day, accept this kind of opacity in sentencing practice, the discussion becomes even more complicated. First, this kind of assessment is basically comparative; that is, one would have to consider whether the problems associated with algorithmic opacity are more prevalent or less so if algorithms are being used than if decisions are made exclusively by humans (see also Chiao, this volume). Second, an overall assessment also requires balancing the pros and cons. For instance, even though algorithmic transparency may, ceteris paribus, be preferable to opacity—indeed, much of the current discussion seems to be based on an "everything else being equal" assumption which, in particular when we are talking about technically caused opacity, may be somewhat naïve—it may still be the case that an opaque algorithm is preferable if it provides more accurate predictions than would be provided without the involvement of such technology (see Ryberg 2019). With regard to this sort of balancing of reasons, the discussion of the challenge of algorithmic transparency still leaves much to be said—both normatively and empirically.

Notes

1. See, e.g., Aas (2004); Carlson (2017); Citron (2008); Citron and Pasquale (2014); Freeman (2016); Kehl et al. (2017); Kim and Routledge (2018); Lepri et al. (2017); Liu et al. (2019); Roth (2016); Simmons (2018); Wisser (2019).
2. In computing, the source code is a list of instructions or statements which a computer programmer writes when developing a computer program. The source code is usually transformed into a machine code that can be executed by the computer.
3. When it comes to insight into the weighting of input factors, one might also distinguish between, on the one hand, the way in which input factors are weighted in a specific case and; on the other, the way input factors have generally been weighted in previous cases. It might be possible to obtain access to the latter information without having access to the former (see, e.g., Lehr and Ohm 2017).
4. For a comprehensive discussion of the use of risk assessments at sentencing, see de Keijser et al. (2019). For a more precise discussion of the ethical significance of accuracy in risk predictions, see Ryberg (2020).
5. This mechanism is what some theorists refer to as "automation bias" (see, e.g., Citron 2008; or Freeman 2016).

6. Obviously, this is not the same as holding that the use of algorithms in the sentencing process could not have such an effect. In fact, it has been suggested that algorithms could be developed precisely for this purpose (see, e.g., Chiao 2018, but also Ryberg 2021). However, this effect follows from the use (and output) of an algorithm, not from the transparency of this tool.

7. Access to this information could imply that a judge detects an inappropriate weighing of input factors in a particular case. Likewise, this sort of transparency could also facilitate a defendant's possibilities of detecting possible misbalances of input factors.

8. A thorough discussion of the possible consequences on perceived procedural fairness would also require a discussion of the (rarely addressed) question as to why procedural fairness is of moral importance. Unfortunately, this question goes beyond the limits of the present chapter. Thus, in the following it will be assumed that perceived procedural fairness is morally important.

9. For a recent publication containing references to other studies, see Lee (2018).

10. For a recent comprehensive discussion of respect in criminal justice, see Watson (2020).

11. Notably, Simmons also believes that this "will require that that the algorithms themselves are transparent" so that judges understand the factors that led to the algorithmic recommendation (2018, 12). However, it is not clear what Simmons's evidence is here. Whether a defendant would feel satisfied by a thorough judicial explanation of the input and output of an algorithm, and perhaps of what justifies its use—even if the inner workings of the algorithm remain opaque—is an empirically open question.

References

Aas, K. F. 2004. "Sentencing Transparency in the Information Age." Journal of Scandinavian Studies in Criminology and Crime Prevention 5: pp. 48–61.

Carlson, A. M. 2017. "The Need for Transparency in the Age of Predictive Sentencing Algorithms." Iowa Law Review 103: pp. 303–329.

Chiao, V. 2018. "Predicting Proportionality: The Case for Algorithmic Sentencing." Criminal Justice Ethics 37: pp. 238–361.

Citron, D. 2008. "Technological Due Process." Washington University Law Review 85: pp. 1249–1317.

Citron, D., and F. Pasquale. 2014. "The Scored Society: Due Process for Automated Decisions." Washington Law Review 89: pp. 1–33.

Cohen, M. 2015. "When Judges Have Reasons Not to Give Reasons: A Comparative Law Approach." Washington and Lee Law Review 72: pp. 483–571.

Demulder, R. V., and H. M. Gubby. 1983. "Legal Decision Making by Computer: An Experiment with Sentencing." Computer/Law Journal 4: pp. 243–303.

Dietvorst, B. J. et al. 2015. "Algorithmic Aversion: People Erroneously Avoid Algorithms After Seeing Them Err." Journal of Experimental Psychology 144: pp. 114–126.

Freeman, K. 2016. "Algorithmic Injustice: How the Wisconsin Supreme Court Failed to Protect Due Process Rights in State v. Loomis." North Carolina Journal of Law and Technology 18: pp. 75–106.

Garcia, P. G. et al. 2018. "Seeing (Movement) Is Believing the Effect of Motion on Perception of Automatic Systems Performance." Human-Computer Interaction (online first): pp. 1–51.

Kehl, D. et al. 2017. "Algorithms in the Criminal Justice System: Assessing the Use of Risk Assessment in Sentencing." Responsive Communities (online).

Keijser, J., J. V. Roberts, and J. Ryberg (eds.). 2019. Predictive Sentencing. Oxford: Hart Publishing.

Kim, T. W., and B. R. Routledge. 2018. "Informational Privacy, A Right to Explanation, and Interpretable AI." IEEE Symposium on Privacy-Aware Computing (online).

Kizilcec, R. F. 2016. "How Much Information: Effects of Transparency on Trust in an Algorithmic Interface." Proceedings of the 2016 CHI Conference on Human Factors in Computer Systems: pp. 2390–2395.

Korbakes, C. A. 1975. "Criminal Sentencing: Should the Judge's Sound Discretion Be Explained?" Judicature 184: pp. 185–191.

Lee, M. K. 2018. "Understanding Perception of Algorithmic Decisions: Fairness, Trust, and Emotion in Response to Algorithmic Management." Big Data and Society, January–June: pp. 1–16.

Lehr, D., and P. Ohm. 2017. "Playing with the Data: What Legal Scholars Should Learn about Machine Learning." University of California Davis Law Review 51: pp. 655–719.

Lepri, B. et al. 2018. "Fair, Transparent, and Accountable Algorithmic Decision-Making Process." Philosophy and Technology 31: pp. 611–627.

Liu, H. et al. 2019. "Beyond State v. Loomis: Artificial Intelligence, Government Algorithmization, and Accountability." International Journal of Law and Information Technology 27: pp. 122–144.

Liu, J. Z., and X. Li. 2019. "Legal Techniques for Rationalizing Biased Judicial Decisions: Evidence from Experiments with Real Judges." Journal of Empirical Legal Studies 16: pp. 630–670.

Rainie, L., and J. Anderson. 2017. "Code-Dependent: Pros and Cons of the Algorithm Age." Pew Research Center, February 8: pp. 1–87.

Roberts, J. V., and M. Hough. 2005. Understanding Public Attitudes to Criminal Justice. Buckingham: Open University Press.

Roberts, J. V., and M. M. Plesnicar. 2015. "Sentencing, Legitimacy, and Public Opinion." In Trust and Legitimacy in Criminal Justice, edited by G. Mesko and J. Tankebe. Dordrecht: Springer, pp. 33–51.

Roth, A. 2016. "Trail by Machine." Georgia Law Journal 104: pp. 1245–1305.

Rudin, C. 2019. "Stop Explaining Black Box Machine Learning Models for High Stakes Decisions and Use Interpretable Models Instead." Nature Machine Intelligence 1: pp. 206–215.

Ryberg, J. 2019. "Risk and Retribution: On the Possibility of Reconciling Considerations of Dangerousness and Desert." In Predictive Sentencing, edited by J. de Keijser, J. Robert, and J. Ryberg, pp. 51–68. Oxford: Hart Publishing.

Ryberg, J. 2020. "Risk Assessment and Algorithmic Accuracy." Ethical Theory and Moral Practice 23: pp. 251–263.

Ryberg, J. 2021. "Sentencing Disparity and Artificial Intelligence." The Journal of Value Inquiry (online first).

Simmons, R. 2018. "Big Data, Machine Judges, and the Legitimacy of the Criminal Justice System." University of California Davis Law Review 52: pp. 1–39.

Springer, A. and S. Whittaker. 2018. "'I Had a Solid Theory Before but It's Falling Apart': Polarizing Effects of Algorithmic Transparency." Human-Computer Interaction (online: arXiv:1811.02163 [cs.HC]).

Spinger, A., and S. Whittaker. 2019. "Making Transparency Clear." Joint Proceedings of the ACM IUI 2019 Workshop, March 20.

Tyler, T. 1988. "Procedural Justice in Felony Cases." Law and Society Review 22: pp. 483–516.

Tyler, T., and E. A. Lind. 1992. "A Relational Model of Authority in Groups." Advances in Experimental Social Psychology 25: pp. 115–192.

Watson, G. 2020. Respect and Criminal Justice. Oxford: Oxford University Press.

Wisser, L. 2019. "Pandora's Algorithmic Black Bow: The Challenge of Using Algorithmic Risk Assessments in Sentencing." American Criminal Law Review 56: pp. 1811–1832.

Zerilli, J. et al. 2018. "Transparency in Algorithmic and Human Decision-Making: Is There a Double Standard?" Philosophy and Technology (online first).

3

Transparency at Sentencing

Are Human Judges More Transparent Than Algorithms?

Vincent Chiao

Transparency is a key attribute of any legitimate sentencing regime. Transparency is usually accomplished by ensuring that sentencing decisions are publicly available and intelligible. Transparency has more recently emerged as an important concern for machine learning sentencing aids. Algorithmic tools, it is alleged, are less transparent than human judges both because the underlying source code can be shielded from public disclosure as a trade secret, and because the manner in which they yield predictions from input data can be extremely difficult for humans, including experts, to interpret. The aim of this chapter is to suggest that insofar as lack of transparency in either of these senses is problematic for algorithmic tools, it is also a problem for human decision-making by judges. Consequently, concerns about transparency have an ambiguous significance in debates about algorithmic sentencing.

A demand for greater "transparency" at sentencing can carry a number of different connotations. As Ryberg notes in his contribution to this volume, although complaints about algorithmic opacity are common, we still lack a clear consensus view as to what exactly algorithmic transparency entails (Ryberg, this volume, MS p.2).[1] The two conceptions of transparency that appear to have generated the most controversy are what I will refer to as the *publicity* and *intelligibility* conceptions of transparency. Critics have argued that algorithmic decision-making is insufficiently public for use in high-stakes legal settings such as sentencing because the source code of an algorithm is often regarded as a trade secret and protected against public disclosure (Wexler 2018; Carlson 2017; Wisser 2019). In addition, critics have argued that algorithms that rely on novel machine learning processes defy explanation and justification by human experts. These algorithms learn on their own how to correlate characteristics of input data to outcomes; the ways

Vincent Chiao, *Transparency at Sentencing* In: *Sentencing and Artificial Intelligence.* Edited by: Jesper Ryberg and Julian V. Roberts, Oxford University Press. © Oxford University Press 2022. DOI: 10.1093/oso/9780197539538.003.0003 in which they do so can be difficult or impossible to account for. This means, critics argue, that we cannot trust these algorithms in high-stakes settings (Kroll et al. 2017; Doshi-Velez et al. 2017).

There is something to be said for both of these conceptions of transparency.[2] In the context of high-stakes legal decisions, such as sentencing, it is intuitive to expect an algorithm's underlying statistical model, its implementation in software, its training data, and the precise way in which it correlates inputs to outputs to be publicly available and readily intelligible, at least to experts. Failure to live up to these standards reasonably generate complaints of "algorithmic opacity."

This chapter complements Ryberg's discussion of transparency by showing that the ethical concerns one might have about algorithmic opacity—publicity and intelligibility—are also problematic in the context of human decision-making, including when judges sentence criminals. Like Ryberg, I start with the principle that proposed changes to the legal process (such as adopting algorithmic sentencing methods) should be evaluated by comparing them to the status quo ante, rather than to a potentially unrealistic, and in any case unrealized, ideal (Ryberg, this volume, p. 40). While there are concerns that one might reasonably raise about an overly shortsighted application of this approach, an incremental, start-where-you-are approach seems sufficiently intuitive to serve as an uncontroversial default in the absence of a developed argument to the contrary.

On this type of incrementalist approach, the relevant question is not whether algorithmic methods are perfectly transparent, it is whether they are *more* or *less* transparent than the status quo—which, in the case of sentencing, is often a fairly open-ended exercise of discretion by a human judge, often under time pressure, with limited ability to learn from mistakes, and little information about overall, system-wide sentencing patterns beyond what can be gleaned from his or her own experience.[3] Surprisingly, critics of algorithmic opacity sometime give the impression that they are sanguine about the level of transparency in human decision-making. Yet judges often give only highly abbreviated and conclusory reasons for their decisions. Moreover, their reasons sometimes appear to exhibit features of post hoc rationalization, as judges are often unaware of what has actually influenced their judgment. Hence, the ethical case for (or against) algorithmic decision-making approaches to sentencing depends on an assessment of the relative merits, along the axes of publicity and intelligibility, of the status quo in sentencing procedure as compared to the status quo supplemented with an algorithmic prediction tool.[4]

Section 3.1 of this chapter considers criticisms of algorithmic opacity based on transparency as publicity. Section 3.2 considers criticism based on transparency as intelligibility. In both cases, I adopt an incrementalist perspective and ask the following: How public, and how intelligible, are comparable human decisions? If, as I argue, human decision-making suffers from significant shortcomings in both dimensions, then the ethical case for or against algorithmic decision-making must become more nuanced, and consider whether a particular algorithmic tool, used for a particular purpose, and equipped with plausibly available forms of explanation and validation, is more or less public or intelligible than judicial decision-making in the status quo equilibrium.

3.1 Publicity

Begin with the idea that a transparent decision-making procedure is one in which every step—that is, each inference, correlation, decision, or other action that contributes to bringing about the ultimate decision—is open to public inspection. Transparency in this sense means there are no secrets. From this point of view, algorithmic opacity is primarily a matter of using trade secret protections to keep proprietary software, its underlying mathematical processes, and training data secret. A commonly proposed remedy is to only permit algorithmic decision-making if trade secret protections are lifted, making the entire operation of the algorithm open to public inspection.[5]

In line with the incrementalist view sketched earlier, the strength of this objection is assessed relative to the status quo baseline. Hence, it is important to consider whether it is the case that every step of a legally significant decision by *humans* is required to be public. As an initial matter, we can consider whether there is a general requirement that judges explain each step in the reasoning leading to their conclusions. The answer is no. In some contexts, including extremely important ones, secrecy is legally permissible. Indeed, sometimes—such as jury deliberations—secrecy is not only permitted but required. Juries neither explain nor rationalize their decisions; they are black boxes by design. At the other end of the litigation process, the United States Supreme Court routinely dismisses certiorari petitions without explanation (Sup. Ct. R. 16.1). Such decisions can be extremely consequential, yet there is no expectation that the justices explain their reasoning. In both of these legal contexts, there is no expectation of transparency.

Looking beyond judges, common law jurisdictions tend not to have a sweeping, categorical requirement that administrative decision makers provide reasons, relying instead on a patchwork of statutory, regulatory, and case law to require reasons in more context-specific ways. For instance, although in Canada there is no universal requirement that administrative decision makers provide reasons (*Baker*, para 37), there is often a statutory duty grounded in a provincial administrative procedure statute (*SPPA* (Ont), ss 3(1), 17(1); *ATA* (B.C.), s 51; *APJA* (Atla), s 7; *ARAJ* (Que), s 8). The same general pattern appears to be true of the United Kingdom: while there is no *general* common law duty on administrators to provide reasons, there are more contextually specific duties grounded in statute or common law (*Ex parte Doody*, 564; *Stefan*, para 22; *Hasan*, paras 19–20; *TIA* (U.K.), s 10(1); *EA* (U.K.), s 38(2); *AWA* (U.K.), s 34(8)(a); *ATCSA* (U.K.), para 11). The Administrative Procedure Act in the United States requires agencies to provide a "brief statement" for denying an application or petition, and authorizes reviewing courts to set aside agency action as arbitrary or capricious, in light of the record (*APA* §§555(e), 706(2)(a); see also *Massachusetts v. E.P.A.*, 533; *State Farm*, 43).

More importantly, however, even when then are reason-giving requirements, courts can be quite flexible in establishing what counts as "reasons" (*Baker*; *Newfoundland Nurses*, para 16; *Unicity Taxi*, para 50). For instance, in *Baker*, a leading Canadian case on procedural fairness, an immigration officer's abbreviated interview notes were regarded as sufficient reasons. Reviewing courts often take a pragmatic approach, looking only to ensure that there is a sufficient basis for understanding why a decision was made: "[e]ven a sentence or two," as one court recently put it, can be sufficient (*Basanti*, para 40). Moreover, even when reviewing lower courts rather than agencies, and even in the contexts of high-stakes decisions for which reasons *are* required, such as criminal sentencing (18 USC §3553(c)), there is nonetheless substantial room for judges to summarily decide disputed issues without spelling out their inferences explicitly or in much detail (see, e.g., *Rita*, 356). In these cases what is being offered to the public is far less comprehensive than the full disclosure of source code that critics of algorithmic transparency demand. So even if proprietary algorithms can be opaque because shrouded in trade secrecy protections, that alone does not show that they would be worse than the status quo.

Would it be an improvement to require every legally binding decision be accompanied by reasons? There is reason to doubt that this would be a useful endeavor. Looking to continental legal systems, scholars have noted the "paradox" that while some European courts are under a statutory requirement to provide written reasons for all decided cases, the "reasons" produced by those courts are frequently so cursory that they barely merit the label (Cohen 2015, 492). As one scholar has archly noted, French legal judgments are "famously concise, lacking any developed findings of fact, almost never referring to past judicial decisions, and containing little that could be considered as serious interpretive or policy analysis" (559). Similarly, although the European Court of Human Rights (ECtHR) is required to give reasons for each of its decisions on the merits, the quality of those reasons "may range from a carefully crafted, individualized opinion to a two-sentence boilerplate opinion form" (564). The ECtHR relies upon "an army of bureaucrats, including about 270 full-time staff attorneys to write opinions, using templates, databases of ready-made clauses, and other shortcuts" (567). Nevertheless, even with a high level of staffing and reliance on boilerplate, as of December 31, 2019, the ECtHR still had a backlog of 59,800 pending applications (ECtHR 2019). Cohen observes that given the very small percentage of its judgments deemed by the ECtHR to be "key" (less than 1%), one might reasonably regard the ECtHR as, in effect, choosing to provide genuine reasons in only a small fraction of cases that it deems important, with the rest decided peremptorily (Cohen 2015, 569).[6] More recently, although the European Union's General Data Protection Regulation has been touted as providing a "right to an explanation" for automated decisions, it is not clear that it actually does so, and/or how substantial an "explanation" is actually required (Wachter et al. 2017; Edwards and Veale 2017). In short, even in jurisdictions that appear to require reason-giving, in practice the reasons provided are frequently far less informative than anything approximating full disclosure of source code.

The impulse to make reason-giving a strict requirement for every consequential legal decision is perhaps analogous to the impulse to require consent for every contractual transaction and suffers from similar limitations. While websites requiring users to click "I agree" are now ubiquitous, it is quite dubious that most people read or understand what they are ostensibly agreeing to, much less have any realistic opportunity to negotiate for different terms (see Van Alsenoy et al. 2014; Edwards and Veale 2017, 66–67). Similarly, requiring courts to provide reasons for everything they do seems fated to turn "reasons" into, essentially, meaningless boilerplate. This is not to condone public obfuscation about the use and background of algorithmic tools, but it is to suggest that what is problematic about such obfuscation cannot be grounded on a general principle of publicity in judicial decision-making (Hannah-Moffat 2013, 17). For in some cases there is no such general principle, and in others what the principle yields in practice seems far less than what is demanded by algorithmic transparency, namely disclosure of the entire decision-making process along with associated training data.

It is worth noting that while advocates frequently suggest that what transparency requires is the removal of trade secret protections for proprietary algorithms, simply opening source code and training data to public inspection suffers from "major limitations" when it comes to uncovering problems, biases, and bugs. As Kroll et al. (2017) observe, "[c]ode can be complicated or obfuscated, and even expert analysis often misses eventual problems with the behavior of the program." Kroll et al. illustrate the point by noting a "potentially catastrophic" security flaw that resulted from a programming mistake that was subjected to over two years of open source, public vetting before being discovered (647).

A more promising avenue is to ensure that an algorithm demonstrates reliability in the relevant contexts, for instance, in populations similar to those where use of the algorithm is contemplated. Assessing the reliability of an algorithm may be possible without actually revealing the source code— for instance, through "model-centric" or "subject-centric" approaches to explainable AI. A model-centric approach to explainable AI (or "xAI") provides explanations about the intentions of the system's designers, training parameters, training data, and tests of outcomes for error or bias. A subject-centric approach provides information about how the system treated similarly placed individuals, as well as how varying this or that feature affects the system's outputs (see Deeks 2019, 1835; Edwards and Veale 2017, 55–59).

Explainable AI approaches also suggest that revealing an algorithm's source code may not be necessary to ensure that an algorithmic device is predictively valid and fair (see, e.g., Kehl, Guo, and Kessler 2017, 28).[7] Consider, for instance, a hypothetical sentencing algorithm that provides users with an interface in which they can manipulate salient case characteristics (criminal record, age, crime of conviction, harm caused, etc.) to see how those manipulations affect predictions for a proportional sentence (Edwards and Veale 2017, 62–63). Compared to a judge's brief and conclusory reasons, given only after she has already made up her mind about what sentence to impose, and with no ability to test how changing this or that variable would affect the outcome, a proprietary algorithm that allows a user to see how manipulating inputs in contexts similar to hers might reasonably be regarded as *more* transparent, and perhaps also more procedurally fair (see Ryberg, this volume, pp. 27–31).

Ironically, France has now penalized efforts to study how *human* judges decide cases. As of this writing, French law penalizes the use of identity data from judges and court staff "having the object or effect of evaluating, analyzing, comparing or predicting their real or supposed professional practices." (*JRA* (France) art. 33 (my translation)). The information that is said to be lacking in computerized algorithms—public understanding of the steps in a decision-making process—turns out to be not only unavailable in the case of human judges, but actually illegal to provide, at least in France. To be sure, this is merely one recent episode in one jurisdiction, not a general trend, but it underscores the more general point that an ostensible requirement that court decisions be backed by publicly known reasons turns out to be more qualified and contentious than it might seem.

Let us take stock. A categorical rejection of proprietary algorithms cannot be based on a putative principle that legally consequential decisions must be backed by a complete set of reasons, for there is no such principle, either de jure or de facto. In some contexts, including those that have high stakes for particular individuals (such as jury trials) or that have broad ramifications (such as petitions asking the Supreme Court to resolve a legal question), the decision-making process is deliberately kept secret. In other contexts, where officials, including judges, are expected to provide reasons for their decisions, those reasons can be extremely terse, conclusory, and consist largely of standardized language, revealing little of the actual process by which a decision was reached. In comparison, explainable AI approaches hold out the promise of significantly greater transparency, even without revealing source code. Arguably, an algorithmic product that is regularly tested for predictive validity and bias provides more objective information on which to base an assessment than the unsystematic, discretionary, and highly discretionary systems of sentencing that continue to predominate in many jurisdictions today. None of this, to be sure, shows that there are no ethical concerns with the use of proprietary algorithms, including concerns related to secrecy. One might, for instance, object to extending trade secret protection to algorithmic tools on the grounds that private firms have inadequate incentives to ensure that their products are genuinely in the public interest, or that public watchdogs will be more effective at catching errors and biases than program designers, and so forth.[8] These types of questions probably cannot be resolved in any kind of general manner, and instead turn on the details of particular contexts; they certainly cannot be resolved simply by insisting that the inferential steps leading up to a legal decision must always be public.

3.2 Intelligibility

One might describe a decision as transparent if the decision maker can explain, to others or at least to him- or herself, how it is that he or she arrived at the decision. Call this transparency as intelligibility. Many of those who have focused their calls for greater transparency in algorithmic decision-making are concerned with transparency in this sense. While "algorithmic" decision-making in one form or another has been present in legal contexts for a long time, what is unique about machine learning algorithms is that they can become sufficiently complex that even experts find it difficult or impossible to interpret how they draw correlations between input data and predicted classifications. Rather than being programmed to use certain characteristics of the inputs as a basis for prediction, machine learning algorithms are able to adjust their parameters as they search to find patterns of correlations. This gives rise to concerns about subjecting people to decision-making processes that no one fully understands (see also Cobbe 2019, 638–639).[9] As Walmsley (2020) puts it, "we have built automated systems that we do not fully understand, that are much faster and more powerful than the human mind, and which are trained on data sets that are too large for us to comprehend." Some have argued that black box models, including ones accompanied by post hoc explanations, should not be used for high-stakes decisions at all, at least when it is possible to achieve similar levels of performance by means of a more readily interpretable model (Rudin 2019).

Once again, however, to assess this complaint it is important to consider the baseline. How well do we understand how judges make their decisions? More generally, how intelligible are human decisions?

Naïve answer: *very*. You know your own mind, including why you decided an issue a certain way. You may or may not be upfront about that to other people, but *you* know your own mind, and in principle you are able to communicate your reasoning and motivations to others. By extension, while a judge may be more or less upfront about his reasons for imposing a particular sentence, in principle he can make the steps leading up to that sentence intelligible by noting them in his reasons for sentence. Ergo, transparency.

Unfortunately, this view is not well supported by evidence. Decades of psychological research support a more circumspect answer. Many aspects of how people process information, from perception to information recall to judgment, are not open to introspection. Moreover, there is a significant gap between the reasons people give for their actions and the factors that actually explain their behavior. Opacity is not simply the result of deliberate dissimulation. In many cases people, including judges, do not know what leads them to decide an issue in a certain way—we do not always know our own minds. Moreover, people may *think* they know their own minds when in fact they do not.

Psychological opacity is a common phenomenon. My aim in the rest of this section is to provide a brief overview of the experimental literature supporting this contention. The overarching point is that even if it can be difficult to understand precisely how a machine learning algorithm reaches its conclusions, much of human decision-making is also often opaque, as people, including judges, often do not understand precisely why they make the decisions they do. Lack of intelligibility is a problem for both algorithmic and human decision-making.

Much of the vast heuristics and biases literature in experimental psychology indicates that human decision-making is often subject to influences lying outside of introspective awareness (Tversky and Kahneman 1981, 457). To take just one example, framing effects—presenting acts as entailing certain or uncertain outcomes, or involving losses rather than gains—have long been known to influence human decision-making (Tversky and Kahneman 1981). Framing effects seem unlikely to be open to introspective awareness, as a person who is aware that two choices are actually the same choice presented in slightly different ways would, presumably, adopt a consistent attitude to both. The same goes for order effects. Presenting an option last in a sequence seems to affect preference, although, strikingly, research subjects not only fail to cite order as a reason for their preference, but sometimes actively deny it (Nisbett and Wilson 1977a). Thus, it is not just that a person's stated reasons may be incomplete; rather they may be positively misleading. The power of heuristics of various kinds is explained by their relatively greater accessibility to cognition than more effortful, calculated forms of reasoning (Kahneman 2003, 699–702).

Other research tackles introspective opacity more directly. Timothy Wilson argues that human behavior "is often determined by . . . implicit motives and non-conscious construals of the world," and "[b]ecause we do not have conscious access to these aspects of our personalities, we are blind to the ways in which they influence our behavior." For instance, a well-known study found that people are prone to misinterpret physiological arousal (i.e., from standing in a dangerous location) for sexual attraction (i.e., toward a female researcher distributing questionnaires) (Dutton and Aron 1974). This suggests that misattribution applies even to judgments of a very subjective and personal nature. In a similar vein, Nisbett and Wilson found that students reacted differently to a professor depending on whether he adopted a warmer or colder demeanor, and rated his attributes (appearance, mannerisms, and accent) accordingly, even though the professor's attributes did not change with his demeanor (Nisbett and Wilson 1977b, 254–256). Most subjects denied that their attitude toward his demeanor affected their attitude toward his attributes, and equivalent numbers said it made them like the professor more rather than less. Subjects also misattributed the causal influence of the professor's attributes, with half or more reporting that his attributes affected their judgment of his demeanor, suggesting that subjects were not aware of what was actually influencing their judgments.

Not only are people sometimes unaware of causal influences on their judgment, in some cases they appear to confabulate reasons that do not exist. For instance, in another well-known study, researchers arranged four identical pairs of pantyhose on a table and asked shoppers to evaluate them and determine their preferences among the pairs. Not only did order exhibit a strong effect (favoring the last pair on the right), but subjects confabulated reasons (sheerness, knit, elasticity) for their preference despite the fact that the pairs were all identical (Wilson 2004, 102–103). These studies, Greene writes, are evidence that "people make choices for reasons unknown to them and they make up reasonable-sounding justifications for their choices, all the while remaining unaware of their actual motives and subsequent rationalizations" (Greene 2008, 36).

These findings extend to contexts that more closely resemble legal decisions. For instance, plainly irrelevant factors appear to influence assessments of blame, causation, and responsibility. If people are inclined to regard someone who causes harm as culpably violating a social norm, they are prone to judge him more harshly for that harm, even it is unconnected to the norm violation. In a typical study, researchers presented subjects with a hypothetical scenario in which a person lost control of a campfire that subsequently spread to his trailer, which turned out to contain dangerous chemicals. The chemicals exploded, and two rescue personnel were killed while responding to the fire. In one version, the person who started the fire used the trailer as a methamphetamine lab, whereas in the other he used it to store fertilizers for a collection of exotic orchids. Subjects were more willing to deem the person as having caused the resulting harm, as having acted intentionally, and as responsible/blameworthy when presented with the "bad" character condition than when presented with the "good" character condition (Nadler and McDonnell 2011). This is striking, as a person's character would seem to be irrelevant to whether he acts intentionally or accidentally, the degree of harm he causes, and his responsibility for doing so.

There is evidence that providing people with the same objective evidence does not eliminate the effect of ideological priors on judgment (Lord, Ross, and Lepper 1979). Suppose that people are shown a video of protesters congregating in front of a building, carrying placards and yelling at passerby, and are asked to determine whether the protesters are "interfering with," "obstructing," "intimidating," or "threatening" people seeking to enter the building. Since people are viewing exactly the same video, presumably it should not matter if the video is described as showing (a) anti-abortion protesters in front of an abortion clinic, or (b) gay rights protesters demonstrating against the military's ban on gays and lesbians at a recruitment center. Surprisingly (or not), there is evidence that people with different cultural/ideological priors (egalitarian versus hierarchical, individualistic versus communitarian) come to divergent conclusions when presented with the same objective facts (Kahan et al. 2012: 878–883).[10] In another study, when researchers asked participants whether an instance of public nudity should be punished, they found that participants' answers were significantly affected by whether or not they agreed with the cause (pro-life or pro-choice) that a hypothetical nude protester was advocating. When asked to explain the basis of their judgments, participants overwhelmingly (52 out of 53) focused on the public nudity aspect rather than the content of the message advocated by the protester (Sood and Darley 2012). This suggests that, the authors write, "the respondents seemed to be unaware of the ideologically biased motives that drove their judgments" (1340).[11] For my purposes here, the important point is not just that the participants were biased in their judgments, but that they were *unaware* that they were biased. Consequently, it is unsurprising that there is a disconnect between the judgments they rendered and the reasons they gave. Their reasons might seem transparent on the surface—we understand their explanations for why they judged as they did—but they are opaque at a deeper level, when we find influences on their judgment that the participants did *not* report.

Our inability to accurately assess why we decide as we do is particularly pronounced in contexts in which we are asked to make multidimensional decisions involving conflicting criteria—a context that perfectly describes sentencing. Our stated reasons for why we decide as we do in such contexts are not always trustworthy as guides to how we actually decided. Researchers have studied similarly multidimensional decisions such as deciding which applicant to hire or admit to a university or to hire for a job. The decisions people actually make in these contexts is not well predicted by their own explicitly stated criteria. After asking subjects to rank applications for university admissions or employment, Norton, Vandello, and Darley (2004) found that the choices people made correlated poorly with the justifications they gave—for instance, choosing an applicant with a lower GPA despite saying that GPA was the most important criterion. The researchers found that when given applications from applicants of different races, racial identity trumped the subjects' own stated criteria. (Subjects—undergraduates at an American university—tended to give preference to minority candidates.) When subsequently interviewed, subjects largely did not mention race as a factor in their decisions, nor did people report greater mental conflict or difficulty deciding when favoring racial identity caused them to override their own stated criteria as compared to those who chose consistent with their stated criteria. This suggests that subjects' explicitly stated criteria, at least in multidimensional decisions, may be functioning more as rationalization than as genuine explanation.

One might point out, reasonably, that these studies do not involve experts, but rather undergraduates in Western, educated, industrialized, rich, and democratic societies. There is reason to worry that findings about this demographic group will not generalize (Henrich, Heine, and Norenzayan 2010). However, since the focus of this section is on the behavior of judges in those same societies, the more specific question is whether judges and experts differ from the typical undergraduate subject of psychological research. For instance, perhaps experts are better able to discern, and marginalize, the influence of irrelevant factors, such as order or framing effects. The evidence is mixed, but there is reason for doubt. Some studies find that more reflective

people, far from being more impartial, are in fact prone to process information in a *more* biased way, particularly when they bear few personal costs
from error (Kahan 2012). More specific to my immediate purpose, studies
of judges have similarly found evidence of psychological opacity in judicial
decision-making. For instance, one recent study found that how sympathetic a party is affects how judges decide cases, even when those cases turn
on purely legal questions—questions, that is, where the sympathy-inducing
traits of a party are strictly irrelevant (Wistrich, Rachlinski, and Guthrie
2015). Researchers have also found that judges, like laypeople, are also susceptible to anchoring effects, suffer from base rate neglect, and exhibit a substantial degree of hindsight bias (Guthrie, Rachlinski, and Wistrich 2007).

Strikingly, anchoring effects have been observed even when the source
of the anchor is clearly irrelevant. A study of sentencing by German judges
presented judges with a hypothetical case file, as well as a high or low
anchoring suggestion, before asking the judges to recommend a fit sentence.
The anchors stemmed from increasingly arbitrary sources, ultimately including having the judges roll dice. Judges who were exposed to a high anchor, even one determined in an obviously arbitrary manner, recommended
substantially longer sentences than those who were exposed to a low anchor (Birte, Mussweiler, and Strack 2006).[12] This study also compared the
performance of judges with significant expertise in criminal law to judges
working in other areas to determine if area expertise insulated against
anchoring effects. They found that "[t]he only notable difference between the
experts and nonexperts is that the experts felt more certain about their sentencing decision ... than the nonexperts ... The certainty experienced by the
judges however was unrelated to their susceptibility to the anchoring bias"
(193–194).

In light of this result, perhaps it is unsurprising that other legally irrelevant factors, such as a sympathetic defendant, turn out to sometimes be more
important to how judges resolve cases than legally relevant factors, such as
precedent (Spamann and Klöhn 2016). A recent study, using sitting judges
and realistic case materials, found that a weak precedent had no impact on
the likelihood that a judge would affirm a conviction, whereas an unsym-
pathetic defendant faced twice the risk of having his conviction affirmed
as compared to a more sympathetic defendant (270). Strikingly, the judges
did not mention the defendant's character in their reasons; ironically, one
judge mentioned the defendant's character only to dismiss it as irrelevant.
The reasons the judges gave emphasized the significance of precedent in

justifying their conclusions, even though the precedents supplied turned out to be inconsequential in affecting how the judges actually resolved the matter. In short, legally irrelevant factors influence judicial decision-making, and judges often do not mention those factors in their reasons, whether out of a desire to obfuscate or simply because the influence was not open to introspective awareness (Liu and Li 2019). Like consumers who deny that their preferences are affected by how goods are displayed while confabulating reasons to distinguish among identical goods, it turns out that the reasons judges give for their decisions cannot always be taken at face value, with the actual influences on the outcome often going unreported.

Defenders of discretionary sentencing by human judges often base their defense on the fine-grained, highly individualized attention that human judges allegedly provide when sentencing. However, sentencing judges, even when possessed of substantial sentencing discretion, tend to impose sentences in highly predictable intervals, a finding that has been observed for well over a hundred years (Dhami et al. 2020; Roberts, Pina-Sanchez, and Marder 2018).[13] While it is perhaps unsurprising that certain intervals occur to the mind more readily than others, that the pattern of criminal sentences so closely tracks predictable number series suggests that judges may not be basing their sentencing decisions entirely on careful scrutiny of the merits of the individual case before them. This conclusion is consistent with prior research that has found (in the bail context) that magistrates, operating under substantial time pressure and with no outcome-based feedback, appear to rely on extremely simple heuristics (in many cases, a heuristic based on a single factor), exhibit significant disagreement in how they treat the same case, and make inconsistent decisions (Dhami and Ayton 2001).[14] Moreover, analysis of their decisions revealed significant discrepancies between the factors that magistrates said were important and the actual influence of those factors on decisions (159). Magistrates nevertheless reported a high level of confidence in their decisions (153).

Finally, there is a large literature indicating that judges, like most people, are subject to a broad range of unconscious influences on their decision-making. For instance, as a class female offenders appear to receive milder sentences than male offenders, controlling for seriousness of the crime, prior convictions, and prior incarceration (Doerner and Demuth 2014; Steffensmeier and Demuth 2006).[15] Black and Hispanic male defendants, in contrast, tend to receive harsher sentences, a pattern that appears to have accelerated in some places after the loosening of sentencing guidelines

(Steffensmeier and Demuth 2006; Yang 2015; but see Wang, Mears, Spohn, and Dario 2013). There is some evidence that attractive people attract lighter punishments (Downs and Lyons 1991).[16] Some researchers have even presented evidence suggesting that the time of day at which a (parole) case is heard affects the outcome, although this finding remains controversial.[17] More generally, the authors of a recent survey of the empirical literature summarized, the reasons judges give for a sentence "can be misleading" and "are not reliable indicators of the considerations and factors that influence judicial sentences," in part because—as noted before—the influence of those factors lie "outside the conscious awareness of the judge" (Goodman-Delahunty and Sporer 2010, 24).

It is time again for stocktaking. While there are surely ethical concerns with relying on intrinsically opaque machine learning algorithms in high-stakes legal contexts, I have endeavored to show that these concerns are not limited to algorithmic decision methods but afflict ordinary human judgment as well. Naïve Cartesianism notwithstanding, decades of psychological research have established that introspective awareness is fallible and afflicted by blind spots, and that the reasons people give are not always the reasons that actually motivate them. While psychologists remain divided as to precisely how much of human decision-making is subject to introspective awareness and control, there is "broad agreement among contemporary psychologists that people are generally unable to fully perceive, and reliably and validly report, the causes of their behavior" (MacCoun 2006, 113). Opacity is ubiquitous, meaning that the ethical problems of relying on processes that we do not (fully) understand must be grappled with directly, rather than by imagining that we can avoid them altogether if we refuse to adopt algorithmic tools in criminal justice.

At this point, one might object that while it may be true that how a person comes to a decision is not fully transparent to him- or herself, but that does not show that human decision-making is *intrinsically* opaque; indeed, the evidence I have amassed suggests that we do have some insight into how human decision-making operates. In contrast, machine learning algorithms are intrinsically opaque, in that even experts cannot explain how the algorithm associates features of input data with predictions.

However, while it is one thing to establish that introspective awareness is not always an authoritative guide to human decision-making, it is another thing altogether to have a fine-grained theory of mind that clearly establishes how human decision-making operates. Neuroscience remains a rapidly developing field, and the etiology of many psychological phenomena remain shrouded in uncertainty. Experts are unable to explain precisely how much of human cognition functions, even while they can explain how inputs (environmental cues) are associated with outputs (behaviors). This is perhaps not so different from xAI approaches that seek to ensure that an algorithmic decision-making process operates consistently, that both inputs (e.g., training data) and outputs (predictions) are unbiased, according to one or another notion of "fairness," and to provide guidance about how variation in inputs correlates with variation in outputs.

To be clear, I do not mean to suggest that humans lack all insight into their decisions, nor that they cannot learn to become aware of, and potentially control, unconscious influences. For instance, legal training and experience does seem to confer a degree of insulation from motivated reasoning, at least when it comes to specifically legal contexts, if not more generally (Kahan et al. 2015). There is also evidence that reason-writing, even if not perfectly revelatory of influences on a judge's decision, does at least reduce bias somewhat (Liu 2018). Notably, requiring judges to write out the rules that apply in a given context *prior* to actually deciding a case appears to yield greater consistency than the more common procedure of providing reasons after a decision has been made (85).[18] The point is rather that discussion of algorithmic opacity should consider the degree to which both human and algorithmic decision-making can be less than fully intelligible, and to consider whether the limitations of human decision-making can be ameliorated by relying on the kinds of explanation and statistical validation that can be provided for algorithmic devices. Opacity, in other words, is not just a problem for algorithms. It is a problem for human judges as well.

3.3 Conclusion

Critics of algorithmic decision-making in criminal justice often complain about a lack of transparency. In some cases, critics are concerned about proprietary algorithms and argue for disclosure of the underlying source code. In other cases, the concern is that we should not rely on inscrutable decision-making processes that we do not fully understand in high-stakes legal settings such as sentencing. Starting from an incrementalist approach to policy evaluation, I have argued that the status quo ante in sentencing—discretionary decisions by judges, sometimes operating under significant time pressure, with limited opportunity for feedback, and little information about aggregate sentencing patterns (other than the judge's own experience)—is itself less than perfectly transparent, both in terms of its publicity and in terms of its intelligibility.

Publicity is not a universal requirement for human decision-making in every legal context. Sometimes legal systems insist on keeping the grounds of a decision secret, and even when they do not, the information that must be revealed often falls far short of anything analogous to full disclosure of every step in an algorithmic decision-making process. Similarly, decades of psychological research have repeatedly demonstrated that people often do not know why they decided as they did; they often given spurious reasons when asked; and either do not mention, or even deny, that a variety of irrelevant factors—from framing and order effects to ideology to random anchors to sympathetic and attractive defendants—influenced their decisions even when it seems clear that they did.

The main claim made in this chapter is that the more pressing ethical question in this area is not whether machine learning algorithms are opaque (they are), but whether they are more or less opaque than human decision-making. I take no view in this chapter as to whether the opacity of human decision-making is "better" or "worse" than the opacity of proprietary and/or inscrutable algorithms as a class. Plausibly, such judgments are context specific, depending on the particular algorithmic tool in question, as well as the baseline norms in a particular jurisdiction for a particular type of decision. However, in forming a contextual judgment of that kind, it is important to focus not only on the ethical limitations of algorithmic decision methods, serious as they are, but also on the ethical limitations of our existing practices, serious as *they* are.

More constructively, the argument of this chapter provides support for proposals to focus less on transparency (whether as publicity or as intelligibility) and attend more to the contestability of algorithmic decision-making (Walmsley 2020). Contestability is relevant at several different points. At the case level, contestability pertains to the ability of the parties, whether accused or Crown, to contest the accuracy of the input data that is fed into an algorithmic tool, akin to their ability to contest the accuracy of the facts upon which a sentencing judge bases sentence. An important relative advantage of human sentencing in this regard is that written reasons, even if imperfect for the reasons noted before, nevertheless provide a basis for an appeals court to review the legality and fairness of a particular sentence. This may be harder to do with regard to an algorithmic tool, although perhaps not an insurmountable barrier; for instance, drawing upon principles of subject-centric xAI, one might require a sentencing algorithm to generate a report of what the algorithm would predict for similarly situated accused, varying this or that feature of the case (e.g., lengthier versus shorter record, a greater versus lesser quantum of damages, etc.). Potentially more importantly, contestability at the system pertains to the ability of civil society to challenge the overall functioning and outcomes generated by an algorithmic tool, for example, by insisting that it be regularly validated on the local population, that it be tested for objectionable carryover of historical biases, and similar pressing group-level concerns. In contrast, sentencing by human judges, particularly in jurisdictions that lack sentencing commissions, remains relatively immune from system-level contestability. Thus, a properly regulated governance framework for algorithmic sentencing arguably has the potential to enhance system-level contestability in some contexts.

Notes

1. For a recent typology of transparency, see Burrell 2016. My account of transparency as publicity and as intelligibility roughly tracks Walmsley's distinction between "outward" and "functional" transparency: Walmsley 2020.
2. There is, in contrast, little to be said for the concern that an algorithm might be too complex for the average person to understand. Law itself is notoriously obscure to laypersons; moreover, when legal officials turn to experts—in the sentencing context, experts such as probation officers, doctors, and therapists—this is precisely because they are likely to have knowledge and experience that laypeople do not have.
3. That said, sentencing norms vary widely across jurisdictions. I focus on traditional discretionary sentencing models for simplicity of presentation. Arguably, guidelines systems can be conceptualized as splitting the difference between purely discretionary and purely algorithmic approaches.
4. Some sentencing factors, such as recidivism risk, are controversial. See Lewis 2020. I take no stand on this type of question; if it is wrong to base sentences on recidivism risk, then it is wrong to use any procedure, algorithmic or otherwise, to assess that risk.
5. This corresponds to the first sense of transparency discussed in Ryberg (this volume). See also Wexler 2018; Carlson 2017; Wisser 2019; Citron and Pasquale 2014, 10, 25.
6. The ECtHR 2019 annual report lists 27 out of 884 judgments rendered that year as "key," or approximately 0.03%.
7. Kehl et al. emphasize the importance of audits by outside researchers, particularly for tools created by for-profit businesses. That seems entirely reasonable. The concern to reveal the weights assigned to particular factors seems unmotivated, however, as

judges often do not reveal those weights, or do so only in very vague ways; moreover, for reasons discussed below, judges' own statements about the weights they assigned to various factors, and even which factors they considered, cannot always be taken at face value.

8. For an instructive cautionary tale about inflated claims by a private firm during the early days of DNA evidence, see Mnookin (2008).

9. This corresponds to the second sense of transparency identified by Ryberg (this volume).

10. As Kahan et al put it, "what [the study subjects] saw—earnest voicing of dissent intended only to persuade, or physical intimidation calculated to interfere with the freedom of others—depended on the congruence of the protesters' positions with the subjects' own cultural values" (884).

11. Other research has found that priming people with high-salience threats (e.g., terrorist attacks) leads to recommendations for harsher punishments, even of crimes that have nothing to do with terrorism, such as sex assault or car theft (Fischer et al. 2007).

12. Mean differences were on the order of eight months in a rape case and about three months in a shoplifting case (191, 193).

13. As Roberts, Pina-Sanchez, and Marder (2018) note, Francis Galton remarked on the tendency of sentences to cluster around salient intervals in an article published in 1895 (note 20).

14. An early study of judges in California found that, despite the judges' stated reasons, in 90% of the cases the judges simply accepted the probation officer's recommendations. See Ebbesen and Konečni 1981; see also Konečni and Ebbesen 1982. Similar results have been found in the United Kingdom: see Dhami 2003 (finding that very simple three-factor heuristics correctly predicted the vast majority of bail decisions.)

15. An older meta-analysis found that gender did not predict verdict, but did impact sentence severity (Mazzella and Feingold 1994, 1327).

16. Studies with students serving the role of mock jurors or sentencing judges have produced similar results: MacCoun 1990; Mazella and Feingold 1994; Sigall and Ostrove 1975.

17. S. Danziger, J. Levav, & L Avnaim-Pesso. 2011. "Extraneous Factors in Judicial Decisions," Proceedings of the National Academy of Sciences 108 (17): 6889–6892; for critical discussion, see A. Glöckner. 2016. "The Irrational Hungry Judge Effect Revisited: Simulations Reveal That the Magnitude of the Effect Is Overestimated." Judgment and Decision Making 11(6): 601–610.

18. The authors also found that judges who delegated reason-writing were more confident in their decisions while in fact being more likely to be influenced by irrelevant factors (86).

References

Alicke, M. D. 1992. "Culpable Causation." Journal of Personality and Social Psychology 63 (3): pp. 368–378.

Burrell, J. 2016. "How the Machine 'Thinks': Understanding Opacity in Machine Learning Algorithms." Big Data & Society 3: pp. 1–12.

Carlson, A. M. 2017. "The Need for Transparency in the Age of Predictive Sentencing Algorithms." Iowa Law Review 103: pp. 303–329.

Citron, D. K., and F. Pasquale. 2014. "The Scored Society: Due Process for Automated Predictions." Washington Law Review 89: pp. 1–33.

Cobbe, J. 2019. "Administrative Law and the Machines of Government: Judicial Review of Automated Public-Sector Decision-Making." Legal Studies 39 (4): pp. 636–655.

Cohen, M. 2015. "When Judges Have Reasons Not to Give Reasons: A Comparative Law Approach." Washington & Lee Law Review 72: pp. 483–571.

Danziger, S., J. Levav, and L. Avnaim-Pesso. 2011. "Extraneous Factors in Judicial Decisions." Proceedings of the National Academy of Sciences 108 (17): pp. 6889–6892.

Deeks, A. 2019. "The Judicial Demand for Explainable Artificial Intelligence." Columbia Law Review 119 (7): pp. 1829–1850.

Dhami, M. K. 2003. "Psychological Models of Professional Decision Making." Psychological Science 14 (2): pp. 175–180.

Dhami, M. K., and P. Ayton. 2001. "Bailing and Jailing the Fast and Frugal Way." Journal of Behavioral Decision Making 14 (2): pp. 141–168.

Dhami, M. K., I. K. Belton, E. Merrall, A. McGrath, and S. M. Bird. 2020. "Criminal Sentencing by Preferred Numbers." Journal of Empirical Legal Studies 17 (1): pp. 139–163.

Doerner, J. K., and S. Demuth. 2014. "Gender and Sentencing in the Federal Courts: Are Women Treated More Leniently?" Criminal Justice Policy Review 25 (2): pp. 242–269.

Doshi-Velez, F., M. Kortz, R. Budish, C. Bavitz, S. Gershman, D. O'Brien, S. Schieber, J. Waldo, D. Weinberger, and A. Wood. 2017. "Accountability of AI under the Law: The Role of Explanation." ArXiv Preprint ArXiv:1711.01134.

Downs, A. C., and P. M. Lyons. 1991. "Natural Observations of the Links between Attractiveness and Initial Legal Judgments." Personality and Social Psychology Bulletin 17 (5): pp. 541–547.

Dutton, D. G., and A. P. Aron. 1974. "Some Evidence for Heightened Sexual Attraction under Conditions of High Anxiety." Journal of Personality and Social Psychology 30 (4): pp. 510–517.

Ebbesen, E. B., and V. J. Konečni. 1981. "The Process of Sentencing Adult Felons." In The Trial Process, edited by B. D. Sales, pp. 413–458. New York: Springer.

Edwards, L., and M. Veale. 2017. "Slave to the Algorithm: Why a Right to an Explanation Is Probably Not the Remedy You Are Looking For." Duke Law & Technology Review 16 (1): pp. 18–84.

Englich, B., T. Mussweiler, and F. Strack. 2006. "Playing Dice with Criminal Sentences: The Influence of Irrelevant Anchors on Experts' Judicial Decision Making." Personality and Social Psychology Bulletin 32 (2): pp. 188–200

European Court of Human Rights, Annual Report 127 (2019), available at: https://www.echr.coe.int/Documents/Annual_report_2019_ENG.pdf.

Fischer, P., T. Greitemeyer, A. Kastenmüller, D. Frey, and S. Oßwald. 2007. "Terror Salience and Punishment: Does Terror Salience Induce Threat to Social Order?" Journal of Experimental Social Psychology 43 (6): pp. 964–971.

Glöckner, A. 2016. "The Irrational Hungry Judge Effect Revisited: Simulations Reveal That the Magnitude of the Effect Is Overestimated." Judgment and Decision Making 11 (6): pp. 601–610.

Goodman-Delahunty, J., and S. L. Sporer. 2010. "Unconscious Influences in Sentencing Decisions: A Research Review of Psychological Sources of Disparity." Australian Journal of Forensic Sciences 42 (1): pp. 19–36.

Greene, J. D. 2008. "The Secret Joke of Kant's Soul." Moral Psychology 3: pp. 35–79.

Guthrie, C., J. J. Rachlinski, and A. J. Wistrich. 2007. "Blinking on the Bench: How Judges Decide Cases." Cornell Law Review 93(1): pp. 1–44.

Hannah-Moffat, K. 2013. "Actuarial Sentencing: An 'Unsettled' Proposition.'" Justice Quarterly 30 (2): pp. 270–296.

Henrich, J., S. J. Heine, and A. Norenzayan. 2010. "The Weirdest People in the World?" Behavioral and Brain Sciences 33 (2–3): pp. 61–83.

Kahan, D. M. 2012. "Ideology, Motivated Reasoning, and Cognitive Reflection: An Experimental Study." Judgment and Decision Making 8: pp. 407–424.

Kahan, D. M., D. A. Hoffman, D. Braman, and D. Evans. 2012. "They Saw a Protest: Cognitive Illiberalism and the Speech-Conduct Distinction." Stanford Law Review 64: pp. 851–906.

Kahan, D. M., D. Hoffman, D. Evans, N. Devins, E. Lucci, and K. Cheng. 2015. "Ideology or Situation Sense: An Experimental Investigation of Motivated Reasoning and Professional Judgment." University of Pennsylvania Law Review 164 (2): pp. 349–440.

Kahneman, D. 2003. "A Perspective on Judgment and Choice: Mapping Bounded Rationality." American Psychologist 58 (9): pp. 697–720.

Kehl, D. L., P. Guo, and S. A. Kessler. 2017. "Algorithms in the Criminal Justice System: Assessing the Use of Risk Assessments in Sentencing," available at: http://nrs.harvard.edu/urn-3:HUL.InstRepos:33746041.

Konecni, V. J., and E. B. Ebbesen. 1982. "The Criminal Justice System: A Social-Psychological Analysis." In An Analysis of the Sentencing System, edited by V. J. Koneckni and E. Ebbessen, pp. 293–332. New York: W. H. Freeman & Co.

Kroll, J. A., J. Huey, S. Barocas, E. W. Felten, J. R. Reidenberg, D. G. Robinson, and H. Yu. 2017. "Accountable Algorithms." University of Pennsylvania Law Review, 165 (3): pp. 633–706.

Lewis, C. 2021. "The Paradox of Recidivism." Emory Law Journal, 70 (6): pp. 1209–1271.

Liu, J. Z., and X. Li. 2019. "Legal Techniques for Rationalizing Biased Judicial Decisions: Evidence from Experiments with Real Judges." Journal of Empirical Legal Studies 16 (3): pp. 630–670.

Liu, Z. 2018. "Does Reason Writing Reduce Decision Bias? Experimental Evidence from Judges in China." Journal of Legal Studies 47 (1): pp. 83–118.

Lord, C. G., L. Ross, and M. R. Lepper. 1979. "Biased Assimilation and Attitude Polarization: The Effects of Prior Theories on Subsequently Considered Evidence." Journal of Personality and Social Psychology 37 (11): pp. 2098–2109.

MacCoun, R. J. 1990. "The Emergence of Extralegal Bias during Jury Deliberation." Criminal Justice and Behavior 17 (3): pp. 303–314.

MacCoun, R. J. 2006. "Psychological Constraints on Transparency in Legal and Government Decision Making," Swiss Political Science Review 12 (3): pp. 83–133.

Mazzella, R., and A. Feingold. 1994. "The Effects of Physical Attractiveness, Race, Socioeconomic Status, and Gender of Defendants and Victims on Judgments of Mock Jurors: A Meta-Analysis 1." Journal of Applied Social Psychology 24 (15): pp. 1315–1344.

Mitchell, O. 2005. "A Meta-Analysis of Race and Sentencing Research: Explaining the Inconsistencies." Journal of Quantitative Criminology 21 (4): pp. 439–466.

Mnookin, J. 2008. "Of Black Boxes, Instruments, and Experts: Testing the Validity of Forensic Science." Episteme 5 (3): pp. 343–358.

Nadler, J., and M.-H. McDonnell. 2012. "Moral Character, Motive, and the Psychology of Blame." Cornell Law Review 97 (2): pp. 255–304.

Nisbett, R. E., and T. D. Wilson. 1977a. "Telling More Than We Can Know: Verbal Reports on Mental Processes." Psychological Review 84 (3): pp. 231–259.

Nisbett, R. E., and T. D. Wilson. 1977b. "The Halo Effect: Evidence for Unconscious Alteration of Judgments." Journal of Personality and Social Psychology 35 (4): pp. 250–256.

Norton, M. I., J. A. Vandello, and J. M. Darley. 2004. "Casuistry and Social Category Bias." Journal of Personality and Social Psychology 87 (6): pp. 817–831.

Roberts, J. V., J. Sanchez, and I. Marder. 2018. "Individualisation at Sentencing: The Effects of Guidelines and 'Preferred' Numbers." Criminal Law Review 2: pp. 123–136.

Rudin, C. 2019. "Stop Explaining Black Box Machine Learning Models for High Stakes Decisions and Use Interpretable Models Instead." Nature Machine Intelligence 1(5): pp. 206–215.

Ryberg, J. 2021. " Sentencing and Algorithmic Transparency," this volume.

Sigall, H., and N. Ostrove. 1975. "Beautiful but Dangerous: Effects of Offender Attractiveness and Nature of the Crime on Juridic Judgment." Journal of Personality and Social Psychology 31 (3): pp. 410–414.

Sood, A. M., and J. M. Darley. 2012. "The Plasticity of Harm in the Service of Criminalization Goals." California Law Review 100 (5): pp. 1313–1358.

Spamann, H., and L. Klöhn. 2016. "Justice Is Less Blind, and Less Legalistic, Than We Thought: Evidence from an Experiment with Real Judges." Journal of Legal Studies 45(2): pp. 255–280.

Steffensmeier, D., and S. Demuth. 2006. "Does Gender Modify the Effects of Race–Ethnicity on Criminal Sanctioning? Sentences for Male and Female White, Black, and Hispanic Defendants." Journal of Quantitative Criminology 22 (3): pp. 241–261.

Tversky, A., and D. Kahneman. 1981. "The Framing of Decisions and the Psychology of Choice." Science 211 (4481): pp. 453–458.

Van Alsenoy, B., E. Kosta, and J. Dumortier. 2014. "Privacy Notices versus Informational Self-Determination: Minding the Gap." International Review of Law, Computers & Technology 28 (2): pp. 185–203.

Wachter, S., B. Mittelstadt, and L. Floridi. 2017. "Why a Right to Explanation of Automated Decision-Making Does Not Exist in the General Data Protection Regulation." International Data Privacy Law 7 (2): pp. 76–99.

Walmsley, J. 2020. "Artificial Intelligence and the Value of Transparency." AI & Society 36, pp. 585–595.

Wang, X., D. P. Mears, C. Spohn, and L. Dario. 2013. "Assessing the Differential Effects of Race and Ethnicity on Sentence Outcomes under Different Sentencing Systems." Crime & Delinquency 59 (1): pp. 87–114.

Wexler, R. 2018. "Life, Liberty, and Trade Secrets: Intellectual Property in the Criminal Justice System." Stanford Law Review 70: pp. 1343–1429.

Wilson, T. D. 2004. Strangers to Ourselves. Cambridge, MA: Harvard University Press.

Wisser, L. 2019. "Pandora's Algorithmic Black Box: The Challenges of Using Algorithmic Risk Assessments in Sentencing." American Criminal Law Review 56 (4): pp. 1811–1832.

Wistrich, A. J., J. J. Rachlinski, and C. Guthrie. 2015. "Heart versus Head: Do Judges Follow the Law of Follow Their Feelings." Texas Law Review 93 (4): pp. 855–923.

Yang, C. S. 2015. "Free at Last? Judicial Discretion and Racial Disparities in Federal Sentencing." Journal of Legal Studies 44 (1): pp. 75–111.

Statutes

18 USC §3553(c) (2012).

Administrative Procedures and Jurisdiction Act, RSA 2000, c A3, s 7 (Alberta).

Administrative Tribunals Act, SBC 2004, c 45, s 51 (British Columbia).

Administrative Procedure Act, §555(e) and §706(2)(A) (USA)

Animal Welfare Act 2006 (UK), s 34(8)(a).

Anti-Terrorism, Crime and Security Act 2001 (UK), Sch 3.

Enterprise Act 2002 (UK), s 38(2).

Justice Reform Act, Art. 33, https://www.legifrance.gouv.fr/eli/loi/2019/3/23/2019-222/jo/article_33.

Statutory Powers Procedure Act, RSO 1990, c S 22, ss 3(1), 17(1) (Ontario).

Tribunals and Inquiries Act 1992 (UK), c 53, s 10(1).

Cases

2127423 Manitoba Ltd v Unicity Taxi Ltd, 2012 MBCA 75*Act respecting Administrative Justice*, CQLR, c J3, s 8 (Quebec).

Baker v. Canada, [1999] 2 SCR 817.

Basanti v. Canada (Citizenship and Immigration), 2019 FC 1068.

Massachusetts v. E.P.A., 549 U.S. 497 (2007).

Motor Vehicle Mfg. Ass'n of the U.S., Inc. v. State Farm Mut. Auto. Ins. Co., 463 U.S. 29 (1983).

Newfoundland and Labrador Nurses' Union v Newfoundland and Labrador (Treasury Board), 2011 SCC 62.

R v Secretary of State for the Home Department, ex parte Doody, [1994] 1 AC 531.

Rita v. United States, 551 U.S. 338 (2007).

Stefan v General Medical Council, [1999] 1 WLR 1293.

The Queen on the Application of Hasan v The Secretary of State for Trade and Industry, [2008] EWCA Civ 1312 at paras 19–20.

4

Sentencing and the Conflict between Algorithmic Accuracy and Transparency

Jesper Ryberg and Thomas S. Petersen

Algorithmic transparency constitutes one of the cardinal issues in the ethical discussion of artificial intelligence. This is true both in relation to the broader societal use of algorithmic tools and in relation to the narrower application of algorithms in sentencing. There are two different reasons as to why an algorithm may lack transparency. As discussed in previous chapters (see Ryberg 2021a and Chiao 2021, this volume), an algorithm may constitute a black box either because it is proprietary—that is, it is protected by trade secrecy—or because it is too complicated for a human to understand. The first cause of opacity could—at least in principle—be easily prevented. This could be done by insisting on the requirement—suggested by several theorists in relation to algorithms used in sentencing—that the inner workings of such algorithms be made fully transparent.[1]

With regard to the second source of opacity—which constitutes the focus of this chapter—there is not an equally straightforward answer. There is little point in insisting that an algorithm should be made transparent if it is too complex and, therefore, by its nature, inherently opaque. Thus, the use of complicated algorithms—such as various types of machine learning algorithms—constitutes a particular challenge. Many theorists have expressed serious concern about the use of such algorithms (see Ryberg 2021b). In fact, it has even been suggested that such black box algorithms should not be used at all in high-stakes decision-making that may have serious impacts on the well-being and lives of citizens—which, of course, is precisely what characterizes sentencing decisions (see, e.g., Rudin 2019; Rudin and Radin 2019).

Jesper Ryberg and Thomas S. Petersen, *Sentencing and the Conflict between Algorithmic Accuracy and Transparency*
In: *Sentencing and Artificial Intelligence*. Edited by: Jesper Ryberg and Julian V. Roberts, Oxford University Press.
© Oxford University Press 2022. DOI: 10.1093/oso/9780197539538.003.0004

In this light, it is not surprising that increasing attention has been directed to the possibility of developing and implementing transparent algorithms. A transparency requirement could be satisfied either by drawing on explainable artificial intelligence (xAI), such as where a second system is post hoc created to explain the first black box system, or by developing and employing systems that are themselves inherently interpretable.[2] However, a frequent assumption has been that the invocation of more transparent algorithms may well not be cost-free. For instance, as Finale Doshi-Veles et al. note, in relation to "explainable algorithmic decision-making," there are concerns that an "explanation would come at the price of some other performance objective, such as decreased system accuracy" (Doshi-Veles et al. 2017, 1). Correspondingly, as explained by computer scientist David Gunning and his colleagues: "There may be inherent conflict between ML [machine learning] performance (e.g., predictive accuracy) and explainability. Often, the highest performing methods (e.g., DL [deep learning]) are the least explainable, and the most explainable (e.g., decision trees) are the least accurate" (Gunning et al. 2019, 1).[3] In fact, as computer scientist Cynthia Rudin has underlined in a recent *Nature* article, the idea of a trade-off between predictive accuracy, on the one hand, and interpretability/explainability on the other, seems to be explicitly or implicitly assumed in most discussions of transparency and machine learning models (Rudin 2019). However, insofar as there is such a conflict, this seems to give rise to a serious dilemma.[4]

In relation to sentencing, it has repeatedly been underlined that some degree of transparency is desirable when algorithms are implicated in decision-making by the courts. However, it is clear that accuracy is usually regarded as the gold standard of a crime predictive tool. If an algorithm is supposed to produce trustworthy risk assessments by predicting the likelihood that offenders will engage in future criminal conduct, then it is crucial that such predictions are very accurate. Therefore, if it is the case that an attempt to avoid black box algorithms in favor of more transparent systems will result in a reduction in predictive accuracy, or if the attempt to reach more accurate crime predictions will lead to a loss in transparency, then one seems to be placed in an uncomfortable situation. The purpose of the present chapter is to reflect on the nature of this dilemma.

As anyone with an insight into philosophical value theory will know, there is ongoing discussion about how conflicts in values should be interpreted and handled. This discussion comprises considerations of questions such as whether all moral values are commensurable, whether some values always trump others, or whether there exist either a plurality of values or simply a single basic value underlying all other value assessments. However, the goal of this chapter is not to enter into such traditional axiological considerations. Rather, the point will be to show that the question concerning the conflict between interpretability and accuracy may sometimes in itself be manageable in the sense that, once one engages in considerations of *why* interpretability and accuracy are desirable in relation to sentencing, the conflict between these two goals may either lack genuine moral significance or be one that can be handled even before one needs to enter more basic axiological considerations of how genuine trade-offs should be resolved. In this sense, the chapter aims to show the significance of engaging in more profound analyses of why some of the standard values that are frequently highlighted in relation to the application of algorithmic guidance—also when it comes to sentencing decisions—are ethically important.

4.1 Overview

In order to develop and sustain these ideas, the chapter will proceed as follows. Section 4.2 considers to what extent a conflict between transparency and predictive accuracy constitutes a genuine ethical problem. Focusing on the ethical significance of transparency, it will be suggested that there may be cases where—even though they do contain such a conflict—this does not, on closer scrutiny, constitute an *ethical* conflict after all. In section 4.3, the same point will be sustained on the ground of considerations concerning the significance of crime predictive accuracy. In section 4.4, it is argued that even in cases involving a morally significant conflict between interpretability and accuracy, it is not necessarily the case that this conflict can only be resolved by engaging in considerations of how interpretability should be weighed against accuracy. There may be other ways of dissolving such conflicts. Section 4.5 outlines some of the theoretical and practical implications of the previous conclusions. Finally, section 4.6 summarizes and concludes.

However, before embarking on these considerations, two minor comments on the scope and assumptions of the discussion should be made. First, we do not discuss whether algorithmic tools should be used in sentencing decisions. For instance, we will not be considering whether predictions of future criminal conduct should play a role at sentencing. Some penal theorists might reject such a role. However, in the following it will be assumed that algorithms designed for this purpose may serve a legitimate goal (see, e.g., Bagaric and Hunter 2021, this volume).[5]

Second, and more importantly, we do not wish to suggest that there is *always* a conflict between the interpretability of an algorithm and the performance of this algorithm in terms of predictive accuracy.[6] Even though, as noted, such a conflict seems to be assumed in many discussions of complicated machine learning models, it has also been underlined that there may sometimes be a tendency to overstate this conflict. For instance, Rudin has recently argued that there is a widespread assumption of such a conflict even when it is not real. As she points out, there are cases where less complex algorithms provide predictions that are just as accurate as more complex black box systems. An example is the algorithm known as Certifiable Optimal Rule Lists (CORELS). This works by looking for if-then patterns in data concerning age and criminal history (the simple machine learning model is the following: if an offender has either >3 prior crimes, or is 18–20 years old and male, or is 21–23 years old and has two or three prior crimes, they are predicted to recidivate within a two-year period, otherwise not (see Rudin and Radin 2019, 4; Angelino et al. 2018)). This model is free and transparent and, notably, seems to produce just as accurate predictions of recidivism as the COMPAS algorithm—widely used in US jurisdictions—which is an inaccessible "black box" operating with 130 + factors. More generally, what Rudin suggests is that an alleged conflict between interpretability and accuracy may sometimes be the result of the fact that researchers are trained in deep learning, but not in interpretable machine learning, and—not least—that it may be easier for private companies to profit from algorithms that are opaque. The inclination to develop interpretable systems at the same performance level may therefore be very limited. Awareness of such tendencies to maintain and overstate a conflict between interpretability and accuracy is, of course, important. For instance, as we will shortly discuss, it may be important in considerations of what requirements the state should place on companies that develop and sell algorithmic tools used in public decision-making. However, in the present chapter the main purpose will be to show that, in addition to these reasons and inclinations to overstate the conflict, there can be reasons to challenge the ethical significance of the conflict even when it is genuine.

4.2 Transparency and Non-significant Conflicts

As a starting point, let us assume that we are faced with a choice between risk assessment algorithms designed to predict the probability that an offender will recidivate. Furthermore, let us assume that there is a genuine conflict between the interpretability and the predictive accuracy of these algorithms in the sense that, if one opts for a less complicated machine learning model, which is more interpretable, this will result in a loss in predictive accuracy and vice versa.[7] In other words, what we have is a genuine conflict between interpretability and accuracy. However, this does not necessarily mean that this conflict is of *ethical* significance. That is, it may still be possible to answer which algorithm is ethically preferable without engaging in any kind of trade-off considerations. The explanation is that the answer is contingent on the question of *why* interpretability is morally salient.

Suppose that the explanation of why interpretability is ethically significant is that insight into how input data result in output predictions is important in order to uphold public confidence and the perceived legitimacy of the criminal justice system. Whether there is empirical evidence supporting this contention is not important here. The explanation is meant only as an illustration (for a more thorough discussion of this argument, see Ryberg 2021a, this volume). On the grounds of this reason, we can imagine that public confidence would decrease if the criminal court made sentencing decisions (partly) on the ground of an algorithm that was inscrutable and evading proper interpretation. However, this need not imply that any variation in the degree of interpretability would be reflected in a corresponding degree of public confidence. For instance, it might be the case that public confidence is simply not sensitive to minor changes in the degree of interpretability or that, once a certain level of interpretability has been reached, any further increases in the adequacy or detail of an explanation is no longer followed by an increase in public confidence. Now, in such situations there will, from an ethical perspective, no longer be an ethical conflict in the choice between the algorithms. If we can choose either between more interpretability/less accuracy or less interpretability/more accuracy then we should ceteris paribus opt for the latter. Even though it involves less interpretability, this does not imply a loss with regard to what makes interpretability morally valuable. In other words, the choice can be made without engaging in any kind of trade-off considerations.

In fact, it is also possible that this reasoning can be repeated at an even more basic level. Suppose we wish to dig even deeper into ethical reasoning by asking why public confidence and trust in the criminal court system is of moral significance. Suppose, for the sake of the argument, that the answer is that public confidence is important in order to uphold public engagement and cooperation with the criminal justice system (e.g., the general willingness to call the police or serve as witnesses). In this case, it might be possible that there is no simple correlation between the level of public confidence and the degree to which people are willing to cooperate with the system. That is, it might be the case that the public willingness to cooperate is either not sensitive to minor change in the level of confidence or that once a sufficient level of confidence has been reached in the public, any further increase in that level will add nothing further to the willingness to cooperate. However, if such were the case, then we would have a situation where a further increase in transparency would not—ethically speaking—add anything of significance. In other words, if we could choose between either more interpretability/ less accuracy or less interpretability/more accuracy then—even if more interpretability would this time be followed by more public confidence—this would still not make this alternative any more desirable because the reason usually supporting the significance of confidence would in this case no longer be increased (i.e., it would not lead to further public cooperation with the criminal justice system). Therefore, once again there would not be a genuine moral conflict. That is, we should opt for less interpretability/more accuracy, not because this is what follows from some sort of trade-off, but simply because the latter alternative is better in one respect without being worse in another.

What these considerations show is that, even if there is a conflict between interpretability and the accuracy of algorithmic tools, the conclusion that an answer to this conflict requires some sort of trade-off is premature. There may be conflicts between interpretability and accuracy—such that an increase in the former implies a decrease in the latter and vice versa—which do not involve a genuine *ethical* conflict. However, this will only be known if one engages in considerations of why interpretability is ethically valuable. It should of course be acknowledged that the previous considerations are hypothetical. We have not argued that the reasons that actually constitute the most plausible explanation of why interpretability of an algorithmic prediction is morally important will behave in such way that they are not necessarily weakened when the level of interpretability decreases. Moreover, there may be several independent reasons sustaining the contention that interpretability is morally important (which makes it less likely that there will be cases in which these reasons will be unaffected by a decrease in interpretability). However, as we shall now see, there may be another type of case in which a conflict between interpretability and accuracy does not involve a genuine ethical conflict.

4.3 Predictive Accuracy and Ethically Non-significant Conflicts

Suppose again that we are faced with a choice between risk assessment algorithms involving either a higher level of interpretability and a lower level of predictive accuracy or vice versa. Suppose also that the lower level of interpretability will be ethically significant in the sense that it implies a decrease in whatever makes algorithmic interpretability ethically important. Would we then be confronted with a genuine ethical conflict that calls for consideration concerning a trade-off between interpretability and accuracy? At first sight, the answer would seem to be affirmative. After all, if predictive algorithms are designed with the very purpose of predicting crime, then it seems obvious to expect that something valuable would be lost (or diminished) if one opts for a less accurate algorithm. How could a more accurate algorithm possibly fail to be ethically preferable to one that is less accurate? Though this prima facie is hard to believe and even though it is standardly assumed in the literature that a more accurate algorithm is preferable to one less accurate—at least when all else is equal—in the following, we argue that this is not necessarily the case.[8] This will, thereby, provide further support to the earlier conclusion that a conflict between interpretability and accuracy need not reflect a genuine ethical conflict.

If an algorithm is used in sentencing decisions, then there will of course usually be serious consequences if it is inaccurate. However, the reason that a more accurate algorithm need not always be ethically preferable to one that produces less accurate predictions, has to do with the fact that ethical assessment of such predictive tools is not only a function of accuracy, but also of the types of error these tools produce. A risk assessment algorithm may make two types of fallacious prediction: false negatives (predictions of no reoffending when this would have occurred) and false positives (predictions of reoffending when this would not have occurred). The question that arises, therefore, is how should these two types of errors be morally assessed? The answer depends upon how precisely risk assessments are used at sentencing. However, suppose *arguendo* that a high-risk assessment results in the imposition of a longer prison term than the one that would have been imposed had the person been considered a low-risk offender.[9] In this case, the consequences of erroneous predictions might be the following.

First, with regard to false negatives, the cost of this prediction would consist in the harm that is caused when the offender recidivates (and which, arguably, could have been prevented had the offender been considered a (true) positive). It will of course be very difficult to estimate the magnitude of this harm in advance, since the risk assessment tool might only predict reoffending—not the type of crime that will be committed. As Rhys Hester rightly notes, "high-risk does not indicate the risk of *what*" (Hester 2019, 218). And even though some risk assessment tools are designed to make predictions of certain categories of crimes—such as violent crime—individual instances of crime in this broad category may well vary significantly in the amount of harm they produce (Ryberg 2020, 255). What is important here is that the cost of false negative predictions consists (mainly) of criminal harm.

Second, when it comes to the costs of false positive predictions, the picture is very different. As noted, the cost of this kind of error will depend upon how the criminal justice system reacts to the risk of future criminal conduct. If it is the case—as we have assumed before—that the fact that a person is considered a high-risk offender implies that he or she will receive a longer prison term, then the cost of an erroneous prediction will amount to the extra harm caused by spending additional time behind bars.

The picture of the harms that follows from erroneous predictions might, of course, be more complicated than suggested by these examples. However, it may suffice to illustrate the point that is important here, namely, that a more accurate risk assessment algorithm need not be ethically preferable to one less accurate. In fact, this can easily be demonstrated. Suppose for the sake of argument that the criminal justice system robustly reacts to false positive predictions of reoffending by imposing on offenders in this category a much longer prison term. Suppose, furthermore, that the crimes committed by those who are false negatives are not overly serious (in fact, this assumption is not unrealistic: as Hester has observed on the grounds of studies in Pennsylvania, "most 'high-risk' offenders are also

low-stake offenders who do not pose a serious threat to public safety"
(Hester 2019, 218)). In this case, a less accurate risk algorithm might be
ethically preferable to one more accurate if its ratio of false positives and
false negatives is such that there is a lower rate of the former type of error
but higher of the latter (see also Ryberg 2020, 255). In simple terms, under
such circumstances, the harm caused by a certain number of minor crimes
might be less than the harm resulting from a minor number of instances
of significantly prolonged periods of imprisonment. Conversely, suppose
instead that the crimes committed by those who reoffend are quite serious
and that the criminal justice system does not react very strictly to predicted
positives. In this case a, less accurate algorithm might be ethically preferable if its balance of false positives and false positives is such that, in comparison to a more accurate algorithm, it produces fewer of the latter errors
and more of the former. Simply put, under such circumstances, a smaller
number of crimes may result in more harm than a larger number of only
moderately extended prison terms.

What these considerations establish is that the ethical assessment of a predictive algorithm is not only dependent on the merits in terms of predictive
accuracy, but also on the error profile of the algorithm and, therefore, that
a more accurate algorithm—when used in high-stake cases such as in relation to sentencing decisions—is not always ethically preferable. As one of
us has argued elsewhere, there are other situations than the earlier outlined
scenarios where less accurate predictions would be preferable to some that
are more accurate.[10] However, there is no need to develop these cases here.
What matters is that if we have a situation in which there is a choice between
a more interpretable/less accurate or a less interpretable/more accurate algorithm, this need not involve a genuine ethical conflict in the sense that the
assessment of which alterative is preferable would require trade-off considerations. Rather, if we have cases such as those outlined before, and if a more
interpretable algorithm is preferable to one that is less interpretable, then
we should simply opt for the more interpretable but less accurate alternative. Contrary to what the choice at first sight seems to imply, this alternative
would be better in one respect without being worse in another. Thus, these
considerations reaffirm the conclusion of the previous section—although for
different reasons. As to the further implications of this conclusion, we will return to these shortly. However, first there is another aspect of the discussion
of how a conflict between transparency and accuracy might be resolved that
should be addressed.

4.4 Resolving Ethical Conflicts between Interpretability and Accuracy

Let us again assume a conflict between the interpretability and accuracy of algorithms used to predict future criminal conduct. Moreover, let us this time also assume that this reflects a genuine conflict between the reasons that make interpretability and accuracy important—that is, in contrast to what we have considered earlier, this is a conflict of ethical significance—such that we cannot choose the less interpretable algorithm without losing something of ethical value and, correspondingly, cannot opt for the less accurate algorithm without facing a genuine ethical loss. As we shall now see, even if all this is the case, it does not necessarily follow that the choice between the two algorithms must require some sort of trade-off between interpretability and accuracy. How can this possibly be?

The simple answer is that there may be other ways of preventing the ethical costs that would follow from the choice of the less interpretable algorithm over the more interpretable algorithm. Suppose, for instance, that the reason that transparency is important in relation to sentencing decisions is that interpretability will have an impact on a defendant's perception of procedural justice (see Ryberg 2021a, this volume). If there is only limited transparency with regard to the reasons that the defendant is considered a high-risk offender, then this will result in a lack of trust in the decisions made by the court. However, there may be other ways of influencing and counteracting the loss of perceived procedural justice. Suppose, as is usually the case, that the predictive algorithm is used as a support system on which a judge can draw in the final decision-making. In this case, it might be possible that remedial efforts by the judge may help in preventing the loss of perceived procedural justice that would, everything else being equal, have followed from the use of the less transparent algorithm. For instance, the judge may make a greater effort to clarify the input factors, to explain why an algorithm constitutes a superior predictive instrument to assessments made by humans, or engage in a dialogue with the defendant, which in other ways could counter concerns. Now, the point of these examples is neither to suggest that there is empirical evidence to the effects of such efforts on the experience of procedural justice—nor to hold that judges always possess the requisite knowledge of the workings of an algorithm—but simply to note that, if perceived procedural justice is affectable by other means, then there may be ways of preventing the loss of procedural justice that would otherwise have followed from the use of the less transparent algorithm had everything else been equal.

Many other examples underlining this point can of course be envisaged. For instance, suppose instead that transparency is important because it increases the likelihood of detecting various types of error in an algorithm (see also Ryberg 2021a, this volume). In this case, it would—everything else being equal—be problematic to use a less transparent algorithm. However, once again everything else need not be equal. It could be the case that it would be possible to detect algorithmic errors by introducing new procedures to subject the algorithm to regular scrutiny and audits by expert teams. If this were possible, one would then have the possibility of opting for the less transparent algorithm without costs, while at the same time gaining the advantages that, presumably, would be associated with the use of a more accurate algorithm.

These examples illustrate that if it is the case that those reasons that make the transparency of an algorithm ethically significant are also affectable in ways other than by changing the level of transparency, then it might be possible to prevent the loss that ceteris paribus would follow from the use of a less transparent algorithm by, in other ways, intensifying or increasing the factors that make transparency ethically important. By introducing procedures designed for this purpose, one would transform the conflict between transparency and accuracy into something no longer a genuine ethical conflict. It might perhaps be objected that this idea of introducing other means to prevent the costs that, everything else being equal, would have followed from the use of a less transparent algorithm is unrealistic. After all, if such means really exist, one should expect that they would have already been introduced in sentencing practice prior to any choices between algorithms of varying levels of transparency and accuracy. However, there is little evidence to support the view that the sentencing process always functions in a way that is ethically optimal (e.g., many commentators have underlined that judges often possess limited knowledge of how the algorithm works and, consequently, that there is often room for improvement). Furthermore, and more importantly, it might be the case that a procedure introduced to prevent the loss that would have followed from the introduction of a less transparent algorithm would only become relevant precisely because there would be such a loss in transparency (for instance, there would be no point in introducing expert audits of an algorithm if, from the outset, they were fully transparent). Thus, this objection does not undermine the main point of this section, namely, to underline the significance of the fact that, in the comparison between more or less transparent algorithms, everything else need not be equal.[11]

4.5 The Significance of Dissolving the Conflict

The point of the discussion so far is not that there are no genuine ethical conflicts between transparency and accuracy. Rather, it has been to show that a conflict need not constitute a genuine ethical conflict and, furthermore, that genuine conflicts may sometimes be resolvable without engaging in trade-offs. But why is this important? Is this just an abstruse academic exercise? In our view, these conclusions are noteworthy for both theoretical and practical reasons.

First, the previous considerations are important in the simple sense that they demonstrate that discussion of transparency and predictive accuracy of algorithmic tools is more complicated than is often realized. It is not uncommon to encounter the view that the transparency of an algorithm is ethically significant, followed by the contention that a more transparent algorithm must be regarded as preferable to a less transparent one. In particular, there is a tendency to assume that a more accurate algorithm must be preferable to one that is less accurate. However, as we have seen, both contentions are premature. Realizing this should introduce more care into theoretical discussions.

Second, the considerations may also have more practical implications with regard to expectations from companies and other parties involved in the development of algorithmic risk assessment tools. Rudin has strongly objected to what she calls the "myth" of the accuracy/interpretability trade-off, which consists of the assumption that a higher degree of interpretability must always be followed by a loss in accuracy and vice versa. In her view, this belief fails to understand that it may be possible to design inherently interpretable systems that produce equally accurate predictions. Since, as we have seen, she believes that this myth is fostered partly by profit considerations of the companies that develop the systems, what she suggests is, firstly, that when it comes to high-stake decisions—such as sentencing decisions—"no black box should be deployed when there exists an interpretable model with the same level of performance" (Rudin 2019, 9). This requirement would make it possible to hold companies accountable when they engage in unnecessary "black boxing." Secondly, she also suggests that when a company introduces a black box model, it should be "mandated to report the accuracy of interpretable modeling methods" (2019, 9). As she argues, if such a requirement is observed one "could more easily determine whether the accuracy/interpretability trade-off claimed by the organization is worthwhile" (2019, 9). However, as we have seen earlier, the assessment of a model's predictive performance is not only a function of its accuracy but also of the types of error it produces. Thus, in order to obtain a more adequate background for assessing whether a company's trade-offs are acceptable, it seems reasonable to expand this proposal by also requiring insight into the error profiles (the ratios of false positives and false negatives) of both the black box model and competing interpretable models. This would provide more appropriate grounds for a comparison.

Third, the fact that it may sometimes be possible to counter the problems associated with a lack of transparency by other means than by merely increasing the level of transparency, also has important practical implications. While Rudin directs attention to the "myth" of accuracy/interpretability trade-offs in order to highlight the problematic tendency to ignore the possibility of "accurate-yet-interpretable" models, there is another myth of the accuracy/interpretability trade-off. This is the tendency to assume that answers to cases involving a genuine conflict between accuracy and transparency must involve engagement in trade-offs. However, as we have seen, this assumption is premature. Once it is realized that transparency is of instrumental value and that the reasons that makes transparency ethically significant may also be affectable in other ways than by changing the level of transparency, it becomes clear that there may be various types of solution to what, on the surface, seems to constitute a transparency challenge. A lack of engagement in the more basic considerations of the reasons that explain why transparency is of ethical significance may blind one to the possibility of alternative solutions. Even though it will require further theoretical elaboration to devise such alternative solutions, this nevertheless shows that the earlier considerations are not merely of theoretical interest. They may very well end up influencing practical decision-making.

4.6 Conclusion

There are two obvious ways of reacting to conflicts between transparency and accuracy of risk prediction algorithms. First, to assume this constitutes an ethical conflict. Second, to assume that this conflict can only be resolved by a trade-off between transparency and accuracy. The purpose of this chapter has been to show that both reactions are premature.

First, it has been argued that even if we have a choice between algorithmic systems involving either a higher level of accuracy and a lower level of transparency or vice versa, this need not constitute an ethical challenge. Insofar as the underlying values that usually make transparency ethically significant are not reduced by opting for the higher level of accuracy, this choice will be ethically trivial; likewise, if the lower level of predictive accuracy does not produce a worse outcome. That is, in such cases the answer to the conflict between transparency and accuracy will be straightforward. Second, even when we are faced with a choice between algorithms that involves a genuine ethical conflict between transparency and accuracy, a solution to this conflict need not entail that either accuracy or transparency be compromised. In some cases, a solution may involve addressing the factors that make transparency ethically significant in ways other than by changing the level of transparency. Finally, it was argued that these considerations have theoretical and practical implications.

Obviously, these considerations do not per se bring us further with regard to the crucial question of how genuine conflicts between transparency and accuracy should ultimately be resolved. However, failure to recognize our conclusions may, as indicated, create the risk that various pitfalls and fallacies will enter the discussion of the legitimate use of crime predictive algorithms—which, by its very nature, is already both ethically and empirically complicated.

Notes

1. See, for instance, the recommendations for the use of risk assessment algorithms in Kehl et al. 2017.
2. For a discussion of the distinction between, and advantages of, interpretability over explainability, see, e.g., Rudin 2019.
3. For a brief overview of performance versus explainability trade-offs for different machine learning techniques, see Gunning et al. 2019.
4. For the purpose of the arguments to be presented in the following, there is no reason to distinguish between explainability and interpretability (for a discussion of this distinction, see Rudin 2019). Thus, for reasons of ease in exposition, we will henceforth simply talk of interpretability.
5. For a defense of the view that consequences should have *some* role to play, even within a full-blown retributivist theory of punishment, see, e.g., Ryberg (2019). For a general

discussion of both the normative and empirical aspects of the use of risk assessments in sentencing, see De Keijser et al. (2019).

6. In some situations, it might even be the case that an increase in interpretability will increase the level of accuracy. For instance, as Deeks suggests: "shedding light on how an algorithm produces its recommendations can help address . . . observers to identify biases and errors in algorithm" (Deeks 2019, 1833). Along the same lines, Rudin holds that in some cases, "the accuracy/interpretability tradeoff is reversed—more interpretability leads to better overall accuracy" (Rudin 2019, 2).

7. We are here assuming that not only accuracy but also interpretability is a matter of degree.

8. The considerations in this section draw on arguments presented in Ryberg (2020).

9. This could be the case either if high-risk offenders are sentenced more severely than offenders would have been punished for the crime in question had risk assessment tools not been applied, or because low-risk offenders are being punished less severely than they would have been punished had such tools not been applied. To avoid misunderstandings, we are not suggesting that it is always the case that a longer punishment of high risk offenders will result in the prevention of more crimes. In real life, there are many problems associated with the use of risk assessments as a factor in the determination of the length of a sentence (see, e.g., de Keijser et al. 2019).

10. These situations comprise cases in which algorithmic tools are used within a sentencing system that punishes offenders too severely, or where the use of one algorithm rather than another will have an impact on the number of offenders whose sentences, at least partly, are determined on the grounds of risk assessments. For a comprehensive discussion of why a less accurate algorithm may under such circumstances be ethically preferable to one that is more accurate, see Ryberg (2020, 256–261).

11. In principle, a parallel argument could also be made with regard to the use of less accurate algorithms. That is, there may be alternative ways of countering the ethical loss that would follow from making sentencing decisions on the grounds of an algorithm that is less rather than more accurate. However, changes that would have such an effect are probably much less realistic. Furthermore, there is no reason to elaborate on such possibilities in order to make the point of this section.

References

Angelino, E. et al. 2018. "Learning Certifiably Optimal Rule Lists for Categorical Data." Journal of Machine Learning Research 18: pp. 1–78.

Bagaric, M. and D. Hunter 2021. "Enhancing the Integrity of the Sentencing Process through the Use of Artificial Intelligence." In Sentencing and Artificial Intelligence, edited by J. Ryberg and J. V. Roberts. New York: Oxford University Press.

Chiao, V. 2021. "Transparency at Sentencing: Are Human Judges More Transparent than Algorithms?" In Sentencing and Artificial Intelligence, edited by J. Ryberg and J. V. Roberts. New York: Oxford University Press.

Deeks, A. 2019. "The Judicial Demand for Explainable Artificial intelligence." Columbia Law Review 119: pp. 1829–1850.

Doshi-Velez, F. et al. 2017. "The Role of Explanation in Algorithmic Trust." online: https://www.semanticscholar.org/paper/The-Role-of-Explanation-in-Algorithmic-Trust-%E2%88%97-Ryan-Doshi-Velez-Budish/6718a458f18e1889385dbf6aaa79236def01465a?p2df.

Douglas, T. et al. 2017. "Risk Assessment Tools in Criminal Justice and Forensic Psychiatry: The Need for Better Data." European Psychiatry 42: pp. 134–137.

Fazel, S. et al. 2012. "Use of Risk Assessment Instrument to Predict Violence and Antisocial Behaviour in 73 Samples Involving 24827 People: Systematic Review and Meta-Analysis." British Medical Journal 345: pp. 1–12.

Gunning, D. et al. 2019. "XAI—Explainable Artificial Intelligence." Science Robotics 4: pp. 1–2.

Hester, R. 2019. "Risk Assessment at Sentencing: The Pennsylvania Experience." In Predictive Sentencing: Normative and Empirical Perspectives, edited by J. de Keiser et al., pp. 213–238. Oxford: Hart Publishing.

Kehl, D. et al. 2017. "Algorithms in the Criminal Justice System: Assessing the Use of Risk Assessment in Sentencing." Responsive Communities (online).

Keijser, J., J. V. Roberts, and J. Ryberg (eds.) 2019. Predictive Sentencing. Oxford: Hart Publishing.

Kim, T. W., and B. R. Routledge. 2018. "Informational Privacy, A Right to Explanation, and Interpretable AI." IEEE Symposium on Privacy-Aware Computing (online).

Kizilcec, R. F. 2016. "How Much Information: Effects of Transparency on Trust in an Algorithmic Interface." Proceedings of the 2016 CHI Conference on Human Factors in Computer Systems: pp. 2390–2395.

Lee, M. K. 2018. "Understanding Perception of Algorithmic Decisions: Fairness, Trust, and Emotion in Response to Algorithmic Management." Big Data and Society, January–June: pp. 1–16.

Lehr, D., and P. Ohm. 2017. "Playing with the Data: What Legal Scholars Should Learn About Machine Learning." University of California Davis Law Review 51: pp. 655–719.

Lepri, B. et al. 2017. "Fair, Transparent, and Accountable Algorithmic Decision-Making Process." Philosophy and Technology 31: pp. 611–627.

Roth, A. 2016. "Trial by Machine." Georgia Law Journal 104: pp. 1245–1305.

Rudin, C. 2019. "Stop Explaining Black Box Machine Learning Models for High Stakes Decisions and Use Interpretable Models Instead." Nature Machine Intelligence 1: pp. 206–215.

Rudin, C., and J. Radin. 2019. "Why Are We Using Black Box Models in AI When We Don't Need To? A Lesson from an Explainable AI Competition." Harvard Data Science Review 1 (2): pp. 1–9.

Ryberg, J. 2019. "Risk and Retribution. On the Possibility of Reconciling Considerations of Dangerousness and Desert." In Predictive Sentencing: Normative and Empirical Perspectives, edited by J. de Keijser et al., pp. 51–68. Oxford: Hart Publishing.

Ryberg, J. 2020. "Risk Assessment and Algorithmic Accuracy." Ethical Theory and Moral Practice 23: pp. 251–263.

Ryberg, J. 2021a. "Sentencing and Algorithmic Transparency." In Sentencing and Artificial Intelligence, edited by J. Ryberg and J. Roberts, pp. 13–33. New York: Oxford University Press.

Ryberg, J. 2021b. "Sentencing Disparity and Artificial Intelligence." The Journal of Value Inquiry (online first).

Simmons, R. 2018. "Big Data, Machine Judges, and the Legitimacy of the Criminal Justice System." University of California Davis Law Review 52: pp. 1–39.

Springer, A., and S. Whittaker. 2018. "'I Had a Solid Theory Before but It's Falling Apart': Polarizing Effects of Algorithmic Transparency." Human-Computer Interaction (online: arXiv:1811.02163 [cs.HC]).

Spinger, A., and S. Whittaker. 2019. "Making Transparency Clear." Joint Proceedings of the ACM IUI 2019 Workshop, March 20.

Tyler, T. 1988. "Procedural Justice in Felony Cases." Law and Society Review 22: pp. 483–516.

Wisser, L. 2019. "Pandora's Algorithmic Black Bow: The Challenge of Using Algorithmic Risk Assessments in Sentencing." American Criminal Law Review 56: pp. 1811–1832.

Zerilli, J. et al. 2018. "Transparency in Algorithmic and Human Decision-Making: Is There a Double Standard?" Philosophy and Technology (online first).

5

Algorithm-Based Sentencing and Discrimination

Kasper Lippert-Rasmussen

5.1 Introduction

Increasingly, US courts are using actuarial recidivism risk prediction instruments in estimating an offender's dangerousness and, thus, the warranted severity of the punishment (Harcourt 2007, 16; Huq 2019, 1074–1076; Slobogin 2018, 507–509; Starr 2014, 805). The relevant algorithms rely on variables such as socioeconomic status, education level, employment status, gender, age, and family and neighborhood characteristics. Typically, they also rely on variables pertaining to past behavior, for example, whether the offender has any previous convictions.[1]

Many find this trend disturbing on the ground that it will result in the fact that two offenders who have committed identical crimes and who do not differ in terms of their individual dispositions to reoffend will typically be punished very differently if one is male, poor, and Black—typically this offender will pose a high actuarial risk of recidivism—and the other is female, rich, and white—typically with a low risk of recidivism.[2] Offenders are punished not simply on the basis of their crime, but also for who they are, where this is defined by statistical properties of the reference classes to which they are assigned (Harcourt 2007, 31–34, 188–189; Slobogin 2018, 13). Others argue that the use of algorithms in recidivism risk assessment eliminates biases in non-actuarially based recidivism risk assessments, notably clinical risk assessment and the impressionistic assessments of judges; reduces the reliance on the inscrutable discretion of judges; and is a cost-efficient form of preventing crime, one which might become even more cost-efficient in the future (Huq 2019, 1050–1052, 1062–1063).

Kasper Lippert-Rasmussen, *Algorithm-Based Sentencing and Discrimination* In: *Sentencing and Artificial Intelligence*. Edited by: Jesper Ryberg and Julian V. Roberts, Oxford University Press. © Oxford University Press 2022.
DOI: 10.1093/oso/9780197539538.003.0005

In this chapter, I shall probe one particular objection to this recent trend: namely, *the discrimination objection* in relation to African Americans in the United States:

> Using actuarial recidivism risk prediction instruments in estimating an offender's dangerousness and thus the warranted severity of the offender's punishment by the courts is discriminatory against offenders who belong to socially salient groups of which it is true that its members are more likely to reoffend, and for that reason unfair and, absent strong countervailing reasons, morally impermissible. (Angwin et. al. 2016; Castro 2019; Hannah-Moffat and Montford 2019, 179; Starr 2014, 803)

Some might challenge the narrow focus which an assessment of this objection invites, arguing that the real-life choice before us is between clinical assessment-based sentencing and clinical-assessment-cum-algorithm-based sentencing. Hence, what we should be asking is which of these two options is morally justified, all things considered. To answer that question, we do not need to know whether algorithm-based sentencing is unfairly discriminatory. Knowledge of the (alleged) truth of the claim—"If either of these two forms of sentencing is unfairly discriminatory, then clinical-assessment-cum-algorithm-based sentencing is less unfairly discriminatory, e.g., because it counteracts implicit, or even explicit, biases of judges and psychiatrists"—suffices.

I agree that this question is important. However, our set of options includes more than just the two posited by this question, for example, if algorithm-based sentencing is unfairly discriminatory, that might be a reason for modifying the way in which we punish if we base punishments in part on algorithm-based assessments of dangerousness (cp. Corbett-Davies et. al. 2017, 8). Moreover, we do not just want to know whether something is morally justified all things considered. We *also* want to know which moral factors bear on the overall moral justifiability of a certain practice. Suppose that there are more options in our option set than the two mentioned in the previous paragraph. In that case, knowledge of the relevant instance of questions of the former type ("Is this practice morally justified all things considered?") can only be acquired through knowledge of the morally relevant factors that speak to that question. One such factor is whether algorithm-based assessments are discriminatory.

In probing the discrimination objection, I take for granted, first, that it is morally justified to punish offenders partly on the basis of how dangerous they are. One might object to sentencing based on actuarial recidivism risk prediction algorithms because one rejects this assumption. However, assessing this objection, which incidentally also applies to sentencing based on clinically based risk assessments, is not my aim here.[3]

Second, there are many different objections to sentencing that is based on actuarial recidivism risk prediction instruments, for example, that these instruments are imprecise as predictors of individual recidivism risk (Angwin et. al. 2016; Starr 2014, 842–850; that they distort sentencing processes by resulting in recidivism considerations being given too much weight relative to considerations about the nature of the crime; or that clinical risk predictions outperform algorithm-based or algorithm-assisted risk predictions (Starr 2014, 807–808). I take no stand on these and other objections and simply assess the practice from the perspective of the discrimination objection. Specifically, with regard to the objection that such instruments are imprecise, I will assume cautiously that recidivism risk assessments are more precise when based both on clinical as well as algorithm-based instruments (but see Starr 2014, 828).[4]

Third, I shall assume that dangerousness—understood as the frequency of recidivism among the reference group to which the offender belongs—is the relevant variable from a penal perspective.[5] Finally, I assume that the use of actuarial recidivism risk prediction instruments for the purpose of sentencing results in crime reduction. Only if the use of such instruments reduces crime does an interesting question from the point of view of penal theory arise; to wit, whether their use is morally permissible.

5.1.1 Overview

In this chapter, I first argue that algorithm-based sentencing is indirectly discriminatory against African Americans (section 5.2). Section 5.3 considers sympathetically the suggestion that, in view of how African Americans might reasonably interpret algorithm-based sentencing, it might amount to direct discrimination. Section 5.4 rebuts a challenge to the view that algorithm-based sentencing is indirectly discriminatory, citing the fact that most crime is, as it were, intra-racial, and thus that the main beneficiaries of algorithm-based sentencing are African Americans. Section 5.5 scrutinizes the view that algorithm-based sentencing is unfairly discriminatory against African Americans on the ground that this practice means that they bear a much greater burden of false positives in relation to the legal system than other groups. I argue that if this objection is sound, then a similar objection applies to the US (as well as to non-US) legal system(s) in general due to differential crime rates across different racially (or otherwise) defined groups. Some might accept this conclusion. However, I am somewhat disinclined to do so, at least on the grounds offered, and, accordingly, while I am inclined to think that algorithm-based sentencing is unfair and discriminatory, I am also inclined to think that it is unfair for reasons other than those articulated by the disproportionate group unfairness objection, however appealing this might seem as an objection to algorithm-based sentencing.

5.2 Direct vs. Indirect Discrimination

In this section, I defend the claim that algorithm-based sentencing is indirectly discriminatory and, more specifically, in a US context probably indirectly discriminatory against African Americans.[6] For that purpose, initially it is important to distinguish between variables that are used in the algorithms and variables that are not. Gender is a variable used in most risk prediction instruments, while race is not.[7] This is so even if, statistically speaking, race might be no less significant than gender.[8] This suggests that while algorithm-based sentencing might be directly discriminatory against men, it is not directly racially discriminatory.

While this might be too simplistic (see next section), this observation points to the need for clarifying the alleged site of discrimination. We need to distinguish between whether *the algorithm itself* is directly discriminatory and whether it is *the application of the algorithm* at sentencing. The fact that race is not a variable used in an algorithm suffices to show that, just like a law that does not refer to race, it is not itself directly racially discriminatory. However, that does not imply that *the use* of the algorithm is not directly discriminatory. After all, it might be used precisely out of ill will against a certain racial group. We could easily imagine that courts using the algorithms were unaware—initially at least—of how sentencing based thereupon has a disparate, adverse impact on African Americans, and if direct discrimination involves some kind of objectionable mental state regarding the discriminatees, for example, hostility, stereotypical overgeneralizations, or sheer indifference, plausibly in such cases algorithm-based sentencing would then not be directly discriminatory (Alexander 1992). Moreover, it might also be the case that some actual uses of algorithm-based sentencing involve no such mental states, but simply the prima facie morally commendable desire to reduce crime by reducing the recidivism rate of offenders, in which case it is hardly directly discriminatory.

In reply, one might point out that it is also the case that race is correlated with many of the variables that are used in most risk prediction instruments, for example, number of prior convictions, being unemployed, or home address in a high-crime area. Accordingly, in the United States, a typical African American offender will be deemed more likely to reoffend by the recidivism risk prediction algorithms than a European American who has committed a similar crime, even if these are not fed any information about the race of the offender. Hence, algorithm-based sentencing leads to African Americans receiving harsher punishments than European Americans for similar offenses, and that, it seems, makes the practice indirectly discriminatory.[9] Thus, while risk prediction instruments used for the purpose of sentencing might involve direct sex discrimination against men—men are more likely to reoffend than women and accordingly, other things being equal, a male offender will be deemed to be at a higher risk of recidivism than a female offender—at most it involves indirect, and not direct, discrimination against African Americans. At least, this is so if we understand the following by indirect discrimination:

> Under many legal systems, an act that imposes a disproportionate disadvantage on the members of a certain group can count as discriminatory, even though the agent has no intention to disadvantage the members of the group and no other objectionable mental state, such as indifference or bias, motivating the act. This form of discriminatory conduct is called "indirect discrimination" or, in the language of American doctrine, "disparate impact" discrimination. (Altman 2020)[10]

Algorithm-based sentencing imposes a disadvantage on African Americans in relation to non-African American offenders in virtue of African American offenders receiving harsher punishments than offenders from the complementary group for identical crimes.[11] Moreover, given the weight we normally attach to putting guilty people in prison for a longer time than is warranted in virtue of their offense etc., this disadvantage is likely to be disproportionate even for significant preventive effects.[12] Hence, it satisfies

Altman's description of indirect discrimination.[13] In fact, many will consider the form of indirect discrimination involved in algorithm-based sentencing a particularly morally objectionable form of indirect discrimination, because the statistical differences between different groups of people—say, African and European Americans—that are fed into the algorithms, which then produce racially disparate predictions of dangerousness, are, while real, the result of past and present unjust discrimination and other forms of injustice (cp. Castro 2019, 407–408; Hannah-Moffat et. al. 2019, 178–179; Tonry 2014, 173). This is also an objection that is not necessarily mitigated even if the relevant predictive instruments are rendered considerably more precise, for example, through extensive machine learning.

5.2.1 The Base-Rate Sentencing Argument

I shall now back up the claim that algorithm-based sentencing as we know it indirectly discriminates against African Americans with a further argument. Suppose that with respect to a certain type of crime, the crime rate is higher for African Americans than for non-African Americans. Suppose also that courts were to use certain proxies—the same that are used for the purpose of assessing recidivism risk—to establish the base-rate probability for any defendant being guilty such that, typically, for an African American defendant, it will take less incriminating evidence to reach the threshold at which it is warranted to convict the defendant. Call this practice "base rate-based sentencing" and the objection to letting the severity of the punishment depend on base-rate reasoning about dangerousness based on an appeal to the injustice of settling whether the defendant is guilty on the basis of base-rate reasoning or the "base-rate sentencing argument."

We can now argue as follows: Base rate-based sentencing is unfairly indirectly discriminatory against African Americans (henceforth: *the sentencing claim*). If base rate-based sentencing is unfairly indirectly discriminatory against African Americans, then so is algorithm-based sentencing (henceforth: *the equivalence claim*). Thus, algorithm-based sentencing is unfairly indirectly discriminatory against African Americans. The sentencing claim is uncontroversial. In a great number of cases, courts have dismissed arguments based on base rate-based reasoning of the sort described here (Starr 2014, 823–836). The equivalence claim seems very plausible. To see why, compare two cases in which offenders receive equally severe punishments:

In the first case, guilt is established independently of any base rate-based reasoning, but the dangerousness is not.

In the second case, guilt is established partly through base rate-based reasoning and, absent such reasoning, the evidence available would not have been sufficient to convict the offender. Moreover, the punishment meted out to this offender is only based on the nature of his crime and not based on any assumptions about dangerousness. The crime for which the first offender is convicted is slightly more serious than the crime for which the second defendant is convicted. Hence, they receive identical punishments.

I believe that there is no basis for saying that one, but not the other, is subjected to unfair indirect discrimination. The equivalence claim offers a superior explanation of this being so. Given the sentencing claim, it follows that algorithm-based sentencing is unfairly indirectly discriminatory against African Americans.

5.2.2 The Avoidability Objection

Some might challenge the suggestion that algorithm-based sentencing is indirectly discriminatory on the basis of what I shall label the *avoidability of wrongful discrimination objection* or, for short, the avoidability objection: the only way to avoid algorithm-based sentencing being unfairly indirectly discriminatory against African Americans—namely, to avoid the disparate negative impact on African Americans—is by adopting a practice whereby non-African Americans receive harsher punishment than comparable African Americans even though their offenses and their risk of recidivism are similar (henceforth: *the unavoidable trade-off claim*). Adopting a practice whereby non-African Americans receive harsher punishment than comparable African Americans (even though their offenses and their risk of recidivism are similar), amounts to wrongful direct discrimination against non-African Americans (henceforth: *the wrongful discrimination claim*). But if the only way to avoid a certain allegedly unfairly indirectly discriminatory practice is to adopt a practice that is wrongfully directly discriminatory against the complementary group, then the allegedly unfairly indirectly discriminatory practice is not unfairly indirectly discriminatory after all (henceforth: *the no-discrimination claim*). Thus, algorithm-based sentencing is not unfairly indirectly discriminatory against African Americans.

In defense of the unavoidable trade-off claim, note that on the assumption that African American offenders are more likely to reoffend than non-African American offenders and insofar as we want to retain algorithm-based sentencing, the only way of avoiding disparate impact on African Americans is by recalibrating our predictive algorithms such that it takes suitably more evidence of danger of reoffending for African American than for non-African Americans in order for the predictive instrument to estimate that the probability of reoffending is, say, high, thereby restoring equality of punishment for similar crimes across African American and non-African American offenders (see footnote 25).[14]

It speaks strongly in favor of the wrongful discrimination claim that a similar discount given to European American offenders would clearly amount to wrongful direct discrimination and that there is no reason why such a discount would suddenly change character vis-à-vis discrimination just because it is awarded African Americans instead (cp. Castro 2019, 417).

In defense of the no-discrimination claim, one might submit that both direct and indirect discrimination are wrongful and that, presumably, there is some way of avoiding engaging in wrongful discrimination. One way of defending this claim appeals to the view that for something to be wrongful, it must be avoidable.

Ultimately, however, the avoidability objection is unsuccessful. I accept that the unavoidable trade-off is true. However, the wrongful discrimination claim is dubious and the no-discrimination claim false. Starting with my reservations about the wrongful discrimination claim note that while, clearly, sentencing African American offenders more leniently than non-African American offenders amounts to discrimination in a generic sense (Lippert-Rasmussen 2013, 15)—roughly, it involves treating members of the two groups differently—it does not follow that such a practice is discriminatory in the more specific sense that people have in mind when they complain about direct or indirect discrimination. Still, many would find it to be a clear instance of racial discrimination if European American offenders who have committed identical crimes but are less at risk of reoffending were systematically punished as severely as African Americans whose crimes are similar and who are at a significantly higher risk of reoffending. In such a case, plausibly, European American offenders could complain on fairness grounds that they are not being treated comparably to African American offenders who committed identical crimes in identical circumstances and are equally likely to reoffend. If this unequal treatment is avoidable, for example, because we have a choice between either using an imperfect algorithm or a more expensive but perfect algorithm, which would allow us to realize both equal predictive accuracy and equal error rates, in the interest of fairness, inter alia, we should expend significant resources to employ the latter predictive instrument.

Consider next the no-discrimination claim, that is, the claim that if the only way to avoid a certain allegedly unfairly indirectly discriminatory practice is to adopt a practice that is wrongfully directly discriminatory against the complementary group, then the allegedly unfairly indirectly discriminatory practice is not unfairly indirectly discriminatory after all. While it might be true of any individual wrongful act that for it to be wrongful it has to be the case that one could have avoided performing it, it is not true that it also has to be the case that one has the option of acting in an alternative way which is not wrongful. It is possible to make conflicting promises such that one must wrongfully fail to fulfill one of them. Thus, I conclude that the avoidability of wrongful discrimination argument fails to undermine the conclusion so far, to wit, that algorithm-based sentencing is indirectly discriminatory against African Americans (among others).

5.2.3 The Gender Objection

A different challenge to the view that algorithm-based sentencing is unfairly indirectly discriminatory—call it *the gender objection*—goes as follows: if algorithm-based sentencing is unfairly indirectly discriminatory against African Americans, then it is also unfairly indirectly discriminatory against men (henceforth: *the transferability claim*). It is not the case that algorithm-based sentencing is unfairly indirectly discriminatory against men (henceforth: *the no-gender discrimination claim*). Thus, it is not the case that algorithm-based sentencing is unfairly indirectly discriminatory against African Americans.

Algorithm-based sentencing is more harmful to male offenders than to female offenders, who tend to have lower rates of recidivism, in a way that is analogous to the way in which it is more harmful to African Americans than to European Americans (Lightbourne 2017, 339; Monahan 2006, 416). This renders the transferability claim plausible.[15] The no-gender discrimination claim has in its favor that few people have complained about algorithm-based sentencing being discriminatory against male offenders, suggesting that few people think it really is unfairly discriminatory against men.[16]

Nevertheless, the plausibility of the transferability claim is deceptive.[17] Compare an analogous claim concerning taxation. It might be true that highly progressive taxation is more harmful to rich people than to poor people in a way which is analogous to indirectly discriminatory taxation disadvantaging, say, non-white South Africans under Apartheid. Yet that does not mean that progressive taxation is indirectly discriminatory against the rich, since the additional harms imposed on the rich might not be morally disproportionate in view of their favorable condition in comparison with other taxpayers. Similarly, if we think of African Americans as a minority subjected to a range of injustices and do not think of men in a similar way, it might be that the additional harms imposed on African Americans by algorithm-based sentencing are disproportionate in a way that the otherwise similar harms—longer prison sentences—imposed by algorithm-based sentencing of men are not.

Setting aside my previous point, one might also dispute that the harms in question are actually similar and argue that the harms suffered by men as a result of male offenders being incarcerated for longer terms are less troubling than the harms suffered by African Americans as a result of African American offenders being incarcerated more years (Fiss 1976; Moreau 2020). Men are not stigmatized as offenders in the way that African American (men) are as a result of penal practices—or to the extent that they are, the stigma is different and less harmful. For those reasons I believe the weaknesses of the transferability claim defeat the gender objection. I conclude that, in the current US context, algorithm-based sentencing appears to be unfairly indirectly discriminatory against African Americans (among others).

5.3 The Munchhausen Argument

According to the challenge that I discuss in this section, even if the use of actuarial recidivism risk prediction instruments is not directly discriminatory when considered in isolation, its use is directly discriminatory when considered in the wider social context of how at least some groups, offenders from which are particularly likely to receive harsher punishments as a result of the practice, perceive such sentencing as directly discriminatory and other groups' awareness of these perceptions (Hosein 2018).[18]

Consider the following quasi-real-life case. Historically, members of a certain minority have been oppressed by their state. Its members have suffered discrimination at the hands of the state and their fellow majority citizens. Moreover, its members are generally worse off on most significant socioeconomic parameters than their majority co-citizens. Finally, many of its members reasonably see the fact that minority members receive harsher punishments—especially harsher punishments reflecting the use of algorithm-based risk assessments—than majority members as a particularly salient manifestation of how, in general, they are treated worse than members of the majority in discriminatory ways.[19] Members of the majority are aware of the fact that this is how members of the minority generally see the facts—rightly or wrongly. While not necessarily being completely insensitive to this fact, they are much less sensitive to it than they would be if some group of majority people had a similar complaint—right or wrong—about a practice that had a similar expressive significance in their eyes. If some majority people saw quota-based affirmative action as a salient expression of how, presently, males are being treated worse than women in ways involving sex discrimination, then majority people would be more receptive to the need to take this perception into account. My claim is that this differential sensibility to the complaints of majority and minority people based on how they perceive their treatment turns something that might otherwise not be a case of direct discrimination into something that is. Or, if you prefer, it means that the use of actuarial recidivism risk prediction instruments reflects something that does constitute direct discrimination—to wit, the willingness to use actuarial recidivism risk prediction for the purpose of sentencing, despite the well-known complaints against the use of such instruments.

I shall refer to this argument as the Munchhausen argument, since according to this argument, it is the fact that something is *seen as* directly discriminatory by putative discriminatees and yet ignored by putative discriminators aware of this perception that makes it directly discriminatory.[20] The Munchhausen argument is consistent with saying that, initially, when algorithm-based sentencing was adopted, it was not directly discriminatory. It acquired this characteristic only after its effects became widely known, because only then did the retainment of the practice become reflective of the relevant differential disposition to take into account majority and minority people's perceptions of social reality.

I have two responses to the Munchhausen argument. First, there is something to the Munchhausen direct discrimination objection. In light of how much attention has been given to "reverse discrimination" complaints in relation to affirmative action and diversity promotion, it is striking how minority perceptions of legal and law enforcement practices have received comparatively little attention and have had little effect on the practices of US courts.[21] Hence, for the surprising reason stated, the practice of algorithm-based sentencing is not only indirectly but also directly discriminatory against African Americans.[22]

Second, however, even if the Munchhausen argument is sound when it comes to African Americans and algorithm-based sentencing, there is a certain sense in which the Munchhausen argument is limited in its scope. Namely, the argument would be rendered unsound if members of the majority could somehow persuade members of the minority that they should see the use of algorithm-based sentencing in a different light, for example, by arguing that the practice benefits minority members.[23] Hence, in response to a Munchhausen-based complaint about algorithm-based sentencing, one can either address the complaint by eliminating the practice, or retain it but reason with the complainants to make them see the practice in a different light. It is, after all, a Munchhausen argument. I shall say more that bears on this question in the next section.

5.4 Proximate vs. Distant Causal Effects

The Munchhausen argument is unlikely to persuade everyone, so in this section I lay it aside and proceed on the assumption that the use of actuarial recidivism risk prediction instruments is not directly discriminatory against African Americans, even if, for reasons explained in section 5.2, in a US context it is still indirectly discriminatory against African Americans. There I submitted that the practice of algorithm-based sentencing imposed disproportionate disadvantages on African Americans and that, given Altman's characterization of indirect discrimination, that suffices to show that the practice is indirectly discriminatory.

Here, however, one might raise the following concern. Assume that it is true of most instances of crime that the victim and the offender are race-identical (cp. Risse and Zeckhauser 2004). If so, there is an additional effect on African

Americans that, arguably, must be taken into account when assessing the use of actuarial recidivism risk prediction instruments, that is, that their use might have much greater positive effects, crime prevention-wise, on African Americans than on European Americans. African Americans are likely to benefit more in terms of the reduction of the risk of being the victim of a repeat offender than European Americans are. Hence, it might be suggested that, overall, algorithm-based sentencing is not even indirectly discriminatory against African Americans (even though it might disadvantage African American *offenders* overall), since, all effects considered, algorithm-based sentencing benefits, rather than disadvantages, African Americans. Indeed, on average it benefits African Americans more than it benefits European Americans.

At this point, proponents of the indirect discrimination complaint could try to salvage it in one of three ways. First, they could draw a distinction between proximate and distant effects and say that only the former matter from the point of view of indirect discrimination. Since, arguably, the more severe punishment of algorithm-based sentencing is a proximate effect thereof, whereas the reduced risk of being a victim of crime is a distant effect thereof, one could sustain the charge of unfair indirect discrimination against African Americans even if, by hypothesis, the distant benefits typically outweigh, prudentially speaking, the proximate costs (see also section 5.5).

Second, they could instead distinguish between different kinds of benefits and harms and argue that it suffices for the complaint of indirect discrimination if in terms of, say, punishments, algorithm-based sentencing disadvantages African Americans irrespective of how it affects them in terms of other benefits/harms.

While both of these argumentative strategies are possible, neither strikes me as particularly plausible insofar as the fact that a practice is indirectly discriminatory is something that gives us a special reason to eliminate this practice. One reason why this is so is the fact that critics who contend that algorithm-based sentencing is indirectly discriminatory often appeal to causally distant effects of the practice to sustain their complaint against indirect discrimination, for example, the effects on employment prospects of legal practices. Another reason is that there is no reason why people should make any principled distinction between proximate and distant causal effects of a practice on them. More distant negative harms might be less likely to materialize, but ascribing significance to this is ascribing significance to the probability of a certain harmful effect occurring, not to whether it is temporally proximate or distant as such. On this view, the justifiability of a practice depends on the totality of its foreseeable consequences—causally proximate or distant—for those subjected to or affected by it.

In part for the reason stated in the previous paragraph, a third reply strikes me as being more plausible than the two previous ones. According to this reply, it is indeed the case that if the only indirect effect of algorithm-based sentencing were a significant reduction of the risk of minority members being victims of crime, this would speak strongly in favor of the relevant form of sentencing not being disproportionately burdensome once we take into account all of its effects, and thus not unfairly indirectly discriminatory to members of that minority. However, one might retort that the case of African Americans is very different:

> [T]he mass incarceration problem in the United States is drastically disparate in its distribution. The unequal distribution is a core driver of its adverse social consequences, because it leaves certain neighborhoods and subpopulations decimated. Black men, for instance, are about fifty times as likely to be incarcerated at some point in their lives as white women are . . . and a 2003 study projected that one in three young black men would be incarcerated at some point in their lives. (Starr 2014, 837; cp. Huq 2019, 1046, 1105–1110)[24]

Given, for instance, the difficulties of finding a job when one has served a prison sentence—the longer the sentence, the greater the difficulties—it would seem reasonable to think that the bad indirect effects on African Americans of algorithm-based sentencing would at least to some degree counterbalance the good effects of reduced recidivist crime (Starr 2014, 839; Tonry 2014, 172). Hence, even if distant causal effects of a practice matter to whether it is indirectly discriminatory, and even if African Americans might be the main beneficiaries of the crime-preventive effects of algorithm-based sentencing, it might nevertheless be indirectly discriminatory against African Americans. However, if that empirical assumption—to wit, the assumption that African Americans in general benefit more than European Americans from longer incarceration of offenders deemed dangerous in algorithm-based assessments—is false, algorithm-based sentencing might not be unfairly indirectly discriminatory against African Americans per se (even if it may be so when it comes to the subgroup of African American offenders).

5.5 The Unfairness to Groups Objection

A common objection to algorithm-based sentencing on the ground that it is unfair to African Americans appeals to different effects of the practice than the ones that we have discussed so far; to wit, that the practice imposes on African Americans a much greater burden of false positives than it does on European Americans and that this unfairness amounts to a form of discrimination. To see how this objection—call it the *unfairness to groups objection*—works, suppose we have a population of 8,000 European Americans and 2,000 African Americans. Suppose, for the purpose of illustration—and for the purpose of illustration only—that the rate of convictions among European Americans is 10% and among African Americans 50%. This means that we have 800 European American convicted offenders and 1,000 African American convicted offenders. Suppose that the rate of recidivism is 50% for both African and European offenders, that is, in absolute numbers we have 400 European American recidivists and 500 African American recidivists. Suppose finally that the recidivism algorithm is 90% accurate, that is, for 100 offenders in 90 cases it will deliver true positives/negatives and in 10 cases it will result in false positives/negatives.

Under those assumptions we have the following distribution of African and European American offenders—the figure in front of "/" represents African Americans and the figure after European Americans. (Ignoring the lowest row and the column furthest to the right both of which sums up numbers in innermost four cells) numbers in the upper left box are true positives; numbers in the lower right box true negatives; numbers in the upper right box false positives; and, finally, numbers in the lower left box are false negatives:

	Actual recidivism	Actual non-recidivism	
Predicted recidivism	450/360	50/40	500/400
Predicted non-recidivism	50/40	450/360	500/400
	500/400	500/400	1000/800

In this case, the risk of experiencing unwarranted lengthy incarceration is 50 (the number of African American offenders who were predicted to recidivate but would not have)/2,000 (the total number of African Americans in the population) for African Americans and 40/8,000 for European Americans. Thus, African Americans are five times as likely as European Americans to suffer unwarranted lengthy incarceration. This is so despite the fact that the test is equally accurate for African and European Americans. The relevant disparity arises simply because African Americans in this example have a higher base rate level of convictions. The unfairness objection says that it is unjust that African Americans have to bear a disproportionate burden (in the form of false positives) of upholding a penal system because of the fact that differential costs are associated with false positives (additional incarceration not warranted by the offenders' dangerousness) and false negatives (costs are imposed not on the offender but on others [cp. Section 5.4]). Hence, algorithm-based sentencing is unfair in my hypothetical example to African Americans because they are made to bear a disproportionate share of "the more burdensome type of errors" relative to European Americans (Hellman 2020, 28).[25]

At this point, some might question whether justice requires something like intergroup fairness when it comes to the ratio of false positives to false negatives, and, thus, whether a charge of unfair indirect discrimination can be based on the relevant unfairness to groups claim. Consider the following argument: if African Americans have a higher crime rate than European Americans, then they are more likely than European Americans to be accused of committing the relevant kind of crime.[26] This is so, for example, as a result of more intense policing of high-crime areas. Moreover, if African Americans are more likely than European Americans to be accused in court of committing the relevant kind of crime, then the ratio of false positives to false negatives is higher for African Americans than for European Americans. That is true in virtue of the fact that courts are fallible and the fact that the risk of a false positive is higher for people who appear in court than for people who do not (for those people it is virtually zero).

Finally, if the ratio of false positives to false negatives is higher for African Americans than for European Americans, then either the use of algorithm-based sentencing is not unfair due to the differential false positives/false negatives ratio across different groups or it is, in which case ordinary penal systems are unfair for a similar reason whenever, as is almost always the case, crime rates vary across different groups. After all, there is no fairness-relevant difference between algorithm-based sentencing and sentencing in general. But, as is widely accepted, it is not the case that ordinary penal systems are unfair for a false positives/false negatives-related reason whenever, as is almost always the case, crime rates vary across different groups.[27] It follows that the use of algorithm-based sentencing is not unfair due to the differential false positives/false negatives ratio across different groups. This conclusion seems surprising in light of the argument in this chapter so far, even though it does not rule out that algorithm-based sentencing is unfair for reasons other than the pertinent one.[28] However, it is unavoidable if a penal system in general need not be unfair whenever different social groups have different underlying crime rates.

The wider implication of this section is less precise than the upshot of the three previous sections, since it takes the form of a dilemma. The first horn of the dilemma says that algorithm-based sentencing is unfair in a way that is indirectly discriminatory due to the group-unfairness objection, in which case ordinary penal systems are unfairly indirectly discriminatory in standard cases where different groups have different underlying crime rates (whether or not algorithm-based prediction tools are used in sentencing). The second horn of the dilemma asserts that it is not the case that algorithm-based sentencing is unfairly indirectly discriminatory due to the group-unfairness objection. These two claims represent a dilemma. The first horn of the dilemma is very radical and revisionary. The second horn is not very attractive either in light of the objections in this and the previous three sections.

One could suggest that we should be more open to the first horn of the dilemma being true on the ground that, in one respect, even though standard legal systems are unfair for reasons similar to the one appealed to in the unfairness to groups objection, they are not unfair all things considered, for example, because fairness to groups must also take into account, say, the negative effects of reducing policing in high-crime areas to equalize the risk of false negatives across groups (cp. Section 5.4). Or they are morally permissible, even if unfair in the relevant respect as well as all things considered (which, however, given the symmetry with algorithm-based sentencing, might not be particularly attractive claims either).

Alternatively, one could try to argue the second horn of the dilemma is more plausible than it might initially seem by noting that while it rules out algorithm-based sentencing being unfair for the reasons brought out in the unfairness to groups objection, it is consistent with the practice being unfair for other reasons. Since I am not sure that this is a plausible way to go either (even though I have doubts about groups as moral subjects, I suspect that this feature of the unfairness to groups objection can be remedied), I conclude simply by noting the dilemma without indicating which way it should be solved.

5.6 Conclusion

In this chapter, I have assessed the recent practice of algorithm-based sentencing from the point of view of discrimination. I have argued that, in a US context, there is reason to think that its use is directly discriminatory against African Americans and even stronger reasons for thinking that it is indirectly discriminatory against African Americans. I also noted why one argument—the group unfairness argument—in favor of this conclusion might imply that legal systems in general are unfair to minorities with higher crime rates despite the absence of any bias against them in the legal system. This appears to be a revisionary implication and underscores the significance of the issue of fairness in algorithm-based sentencing.[29]

Notes

1. On some views, uses of the two kinds of variables are morally different in that the use of variables reflecting past choices respects the offenders qua autonomous beings in a way that the use of other variables does not (Wasserman 1991; Eidelson 2015; Castro 2019, 412–414). However, it is contentious whether some socioeconomic variables do not also reflect choices made by the offender, e.g., education, and whether variables pertaining to past behavior always (only) reflect autonomous choices, e.g., because, under some circumstances, persons can be forced to offend.
2. I set aside whether the data on which probabilities of recidivism are calculated reflect underlying real rates of recidivism (as opposed to biased police practices, etc.).
3. This is not to say that I will not discuss any objection to algorithm-based sentencing which might not also apply to other forms of sentencing. Many, but not all, objections which apply to one apply to the other as well (Enoch et. al. 2012). Additionally, the objection discussed in section 5.3 applies to algorithm-based sentencing, but not to clinical assessment-based sentencing, because of differences in how the two are perceived.
4. Greater precision in assessments of dangerousness might not lead to less unjust punishments (Ryberg 2020). I set aside this complication.
5. Actually, this assumption is false (Starr 2014, 855–862). If we want to incarcerate offenders with a high risk of reoffending for a longer period of time in order to reduce crime, then what we should be interested in is a comparison of the level of crime with and without algorithm-based sentencing. This factor is pried apart from the former in

cases where longer incarceration results in high-risk offenders engaging in even more crime once released, e.g., because of the increased opportunities to form contacts with other offenders in prison useful for engaging in crime once outside prison, or, for that matter, while crimes committed in prison. Given the crime reduction aim, our concern should be with the elasticity of recidivism in relation to length of incarceration (Starr 2014, 858). This important point is one that is independent of a concern for the unfairly discriminatory nature of algorithm-based sentencing and, accordingly, I set it aside here.

6. I take no stand on whether it is *more* discriminatory than clinical assessments. Even if it were not, the fact that it is discriminatory would still be a prima facie objection to algorithm-based sentencing.

7. Cp. *State v. Loomis*, 881N.W.2d 749 (Wisc. 2016) at 766. People who take a sympathetic view of the use of algorithms for sentencing purposes are mostly skeptical of the use of race as a predictive factor even when its use would improve the accuracy of the predictions made (cp. Hellman 2020).

8. Some algorithm-based instruments have used race as a variable, but race has the legal status of a suspect classification in the United States and, thus, its use warrants strict scrutiny, which is one reason why no presently used algorithms processes information about the race of the offender.

9. This is not to say that we should worry less about racial biases in algorithm-based sentencing than we should if it amounted to direct discrimination. Here I am non-committal on whether indirect discrimination is less or exactly as morally objectionable as direct discrimination (see Lippert-Rasmussen 2013, 67–68; Moreau 2020).

10. Altman's characterization states that the presence of any objectionable mental states is not a necessary condition for the presence of indirect discrimination, not that the absence of such states is a necessary condition for the presence of indirect discrimination.

11. It does not impose a disadvantage on each and every African American. However, ceteris paribus on average it makes African Americans worse off and, possibly, that suffices for saying that, in the relevant, indirect discrimination-constituting way, the practice makes African Americans worse off (cp. Lippert-Rasmussen 2013, 61–65). Similarly, employment practices that disadvantage women, because they make it harder to get a job if there is a chance that you will become pregnant, are indirectly discriminatory against women even if women who cannot become pregnant were not disadvantaged by the practice.

12. If algorithm-based sentencing is only used to lessen punishments, then the present point does not apply. However, African Americans would still be disadvantaged, compared to members of other socially salient groups, by the practice and that might suffice for the charge of indirect discrimination (Lippert-Rasmussen 2014).

13. The quote reads "*can* count as discriminatory," so depending on the additional conditions that must be satisfied for it to be actually discriminatory, algorithmic sentencing of the sort in question might not be so.

14. See the defense made in favor of the use of COMPAS, https://www.washingtonpost.com/news/monkey-cage/wp/2016/10/17/can-an-algorithm-be-racist-our-analysis-is-more-cautious-than-propublicas/?noredirect=on&utm_term=.941b2062672d.

15. Assuming, however, that algorithm-based sentencing compounds prior injustice against African Americans but not against men, and assuming that there is a distinct duty not to compound prior injustice, this might be a reason to reject the transferability claim (cf. Hellman forthcoming, 4; Hellman 2020, 31–32; see also Hellman forthcoming, 35). I am skeptical about the existence of such a distinct duty, but to the extent that there is one, this would support my skepticism about the gender objection.

16. Some might suggest that this fact is not explained by the fact that people do not consider algorithm-based sentencing of men unfairly discriminatory against them, but by the fact that even though they think it is unfairly discriminatory against men, they also think it is justified by its overall effects. One weakness of this suggestion is that people generally think considerations about fairness are very important when it comes to the overall moral justification of punishment.

17. Some might say the same about the no-gender discrimination claim. I take no stand on this claim, noting that for the gender objection to fail, it suffices if one of its premises is false.

18. This label alludes not to Munchhausen Syndrome, but to the main character in *Rudolf Erich Raspe's* 1785 book *Baron Munchausen's Narrative of his Marvelous Travels and Campaigns in Russia,* in which Baron Munchhausen pulls himself out of a bog by pulling his own hair and, thus, lifting himself (and his horse) up and onto safer grounds.

19. By "reasonably seeing" I intend to convey that, relative to the evidence, etc., available to typical minority members, a good case can be made from their perspective for seeing the practice in that way. Hence, the case need not be conclusive and it need not be the case that the way in which it is reasonable for minority members to see the practice is the right way to see it.

20. This element is not crucial to something like the present line of argument. If majority people came to see algorithm-based sentencing as directly discriminating against minority people even if minority people did not see it that way, then that too might suffice for rendering algorithm-based sentencing directly discriminatory. Thus, the present line of argument generalizes to other cases.

21. The majority is, well, the majority, and it is an open question how numbers should affect what amounts to unbiased public attention.

22. Recall from section 5.2 that it is possible for a practice to be directly and indirectly discriminatory at the same time.

23. That this is the chosen response might in itself amount to a form of discrimination if a different approach would have been adopted in response to similar complaints from majority people.

24. Huq (2019, 1114–1115, 1124) agrees that "net costs or benefits for" minorities, including indirect effects, determine whether algorithm-based sentencing is fair to minorities. He just thinks that, at least in a wide range of cases, the relevant balance speaks against algorithm-based sentencing with disparate racial impact.

25. To make the algorithm less unfair in this sense, we could tinker with it such that it becomes less likely to predict that African American offenders will reoffend. If we, as it were, move 400 African American offenders that the test initially predicts will reoffend to the group that the modified algorithm predicts will not reoffend by

strengthening the requirements that must be met for the algorithm to predict that an African American offender will reoffend. Since the test is 90% accurate, 360 of those offenders are actually recidivists and 40 are not, we get:

	Actual recidivism	Actual non-recidivism	
Predicted recidivism	90/360	10/40	100/400
Predicted non-recidivism	410/40	490/360	900/400
	500/400	500/400	1000/800

Now African Americans are exactly as likely as European Americans to suffer unwarranted long incarceration (10/2000 = 40/8000). However, another discrepancy has arisen. If you are dangerous, that is, if you will actually reoffend, you have much better prospects of getting off "too lightly," that is, be deemed not dangerous while in fact you are, if you are African American (410/500) than if you are European American (40/400). Some might think that this amounts to a form of reverse racial discrimination against European Americans (cp. Chiao 2018, 240). This example also provides a simple illustration of a result that has been demonstrated formally elsewhere (Kleinberg et. al. 2016), that is, except under very special circumstances, when base rates of convictions vary across two groups, it is impossible to realize both of the following two desiderata: (1) that the likelihood that if one's algorithm predicts that one will (not) reoffend, then one will actually (not) reoffend is the same across the two groups; and (2) that the likelihood that if one will actually (not) reoffend, then one's algorithm will predict that one will (not) reoffend is the same across the two groups.

26. For readability I omit the "other things being equal" clause in the remaining premises and the conclusion.

27. Some might say that this claim is problematic, since it suggests that something like predictive parity across groups captures the relevant fairness concern, and the case of algorithm-based sentencing shows that this is not all that matters fairness-wise. Hence, we should be open to a similar suggestion in relation to ordinary sentencing practices, for example, that I am being treated unfairly by the penal system if I live in a part of town where there is a higher crime rate and where, for that reason, police patrol more often and, thus, I face a higher risk of being innocently convicted than people living in parts of town where crime rates are lower and police presence lower as a result.

28. Under the present assumption, the impossibility result mentioned in footnote 25 generalizes to the penal system in general.

29. Previous versions of this paper were presented at Aarhus University, June 24, 2019; University of Oxford, September 27, 2019; University of Toronto, November 16, 2019; University of Copenhagen, January 25, 2020. I thank Reuben Binns, Vincent Chiao, Tom Douglas, Ben Eidelson, Catherine Evans, Moti Gorin, Axel Gosseries, Kalle Grill, Sune Holm, Adam Hosein, Frej Klem Thomsen, Niko Kolodny, Søren Flinch Midtgaard, Deborah Hellman, Sophia Moreau, Lauritz Aastrup Munch, Jennifer

Nedelsky, Robert Noggle, Viki Pedersen, Jesper Ryberg, Gina Schouten, Anna Su, Jens Tyssedal, Carissa Veliz, Daniel Viehoff, Nicholas Vrousalis, and Hazem Zohny for helpful comments. This work was funded by the Danish National Research Foundation (DNRF144).

References

Alexander, L. 1992. "What Makes Discrimination Wrongful?" University of Pennsylvania Law Review 141 (1): pp. 149–219.

Altman, A. 2020. "Discrimination." Stanford Encyclopedia of Philosophy: https://plato.stanford.edu/entries/discrimination/

Angwin, J., J. Larson, S. Mattu, and L. Kirchner. 2016. "Machine Bias." ProPublica May 23: https://www.propublica.org/article/machine-bias-risk-assessments-in-criminal-sentencing.

Castro, C. 2019. "What's Wrong with Machine Bias?" Ergo 6 (15): pp. 405–426.

Chiao, V. 2018. "Predicting Proportionality: The Case for Algorithmic Sentencing." Criminal Justice Ethics 37 (3): pp. 238–261.

Corbett-Davies, S., E. Pierson, A. Feller, S. Goel, and A. Huq. 2017. "Algorithmic Decision Making and the Cost of Fairness." CoRR, abs/1701.08230. Retrieved from http://arxiv.org/abs/1701.08230.

Eidelson, B. 2015. Discrimination and Disrespect. Oxford: Oxford University Press.

Enoch, D., L. Spectre, and T. Fischer. 2012. "Statistical Evidence, Sensitivity, and the Legal Value of Knowledge." Philosophy and Public Affairs 40 (3): pp. 197–224.

Fiss, O. M. 1976. "Groups and the Equal Protection Clause." Philosophy & Public Affairs 5 (2): pp. 107–177.

Hannah-Moffat, K., and K. S. Montford. 2019. "Unpacking Sentencing Algorithms: Risk, Racial Accountability, and Data Harms." In Predictive Sentencing: Normative and Empirical Perspectives, edited by J. de Keijser et al., pp. 175–196, Oxford: Hart Publishing.

Harcourt, B. 2007. Against Prediction. Chicago: University of Chicago Press.

Hellman, D. Forthcoming. "Sex, Causation, and Algorithms."

Hellman, D. 2020. "Measuring Algorithmic Fairness." Virginia Law Review 106 (4): pp. 811–866.

Hosein, A. O. 2018. "Racial Profiling and a Reasonable Sense of Inferior Political Status." Journal of Political Philosophy 26 (3): pp. 1–20.

Huq, A. Z. 2019. "Racial Equity in Algorithmic Criminal Justice." Duke Law Journal 68: pp. 1043–1134.

Kleinberg, J., S. Mullainathan, and M. Raghavan. 2016. "Inherent Trade-Offs in the Fair Determination of Risk Scores." arXiv: 1609.05807v2.

Lightbourne, J. 2017. "Damned Lies and Criminal Sentencing Using Evidence-Based Tools." Duke Law & Technology Review 15: pp. 327–343.

Lippert-Rasmussen, K. 2013. Born Free and Equal? Oxford: Oxford University Press.

Lippert-Rasmussen, K. 2014. "Indirect Discrimination Is Not Necessarily Unjust." Journal of Practical Ethics 2 (2): pp. 33–57.

Monahan, (2006) "A Jurisprudence of Risk Assessment." Virginia Law Review 92: pp. 391–435.

Moreau, S. 2020. Faces of Inequality. New York: Oxford University Press.

Risse, M., and R. Zeckhauser. 2004. "Racial Profiling." Philosophy & Public Affairs 32 (2): pp. 138–143.

Ryberg, J. 2020. "Risk-Based Sentencing and Predictive Accuracy." Ethical Theory and Moral Practice 23: pp. 251–263.

Slobogin, C. 2018. "Principles of Risk Assessment for Researchers and Practitioners." Behavioral Sciences & the Law 36: pp. 507–516.

Starr, S. 2014. "Evidence-Based Sentencing and the Scientific Rationalization of Discrimination." Stanford Law Review 66: pp. 803–872.

Tonry, M. 2014. "Legal and Ethical Issues in the Prediction of Recidivism." Federal Sentencing Reporter 26 (3): pp. 167–176.

Wasserman, D. 1991. "Morality of Statistical Proof and the Risk of Mistaken Liability." Cardozo Law Review (13): pp. 935–976.

6

Learning to Discriminate

The Perfect Proxy Problem in Artificially Intelligent
Sentencing

Benjamin Davies and Thomas Douglas[1]

6.1 Introduction

Traditional tools for predicting recidivism—often called actuarial risk assessment instruments—employ a fixed number of human-selected variables
and a regression-based algorithm to classify the risk that an individual will
reoffend. A commonly used example is the Violence Risk Appraisal Guide
(VRAG), which employs 12 variables, including age, history of alcohol abuse,
and marital status, to classify offenders into one of nine risk categories for violent recidivism.

Recently, there has been much interest in, and work to develop, more sophisticated machine learning-based recidivism prediction tools (Berk and
Hyatt 2015). Based on a large set of "training data" about a population of
offenders, including information about who went on to recidivate,[2] a data
mining algorithm would derive a model that can be deployed to assess recidivism risk in other populations.

Recidivism prediction tools, whether of the traditional variety ("traditional tools") or developed through machine learning ("ML tools"), are commonly criticized for being biased against members of certain racial groups.
In a well-known example, *ProPublica* criticized the COMPAS algorithm for
wrongly predicting recidivism much more commonly in Black Americans
than white Americans (Angwin et al. 2016; see also Angwin and Larson
2016; Chouldechova 2017; Dieterich et al. 2016). In fact, recidivism prediction tools exhibit many different kinds of bias (Barocas and Selbst 2016; Berk
et al. forthcoming; Chouldechova 2017; Hacker 2018; Zehlike et al. 2020),
not all of which can be simultaneously avoided (Berk et al. forthcoming;
Chouldechova 2017; Corbett-Davies et al. 2017; Kleinberg et al. 2017).

Benjamin Davies and Thomas Douglas, *Learning to Discriminate* In: *Sentencing and Artificial Intelligence*.
Edited by: Jesper Ryberg and Julian V. Roberts, Oxford University Press. © Oxford University Press 2022.
DOI: 10.1093/oso/9780197539538.003.0006

However, it is often assumed that they can straightforwardly avoid one important kind of bias: direct discrimination on the basis of race.[3]

6.1.1 Overview of the Chapter

In this chapter, we explore the justifiability and significance of this assumption, with reference specifically to ML tools. We first (section 6.2) describe how traditional tools can be designed to avoid direct racial discrimination. We then (section 6.3) identify and describe a problem for attempts to extend this strategy to ML tools: though designers of ML tools may, strictly speaking, be able to avoid direct racial discrimination, it is not clear that they can avoid its *wrongness*. In the subsequent three sections, we pursue this thought by distinguishing various explanations for the wrongness of discrimination, in each case asking what the explanation implies for the use of ML tools. These explanations advert to procedural unfairness (section 6.4), bad outcomes (section 6.5) and disrespect (section 6.6). In section 6.7, we conclude, and draw out some practical implications of our argument.

6.2 Direct Racial Discrimination and Traditional Tools

We will use the term "direct discrimination" to refer only to direct *racial* discrimination, and we will take it that *A* engages in direct racial discrimination against *B* when *A* treats *B* less favorably than she treats or would treat comparator individual(s) *C*, (partly) on the basis of *B*'s membership of racial group *G*.[4] Direct discrimination (sometimes called "disparate treatment") is typically contrasted with indirect discrimination (or "disparate impact"). At a rough approximation, indirect racial discrimination is treatment that does not constitute direct racial discrimination, but does have a disproportionate negative impact on members of one or more racial groups.

In line with most existing literature, we assume that using a recidivism prediction tool would constitute direct discrimination against members of a racial group if (a) the tool employs membership of that group as a predictor of recidivism, and (b) predicted recidivism is used as a basis for unfavorable treatment. The focus of this volume is on criminal sentencing, and when recidivism prediction tools are used in sentencing, predictions often *are* used as a basis for unfavorable treatment: those classified into high-risk categories are subjected to longer or otherwise harsher sentences. So (b) is often satisfied, and we will henceforth simply assume it to be satisfied. However, (a) is not normally satisfied by traditional tools, which typically do not employ race as a predictive variable (Starr 2014, 811–812, 824).[5] Thus, the use of traditional tools is typically not directly discriminatory—at least, not by virtue of employing race as a predictor within the tool.

The use of traditional tools might still constitute direct discrimination for reasons extrinsic to the tool.[6] For example, a policymaker might decide to employ a particular tool in part because she is indifferent to the harms it will impose on a particular racial group. Moreover, a traditional tool might be objectionable because risk scores produced by the tool track—and perhaps amplify the effects of—prior direct discrimination.[7] This may occur because, for example, the data on recidivism used to produce the tool were the product of directly discriminatory policing or juridical practices (e.g., Lum and Isaac 2016) or because past direct discrimination causally contributes to recidivism in its victims and this is captured by the data (e.g., Lippert-Rasmussen 2014, 283–300).[8] Finally, use of a traditional tool could be—and we suspect often is—*indirectly* discriminatory, for example, because it has a greater negative impact on already disadvantaged racial groups than others, and lacks any benefit sufficient to justify this unequal impact.[9] However, if membership of G is not used as an explicit predictor, it is in principle possible to use traditional tools without engaging in *direct* discrimination. Moreover, this might be thought a significant result, for direct discrimination is often thought to involve forms of wrongdoing over and above those present in indirect discrimination.[10]

6.3 Direct Racial Discrimination and ML Tools

Could designers of ML tools avoid direct discrimination in a similar way? The question might initially seem obtuse. After all, it is straightforward to exclude race from the list of predictors employed by an ML tool. This can be done by withholding information about race from the tool during the training phase.

However, supposing there is a correlation between race and measured recidivism in the training data, an ML tool will, given enough data and in the absence of "de-biasing,"[11] likely "learn" a proxy for race—a combination of other factors that to some degree captures the correlation between race and measured recidivism.[12] Traditional tools often contain such proxies too, but what sets ML tools apart is that, given the large amount of data they can be fed, they may learn a *perfect* proxy for race—a combination of variables that *fully* captures the correlation between race and measured recidivism, such that including race over and above this combination would have *no effect* on risk classifications.[13] If a perfect proxy were developed, we might legitimately wonder whether direct discrimination had been avoided in any more than name. Indeed, we might wonder whether it had really been avoided at all.

There are two distinct questions here. First, would deploying an ML tool that includes a perfect proxy for race *literally be* directly discriminatory by reason of including that proxy? Is treating unfavorably on the basis of a perfect proxy for race just one way of treating unfavorably on the basis of race? This will depend in part on how we interpret "treating unfavorably on the basis of race." On one reading, A treats B unfavorably on the basis of race if and only if the *concept* of race figures in the causal process that leads to unfavorable treatment.[14] This need not be the case when A treats B unfavorably because B is picked out by a perfect proxy for race. On another reading, however, the causal role of the *concept* of race is irrelevant. What matters is the causal role of race itself—whether B is treated unfavorably because B is in fact of a certain race.[15] If race *causes* the characteristics that serve as the perfect proxy for race, then use of the proxy will, on this reading, constitute direct discrimination.[16]

Although philosophically interesting, we set aside this metaphysical issue and focus on a second question: even if deploying an ML tool that includes a perfect proxy for race would, strictly speaking, avoid direct discrimination, might it nevertheless be morally wrong[17] for similar reasons and to a similar degree as had it included race and thus been directly discriminatory?

In what follows, we distinguish various explanations commonly given for the wrongness of discrimination, broadly construed, and consider what these imply for the wrongness of using an ML tool that excludes race as an explicit predictor but contains a perfect proxy for race; we call the use of such a tool "perfect proxy profiling." Throughout, in assessing the wrongness of perfect proxy profiling, we will keep two comparators in view: the use of a traditional tool that excludes race as an explicit predictor but contains an imperfect proxy for race ("imperfect proxy profiling"); and the use of an ML tool that *includes* race as an explicit predictor ("explicit profiling"), and which thus directly discriminates. This is because we are motivated by two questions. First, does the move from imperfect proxy profiling (via traditional tools) to perfect proxy profiling (via ML tools) bring us closer, morally speaking, to direct discrimination? And second, does it bring us all the way?

With respect to the first question, we will argue that, on some explanations of the wrongness of discrimination, perfect proxy profiling is, or is likely to be, more seriously wrong than imperfect proxy profiling;[18] if ML tools were to learn a perfect proxy for race, that would be a problem.[19] With respect to the second, we will suggest that, on some explanations, perfect proxy profiling could, depending on the underlying empirical facts, be as wrong as explicit profiling. This implies that, if we exclude race as an explicit predictor only for it to be replaced by a perfect proxy, we will have done nothing to mitigate that wrongness.[20]

Before turning to these arguments, a preliminary remark concerning our terminology. Our ultimate interest in what follows will be in whether, when, and why the *use* of recidivism prediction tools would be discriminatory, and therefore wrong. However, we will sometimes describe the tools themselves as discriminatory (or not).[21] We do not mean thereby to suggest that algorithmic tools are agents, that they can act wrongly, or that they can be discriminatory in any non-derivative sense.[22] When we say that a tool is discriminatory, we mean only that using it to determine sentence harshness would be discriminatory, and in virtue of features of the tool, rather than features of the particular, contingent way in which it is used.

6.4 Procedural Unfairness

We begin with the view that discrimination is wrong because it is procedurally unfair. Procedural unfairness can be contrasted with substantive unfairness (which we consider in section 6.5): procedural unfairness concerns the process via which goods and ills are allocated to different people, whereas substantive unfairness concerns the resulting pattern of distribution of these goods and ills. If an interviewer discounts a candidate's strengths because of her race, this is procedurally unfair, yet it is consistent with things turning out as they should, for example because the candidate is rightly hired anyway. Conversely, a selection procedure, such as preferring candidates with better formal qualifications, may seem procedurally fair, yet lead to a pattern of distribution that is substantively unfair, for example because people who never had the chance to complete their education are excluded from the most attractive jobs.

One view of procedural fairness is Aristotle's instruction to "treat like cases alike" (Gosepath 2007),[23] which is normally taken to imply that fairness requires that any two individuals are treated equally unless there is a *morally relevant* (in the context) difference between them (Halldenius 2018).[24] Several attempts to explain the wrongness of discrimination can be thought of as variants on this view, differing only in which differences they take to be morally relevant.

For example, explicit profiling has been criticized on the ground that it treats some less favorably than others on the basis of facts which they cannot or could not control (Boylan 2008; Gardner 1998). We could think of these critiques as asserting the Aristotelian criterion of fairness conjoined with the view that differences in uncontrollable factors are morally irrelevant. Others suggest that explicit profiling is objectionable because it treats some less favorably than others on the basis of differences in group membership, not individual characteristics (Miller 1999, 169; Shin 2018; Thomas 1992). The underlying thought may be that group-based differences are morally irrelevant.

What do these explanations imply for the wrongness of perfect proxy profiling?

Assume, first, the control explanation: explicit profiling is wrong when and because it treats some less favorably than others based on factors beyond the control of both.[25] How would perfect proxy profiling compare to explicit profiling on this explanation? And how would it compare to imperfect proxy profiling? In most cases all three types of profiling will be wrong. Explicit profiling employs at least one uncontrollable factor as a predictor: race. Neither perfect proxy profiling nor imperfect proxy profiling uses precisely that factor, but both normally employ other factors that are beyond an individual's control, such as age and history of parental offending. It would be possible to design a tool that employed only controllable factors such as marital status and individual history of offending. However, we are not aware of any widely used or advocated tool that takes this approach. In practice, all three types of profiling will employ uncontrollable factors, so, on the control explanation, all three are procedurally unfair. There is, of course, a further question of *how* unfair they are. Perhaps it could be argued that one type of profiling is more procedurally unfair than another if it employs more uncontrollable factors, employs a higher proportion of uncontrollable factors, or overall allows uncontrollable factors to more strongly influence treatment. However, we see no reason to suppose in advance that explicit profiling, perfect proxy profiling, and imperfect proxy profiling differ in these ways; whether they do will be contingent on precisely which predictors end up in the predictive model.

Consider now the individuality explanation: explicit profiling is wrong when and because it fails to treat people as individuals. This explanation can be understood in various ways,[26] but in our view, the most plausible understanding is offered by Thomas (1992). Thomas suggests that a problem with explicit profiling is that it employs an unjustifiably coarse predictor (race), ignoring other factors that could and should be used to make finer-grained predictions.[27] Understood thus, the individualist objection seems less powerful against ML tools (whether or not they explicitly employ race) than it is against traditional recidivism prediction tools. ML tools can be given a very large set of data, and so can make finer-grained predictions than traditional tools. However, the explanation does not clearly distinguish perfect proxy profiling or explicit profiling; both are likely to employ (similarly) fine-grained predictions.

In sum, neither the control explanation nor the individuality explanation clearly establishes that perfect proxy profiling is more wrong than imperfect proxy profiling, or less wrong than explicit profiling.

6.5 Negative Outcomes

A second type of explanation for the wrongness of discrimination adverts to its unfair, unjust or otherwise disvaluable outcomes. In this section, we first (section 6.5.1) set out some specific versions of this explanation, distinguished by the nature of the outcomes they invoke, before (section 6.5.2) considering what they imply for the wrongness of perfect proxy profiling vis-à-vis imperfect proxy profiling and explicit profiling. Throughout, we will, for ease of exposition, present the explanations as appealing to the *badness* of outcomes, though, as indicated before, these explanations sometimes appeal to some more specific disvalue, such as injustice. We will also present the explanations as maintaining that *individual instances* of profiling are wrong when and because they produce bad outcomes, although there are also "collective" variants of the explanations. Individual acts of profiling that do not cause any bad outcome in isolation may form part of a broader pattern of acts that does cause bad outcomes. In such cases, it may be right to legislate against all such profiling, thus making individual cases wrongful simply because they are rightly legally proscribed (Arneson 2006; Gardner 1998, 2017). Alternatively, it may be that individual instances of profiling can be wrong, even if neither individually harmful nor legally prohibited, by virtue of the role that they play in a wider pattern of practices that produces bad outcomes. For example, perhaps engaging in profiling makes one *complicit* in a wrong committed collectively by all who profile.[28] We will not pursue these possibilities.

6.5.1　Variants of the Explanation

One outcome-based explanation for the wrongness of discrimination—the proportionality explanation—maintains that it contributes to some racial group being under-represented in advantaged positions in society, or over-represented in disadvantaged positions.[29] For instance, explicit profiling may be wrong when and because, partly as a result of the profiling, Black people make up a larger share of the population of offenders classified as "high risk" than of the population at large.[30]

Sometimes, disproportionality does not seem bad in any way. As Binns (2018, 1) notes, there is a statistical disproportion in predicted recidivism between men and women, explained partly by the fact that men really are much more likely to recidivate (see also Castro 2019, 408).[31] It is not obvious that there is anything bad about this.

Nevertheless, disproportionality is *often* bad, at least instrumentally.[32] For example, it may contribute to stereotypes that will limit future equality of resources, well-being, or opportunity. Lever (2017) suggests that profiling may lead to harmful essentialist ideas of race on which certain races have inherent predispositions to certain kinds of crime, while Solanke (2017) takes the central wrong of discrimination to be its stigmatizing effect.[33]

Disproportionality may also be instrumentally disvaluable because it aggravates some past or ongoing group-level injustice (e.g., Yost 2017, 273–282). Suppose that racial group G has been subject to systematic oppression in the past, as a result of which G-members face stronger incentives to commit crime than others, and thus have offended at higher rates. Suppose further that, as a result of their higher offending rates, members of this group are overrepresented among those deemed to be at high risk of recidivism, and thus among those subjected to the harshest criminal sentences. In this case, the harsher than average treatment meted out to *G*-members plausibly aggravates the injustice of the prior oppression by increasing its harmfulness.

We can think of the proportionality explanation as a specific version of a more general type of explanation: discrimination is wrong when and because it results in (or is part of a wider practice that results in) an unjust, unfair, or otherwise undesirable pattern of distribution of goods and ills. Some explanations of this type focus, like the proportionality explanation, on the distribution of goods and ills across *groups*. Others focus on their distribution across *individuals*. For instance, one influential view (Knight 2018; Lippert-Rasmussen 2014) holds that discrimination is wrong when and because it fails to produce the best available pattern of inter-individual distribution, as judged by *desert-weighted prioritarianism* (a theory according to which advantages enjoyed by individuals are more morally valuable (i) the worse off the individual is, and (ii) the more deserving they are).

Another type of explanation appeals to bad outcomes that can readily be understood in non-distributional terms.[34] For example, Hosein (2018) notes that explicit profiling drives a distrust of the state among members of profiled groups. He further argues that the extent of this distrust may create a situation where individuals from minority ethnic groups are alienated from their own political society and institutions. Such distrust and alienation are bad outcomes regardless of how they are distributed, though the fact that they are unequally distributed may make them worse.[35]

There are also psychological harms to the individuals who are explicitly profiled. These include the psychological effects on the individual who suffers discrimination. But they also include effects on others, including victims' loved ones and members of the group who expect future discrimination. Psychological harms identified as grounding the wrongness of discrimination include humiliation (Boylan 2008; Bou-Habib 2011), anger and resentment (Alexander 1992; Kennedy 1997), distress (Brown et al. 2000), and fear (Lever 2017; Zack 2005, 59).

6.5.2 Implications for Perfect Proxy Profiling

How does perfect proxy profiling compare to imperfect proxy profiling and explicit profiling when judged against the various outcome-based explanations surveyed above? The short answer is, "it depends"—on which specific explanation we consider, the nature of the tool employed, and the context in which it is used. Thus, we will not, in this section, seek to derive any straightforward, general answers to these questions. Instead, we describe four considerations that will be relevant to answering them.

The first consideration is relevant to the comparison between imperfect proxy profiling using traditional tools, on the one hand, and perfect proxy profiling or explicit profiling using ML tools, on the other. Whether a move from traditional tools to ML tools will exacerbate the bad outcomes discussed in the previous subsection depends in part on whether traditional tools under- or overstate the correlation between race and measured recidivism. It is tempting to think that, since traditional tools contain only an imperfect proxy for race, they must understate any correlation. This is incorrect.

Consider the following hypothetical. There is a positive correlation between membership of racial group, G, and measured (not necessarily actual) recidivism. However, this is explained by several specific correlations that work in opposing directions, with some weakening the overall correlation, and others strengthening it. For example, perhaps G-membership is correlated with economic deprivation, which makes recidivism more likely, but also with strong familial and community relationships, which make recidivism less likely. A traditional tool containing only an imperfect proxy for G-membership might overestimate the positive correlation between G-membership and recidivism because, say, the objective, demographic variables used in the tool capture economic factors well, but don't capture the strength of familial or community relationships. By contrast, an ML tool that either explicitly employed or contained a perfect proxy for G-membership would capture both factors. It would thus yield a weaker correlation between G-membership and predicted recidivism. In this context, a move from the traditional tool to an ML tool would likely mitigate some of the outcome-based concerns mentioned earlier. For example, G-members would be *less overrepresented* among those predicted to reoffend by the ML tool than among those predicted to reoffend by the traditional tool.

In other contexts, however, a move from traditional tools to ML tools could strengthen the correlation between race and predicted recidivism. For instance, suppose that social deprivation causally contributes to measured recidivism and that a correlation between such deprivation and race fully accounts for the correlation between race and measured recidivism. Suppose further that a traditional tool employs an official measure of deprivation as a predictor, but that this measure understates the degree to which deprivation is racialized, say, because it is poor at identifying the types of deprivation that are particularly common in minority racial groups. In this context, the traditional tool will understate the correlation between race and measured recidivism. By contrast, an ML tool that explicitly employs or perfectly proxies race will capture the stronger correlation between race and measured recidivism. It will thus exacerbate some outcome-based objections. For example, it will deliver even more disproportionate results.

A second consideration relevant to our moral comparison is the *claim to advantage* of those who are harmed by the adoption of one type of profiling in preference to another.

Suppose, for example, that a move from imperfect to perfect proxy profiling would tend to disadvantage G-members; it would slightly increase the proportion of G-members predicted to recidivate, and slightly decrease the proportion of others predicted to recidivate. And suppose that desert-weighted prioritarianism is the correct distributive theory: a person's claim to advantage is stronger the worse off she is, and the more deserving she is. Under these assumptions, the move to perfect proxy profiling will likely exacerbate distributive concerns if G-members are on average worse off and more deserving than others, and mitigate them if G-members are on average better off and less deserving than others.

A third consideration relevant to our moral comparison is the objectivity of the outcomes invoked by the particular outcome-based explanation of the wrongness of discrimination. Some of the bad outcomes surveyed earlier are objective in the sense that they are wholly independent of anyone's contingent beliefs about or other attitudes toward the profiling and its consequences. Suppose, for example, that the relevant bad outcome is simply that some racial groups are overrepresented among those predicted to recidivate. Whether a particular form of profiling produces this bad outcome is objective in the sense we have just described. Indeed, the outcome could occur even if no one knew or suspected that any profiling had taken place.

Others among the bad outcomes cited by the explanations surveyed earlier are *subjective*—their occurrence is dependent on contingent beliefs about or other attitudes toward the profiling. Perhaps the most obvious examples are psychological harms. Whether and to what degree a person subjected to profiling is humiliated by that profiling will, for instance, depend not only on the racial distribution of risk classifications but also on what people believe about this distribution and how it is determined. Someone categorized as high risk due to explicit profiling is less likely to feel humiliated if they falsely believe the profiling tool neither explicitly employed nor tracked race.

This distinction is particularly relevant to the comparison between perfect proxy profiling and explicit profiling. To our knowledge, all of the objections to profiling that invoke bad *objective* outcomes invoke outcomes that are mediated wholly by the way in which risk classifications (or misclassifications) are distributed across racial groups. Yet perfect proxy profiling and explicit profiling, by definition, produce the same (mis)classifications. So they will fare equally when judged against these objections.

The same conclusion cannot, however, be drawn with respect to objections that invoke bad *subjective* outcomes. Although perfect proxy profiling and explicit racial profiling produce the same distributions of risk (mis) classifications across racial groups, they might nevertheless be perceived differently and thus, for example, give rise to different psychological harms.

The fourth and final consideration is the *publicity* of the profiling. This is relevant only to explanations that invoke subjective outcomes. As noted earlier, if people do not know that profiling takes place, they are presumably less likely to be humiliated by it than if the profiling is known. Similarly, if people do not know that profiling takes place, this will likely weaken the tendency of profiling to promote widespread beliefs about the link between race and crime, so stigmatization will be less likely.

There are thus some reasons to think that a move from imperfect proxy profiling via traditional tools to perfect proxy profiling via ML tools might mitigate some of the bad outcomes mentioned earlier. While any profiling can be done secretly,[36] the workings of complex ML-derived algorithms are less accessible to the average person than traditional tools employing a small number of predictive variables, such as VRAG. Thus, it might be that an ML-derived algorithm learned a perfect proxy for race, and made sentencing recommendations on this basis, without many people knowing about it.

To the extent that discrimination is wrong by virtue of its subjective outcomes, if an ML tool developed a perfect proxy for race unbeknown to most people *and* this meant that some bad outcomes were avoided, the profiling would *in one respect* be less wrong than a comparable, publicly open method of profiling. However, it may still be more wrong overall, since profiling people in ways that cannot be subjected to reasonable public scrutiny contravenes a purported publicity requirement for democratic states (Rawls 1996, 68–69).[37]

6.6 Disrespect

A final influential family of explanations for the wrongness of discrimination centers on respect (Beeghly 2018). Some of these explanations appeal to what we call "mental state disrespect": discrimination is wrong when and because discriminators act on the basis of disrespectful attitudes or fail to act on the basis of respectful attitudes. For instance, discriminators might view members of racial minorities with unjustified hatred (Garcia 1996); inaccurately judge them to have less than equal moral worth (Alexander 1992); be culpably indifferent to their suffering (Alexander 2010, 203); or simply fail to take account of them as their moral worth demands (Eidelson 2015).[38] As noted in the introduction, while such possibilities are important, they do not raise any particular issue for perfect proxy profiling. Such profiling is plausibly no more or less likely to be based on (dis)respectful attitudes than imperfect proxy profiling. It is also, we think, not obvious that (imperfect or perfect) proxy profiling would fare any better than explicit profiling with respect to mental state disrespect. It seems initially plausible that agents motivated by the most disrespectful attitudes would be more likely than agents with better attitudes to employ explicit profiling, since they are less likely to see it as wrong. But there are reasons to doubt this; given strong legal protections against, and social disapproval of, explicit profiling, such agents might in fact be attracted to proxy profiling as a way of masking their disrespectful attitudes (Barocas & Selbst 2016, 692–693).

We will not further pursue the thought that the use of recidivism prediction tools might be disrespectful on a mental state account. Instead, we focus on an objective understanding of disrespect. Accounts that view discrimination as wrong because it is objectively disrespectful have been influential (Glasgow 2009, 2015; Hellman 2008, 2018; Scanlon 2008; Shin 2018). While such accounts vary in their detail, they share a commitment to the idea that discrimination can be disrespectful, and therefore wrong, because of its *objective social meaning*—for example, because it sends the message that members of a particular racial group are inferior—even if there is no disrespectful attitude (or lack of a respectful attitude) behind it. Actions can have an objective social meaning—where objectivity implies independence from any particular individual's contingent mental states—due to various social and historical facts, including facts about how (reasonable) people typically respond when such acts are performed.

Consider, for instance, purchasing a product in a shop. What it means to hand over pieces of metal, paper, or plastic is not independent of belief altogether, but its meaning does not depend on the *particular* intentions of specific individuals. If Marilyn hands over some legal tender, and a shopkeeper lets her take away some chocolate, Marilyn has *bought* that chocolate regardless of what she believes has happened or intended to happen. Similarly, proponents of the objective meaning explanation say, a discriminatory act can have a disrespectful meaning even if the discriminator has exemplary attitudes, and even if the victim neither knows nor suspects the act to be discriminatory (Glasgow 2015, 121). For example, it may have the meaning because many victims reasonably believe that acts of this type are normally motivated by objectionable attitudes.

Suppose the social meaning account of disrespect is correct.[39] This raises the issue of what the social meaning would be of using an ML tool where (a) the tool contains a perfect proxy for the offender's racial group, and (b) the tool classifies the offender as high risk partly on the basis of this proxy.

One option is to see ML tools as both novel and unique, and hence currently lacking any social meaning. On this view, while the use of ML tools might over time *develop* a social meaning, it currently lacks one. This would mean, a fortiori, that perfect proxy profiling cannot be objectively disrespectful.

However, racial profiling and offender risk assessments based on traditional tools are now familiar practices, and it is plausible to think that the social meaning of these practices would immediately extend to the use of ML tools. The interesting question is whether the meaning of perfect proxy profiling (via use of an ML tool that excludes race as an explicit predictor) would be closer to that of explicit profiling (via use of an ML tool that includes race as an explicit predictor), or to that of imperfect proxy profiling (via use of a traditional tool). We suspect that it would be closer to the former. This can be supported by considering the following imaginary example.

Suppose that there are only two towns—Springfield and Shelbyville—in a sparsely populated region of the USA. The residents of Springfield regard all residents of the closest town, Shelbyville, with hatred, simply because they are from Shelbyville. However, no Springfielder has ever been to Shelbyville, while Shelbyvillians—knowing about their neighbors' attitudes—avoid Springfield. All residents of both towns are thus unaware that all residents of Springfield are white, while all residents of Shelbyville are Black. One day Bart, a Springfielder, decides to go to Shelbyville to steal their town monument. On arrival, he realizes the facts about the racial divide. He also learns the reasons for the divide: several generations earlier, a combination of explicit racism on the part of white residents and racialized economic disadvantage suffered by Black residents caused Black Springfielders to leave and establish Shelbyville. While these facts were not actively hidden in subsequent generations, they were not widely discussed, and so most residents of both towns are unaware of their joint history. When Bart gets back to Springfield, he tells all his friends these facts, and soon most Springfielders know them. Yet their negative attitudes persist.

Both before and after Bart's visit, Springfielders engage in some actions—such as avoiding Shelbyville and expressing hatred for Shelbyvillians—that are motivated in part by their hatred of Shelbyvillians. What should we say about the social meaning of these actions? Before Bart's visit, Springfielders hate Shelbyvillians, but no resident of either town has reason to think that "Shelbyvillian" is coextensive with "all and only the Black residents of my local region," nor that it picks out a group whose forebears were victimized by Springfielders. While actions motivated by this hatred might have a morally questionable social meaning, it is very doubtful that they express racial disrespect. But once Bart and most other Springfielders realize the racial extension of their attitudes, and the underlying historical facts, things plausibly change. Saying "I want nothing to do with anyone from Shelbyville" very plausibly takes on a racially disrespectful meaning now that it is widely known that it covers all and only the Black residents of one's local region, and that Black people have historically been disadvantaged, in part due to explicit racism on the part of one's own predecessors. Moreover, it is plausible that it takes on this meaning even in cases where the particular person making the utterance is one of the few Springfielders who still does not know the relevant racial and historical facts, and even where this ignorance is blameless.

Similarly, our view is that, at least once it becomes clear and widely known that an ML tool has learned a perfect proxy for membership of a racial group known to have been subject to systematic and racially motivated oppression, use of the tool would plausibly come to express distinctively racial disrespect. At least, we think this would plausibly be so if use of the tool is accompanied by no efforts to mitigate its racialized meaning or disparate racial impacts, and if members of the oppressed racial group reasonably regard use of the tool as manifesting an indifference to the past injustice on the part of those who designed or use the tool (whether or not it in fact manifests such an indifference).[40] Indeed, it seems plausible that use of the tool in this context would be just as disrespectful as would using a tool that explicitly uses membership of the racial group in question, holding fixed the attitudes of those who designed and use the tool.

By contrast, the presence of a racially disrespectful social meaning becomes far less clear when the proxy is imperfect and understates the correlation between race and measured recidivism. Consider a variant of the Springfield-Shelbyville case in which some migration of Black people from Springfield to Shelbyville still occurred, and for the same reasons, but many Black people remained in Springfield, and many white people also migrated to Shelbyville for reasons unconnected to race. As a result, Springfield is only 55% white, and Shelbyville 55% Black. In this version of the case, it is less clear that the Springfielders' hatred-motivated actions have a racist meaning once the facts are widely known. Similarly, it is not clear to us that continuing to use a traditional recidivism prediction tool after discovering that one of the predictors it employs is weakly correlated with race has the same social meaning as continuing to use a tool discovered to contain a perfect proxy for race.

To be clear, we are not suggesting here that use of an imperfect proxy would never express racial disrespect or even that it would always express *less* disrespect than use of a perfect proxy.[41] Rather, our claim is that, at least in some cases—most likely when the proxy is weak—it would express no or less disrespect. This, then, may be one respect in which perfect proxy profiling is more seriously wrong than at least some instances of imperfect proxy profiling.

6.7 Conclusion and Implications for Sentencing

We have considered three different types of explanation for the wrongness of discrimination, adverting respectively to procedural unfairness, bad outcomes, and disrespect. What do these explanations imply for the wrongness of ML-based perfect proxy profiling in criminal sentencing, vis-à-vis ML-based explicit profiling, and imperfect proxy profiling using traditional tools?

One version of the appeal to procedural unfairness holds that discrimination is wrong when and because it treats some less favorably than others on the basis of factors beyond their control. This explanation does not clearly distinguish perfect proxy profiling from imperfect proxy profiling or explicit profiling; they all employ uncontrollable factors as predictors and there is, we think, no reason to suppose in advance of looking in detail at a particular tool that one type of tool will rely more heavily on such factors than another. Another version holds that discrimination is wrong when and because it fails to treat people as individuals. This explanation again fails to clearly distinguish perfect proxy profiling from explicit profiling. However, it may suggest that both, being ML-based, are typically less wrong than imperfect proxy profiling using traditional tools, since ML tools would normally employ finer-grained predictors.

Consider next explanations that appeal to bad outcomes. It is difficult to draw any straightforward and generalizable conclusions regarding the implications of these explanations for the three types of profiling under consideration. However, one relatively clear implication is that perfect proxy profiling will fare no better or worse than explicit profiling with respect to explanations that invoke bad *objective* outcomes. Another is that, to the extent that imperfect proxy profiling understates the correlation between race and measured recidivism, a move to ML tools that either include race or a perfect proxy for it will tend to strengthen racial disproportionality, increasing the degree to which members of the group picked out by the proxy are overrepresented among those assigned the highest risk classifications, and thus among those given the harshest sentences. It will thus tend to exacerbate the (further) bad outcomes, such as stigmatization, to which such disproportionality often contributes.

Consider, finally, disrespect-based explanations. None of the three types of profiling under consideration need involve mental state disrespect, and it is an open empirical question which is or are more likely to do so; however, all could involve social meaning disrespect. We suggested that, in certain contexts, perfect proxy profiling would plausibly be more disrespectful, with regard to its social meaning, than imperfect proxy profiling, and indeed that it may be as disrespectful as explicit profiling.

What implications might our arguments have? Let us briefly mention four.

First, our arguments cast doubt on the thought that, as we move from traditional to ML tools, we should retain the practice of excluding race from our predictive models. On none of the explanations that we have surveyed is it *obvious* (though on some it is *arguable*) that perfect proxy profiling using ML tools is, or is typically, less seriously wrong than explicit profiling using such tools. This suggests that, if an ML tool would indeed learn a perfect proxy for race, preventing it from explicitly employing race may not mitigate its wrongness.

Second, some of the views that we have considered are reassuring about the move from traditional to ML tools, whether or not those latter tools explicitly employ race. If the appeals to procedural fairness and/or mental state disrespect exhaust the wrongness of discrimination, there may be no reason to fear the move from traditional to ML tools, since, on these views, neither perfect proxy profiling nor explicit profiling via ML tools is clearly more seriously wrong than imperfect proxy profiling.

Third, on other views, however, the move to ML tools is of concern. Suppose that explanations appealing to bad outcomes or objective social meanings account for some of the wrongness of discrimination. On these views, imperfect proxy profiling is already morally problematic, but a move to either explicit or perfect proxy profiling exacerbates some of these problems. This suggests that the move to ML tools may bring with it a greater need for de-biasing measures.

Finally, a fourth possible implication of our arguments is that they may cast doubt on one objection to such de-biasing. De-biasing methods typically require that the recidivism prediction tool explicitly take race into account, for example, in order to adjust classifications or segment analysis on the basis of race (e.g., Corbett-Davies and Goel 2018, esp. 2, 14). One possibility, for example, is to set a different risk threshold for deeming a person to be high risk depending on their racial group.[42] Yet factoring race into tools is sometimes thought problematic, perhaps because it is taken to involve direct discrimination.[43] Hellman (2020) challenges this view at the level of law, arguing that explicitly employing race in an algorithm will not always be unlawful in the United States.[44] Our analysis suggests another kind of response. Even if de-biased algorithms would be directly discriminatory, that might not give us a decisive moral reason to eschew them, since "raw" (i.e., not de-biased) algorithms may be morally wrong in similar ways and to a similar degree. This will be plausible if direct discrimination is wrong by virtue of its disrespectful social meaning, bad objective consequences, procedural unfairness, or some combination of these. We argued that none of these factors clearly distinguish perfect proxy profiling from explicit profiling.

Notes

1. We thank, for comments on earlier versions of this chapter, Gabriel De Marco, Adam Omar Hosein, Maximilian Kiener, Kasper Lippert-Rasmussen, Frej Klem Thomsen, and the editors of this collection. For her research assistance, we thank Tess Johnson.

For their funding, we thank the European Research Council (Consolidator Award 819757).

2. This data might include, for example, "information about all contacts, of any sort, with police, social services, health services, and child welfare services" and "data from "dragnet surveillance tools," [and] closed-circuit television ("CCTV") cameras used to acquire and track license plate numbers" (Huq 2019, 1061).

3. Hacker (2018, 1151–1152).

4. Our definition here is inspired by that contained in European law. See, for example, Council Directive 2000/43/EC (2000) Art. 2, 2(a).

5. See also Berk and Hyatt (2015, 226); Corbett-Davies et al. (2017, 797, 804); Frase (2014, 149); Hellman (2020, 848); Kroll et al. 2017, 682, 685); Monahan (2014); Slobogin (2012, 13–14).

6. This point is made by Lippert-Rasmussen, this volume.

7. Here we mention only two mechanisms via which this may occur. For others, see Barocas and Selbst (2016, 692–693); Calders and Žliobaitė (2013).

8. Use of the tool in this context might, for example, make the tool-user *complicit* in the earlier discrimination.

9. See Lippert-Rasmussen, this volume, for discussion.

10. This is suggested by the fact that direct discrimination is generally regulated separately from—and indeed often more stringently than—indirect discrimination (see, for discussion, Khaitan 2015). The thought underpinning this regulatory separation is, we suspect, that direct discrimination is, other things being equal, more seriously or at least differently wrong than indirect discrimination. We are not ourselves committed to this view, and indeed our subsequent arguments imply that it is false on certain explanations of the wrongness of direct discrimination. However, we suspect many would accept it. Indeed, it is sometimes suggested that indirect discrimination is only of concern insofar as it is evidence of direct discrimination (e.g., Lim 2019, 912–913).

11. By "de-biasing," we mean alteration of a recidivism prediction tool, or the data fed into it, to improve the distribution of risk (mis)classifications across racial groups. For discussion of particular de-biasing techniques see, for example, Custers et al. (2013, 223–270); Dwork et al (2012); Hardt et al. (2016). For reviews of various strategies, see Berk et al. (2021, 24–32); Corbett-Davies and Goel (2018, 8); Hacker (2018, 1176–1177); Kroll et al. (2017, 682–692); Lepri et al. (2018, 615–618).

12. Barocas and Selbst (2016, 721, 728); Calders and Žliobaitė (2013, 54); Hardt et al. (2016, 1); Hacker (2018, 1149); Huq (2019, 1053, 1099–1100); Royal Society (2017, 92).

13. This phenomenon is often referred to as "redundant encoding." See, for discussion, Barocas and Selbst (2016, 695); Dwork et al. (2012, 226); Hacker (2018); Zimmermann et al. (2020).

14. This is what philosophers would call a "*de dicto*" ("about what is said") reading.

15. This is what philosophers would call a "*de re*" ("about the thing") reading.

16. See Thomsen (2018a, 24) and Khaitan (2015, 36–37) for discussion of similar distinctions.

17. Throughout, we use "wrong" to mean "*pro tanto* wrong," i.e., in one way wrong, unless otherwise specified.

18. We will sometimes say "more wrong" in place of "more seriously wrong." We understand both to mean "possesses a greater degree of *pro tanto* wrongness."

19. It tends to be assumed in the literature that the development of a perfect proxy for race would be a problem. See, for example, Hacker (2018, 1148–1149); Moritz et al. (2016, 1). The main contribution of this chapter is to begin to explain *why* it is a problem.

20. See, for a similar view, Huq (2019, 1094).

21. See also Lippert-Rasmussen, this volume.

22. Although we do consider this possibility in section 6.6.

23. See also Gardner (1996).

24. For discussion and criticism of this principle, see Thomsen (2018b).

25. For critical discussion, see Heinrichs (2007, esp. 105–106).

26. For critical discussion, see Beeghly (2015, 686–688); Castro (2019, 409–411); Eidelson (2015, ch. 5); Hellman (2008, 128); Lippert-Rasmussen (2011, 51–52; 2014, 275–278); Mogensen (2019, 456); and Segev (2018).

27. For critical discussion, see Lippert-Rasmussen (2011, esp. 49–53).

28. For a study of individual wrongdoing through complicity in collective wrongdoing, see Kutz (2000).

29. See Lammy (2017) for discussion of disproportionality in the United Kingdom's criminal justice system.

30. For discussion, see Lippert-Rasmussen (2014, ch. 7).

31. For an argument to the effect that disproportionality is not bad *in itself*, see Lippert-Rasmussen (2008).

32. Disproportionality is often also good evidence of other injustices, such as the presence of institutional barriers or biases that disrupt equality of opportunity (Lippert-Rasmussen 2014, 199; Yost 2017, 272–273), or the clustering of various types of disadvantages on members of a group (Castro 2019). In the context of recidivism prediction, disproportion between racial groups in those deemed to be highest risk might be suggestive of biased policing practices, or of the clustering of forms of social deprivation that tend to promote crime.

33. See also Walton (1989) and Bierria (2020).

34. For discussion of a range of such outcomes, see Thomsen (2011, 105–107).

35. Hosein (2018, e1) suggests that this alienation may create a de facto "inferior political status" (see also Alexander 2010; Crenshaw 1989).

36. For instance, Angwin et al. (2016) note that Northpointe, the provider of COMPAS, "does not publicly disclose the calculations used to arrive at defendants' risk scores."

37. Precisely how to satisfy this requirement for the workings of an ML tool is complex. It would not suffice to simply release the code that controls the algorithm's development, for there is an important difference between being "open," by releasing as much information as possible, and being "transparent," by facilitating genuine public understanding (O'Neill 2006).

38. See Gardner (1998); Lippert-Rasmussen (2014); Segall (2012); and Shelby (2002) for critical discussion.

39. See Lippert-Rasmussen (2014) and Eidelson (2015) for critical discussion, and Glasgow (2015) for a response to Lippert-Rasmussen.

40. Some might make the stronger claim that, even if no one knew about or suspected the presence of the proxy, perfect proxy profiling would have a disrespectful social meaning in this context. We remain neutral on this claim, but note that, given what is already known about machine learning, the presence of a perfect proxy is likely to be suspected by at least some members of any society that employed perfect proxy profiling.

41. Adam Omar Hosein [personal communication] rightly notes that saying, "I would never be friends with someone from Brixton" plausibly expresses disrespect for Black people even though the population of Brixton is far from 100% Black.

42. For discussion, see Hellman (2020, 848–853).

43. Corbett-Davies et al. (2017, 805): "[E]xplicitly including race as an input feature raises legal and policy complications, and as such it is common to simply exclude features with differential predictive power." Huq (2019, 1057): "the use of racially bifurcated thresholds would raise constitutional concerns akin to those engendered by affirmative action programs."

44. Although, she acknowledges (2020, 848–853) that it will be unlawful in cases where the threshold for high risk is set differently for different racial groups. See also Huq (2019, 1098).

References

Alexander, L. 1992. "What Makes Wrongful Discrimination Wrong? Biases, Preferences, Stereotypes, and Proxies." University of Pennsylvania Law Review 141: pp. 149–220.

Alexander, M. 2010. The New Jim Crow: Mass Incarceration in the Age of Colorblindness. New York: The New Press.

Angwin, J., and J. Larson. 2016. "ProPublica Responds to Company's Critique of Machine Bias Story." ProPublica, July 29. https://www.propublica.org/article/propublica-responds-to-companys-critique-of-machine-bias-story [Accessed July 31, 2020].

Angwin, J., J. Larson, S. Mattu, and L. Kirchner. 2016. "Machine Bias." ProPublica, May 23. (Accessed July 31, 2020) https://www.propublica.org/article/machine-bias-risk-assessments-in-criminal-sentencing.

Arneson, R. 2006. "What Is Wrongful Discrimination?" San Diego Law Review 43 (4): pp. 775–808.

Barocas, S., and A. D. Selbst. 2016. "Big Data's Disparate Impact." California Law Review 104 (3): pp. 677–690.

Beeghly, E. 2015. "What Is a Stereotype? What Is Stereotyping?" Hypatia 30 (4): pp. 675–691.

Beeghly, E. 2018. "Discrimination and Disrespect." In The Routledge Handbook of the Ethics of Discrimination, edited by Kasper Lippert-Rasmussen, pp. 83–96. Abingdon: Routledge.

Berk, R., and J. Hyatt. 2015. "Machine Learning Forecasts of Risk to Inform Sentencing Decisions." Federal Sentencing Reporter 27 (4): pp. 222–228.

Berk, R., H. Heidari, S. Jabbari, M. Kearns, and A. Roth. 2021. "Fairness in Criminal Justice Risk Assessments: The State of the Art." Sociological Methods & Research 50 (1): pp. 3–44.

Bierria, A. 2020. "Racial Conflation: Rethinking Agency, Black Action, and Criminal Intent." Journal of Social Philosophy. doi:10.1111/josp.12331.

Binns, R. 2018. "Fairness in Machine Learning: Lessons from Political Philosophy." Proceedings of Machine Learning Research 81: pp. 1–11.

Bou-Habib, P. 2011. "Racial Profiling and Background Injustice." Journal of Ethics 15: 33–46.

Boylan, M. 2008. "Racial Profiling and Genetic Privacy." Center for American Progress, Washington, DC, July 9. https://www.americanprogress.org/issues/courts/reports/2008/07/09/4728/racial-profiling-and-genetic-privacy/ [Accessed July 31, 2020].

Brown, T., D. Williams, J. Jackson, H. Neighbors, M. Torres, S. Sellers, and K. Brown. 2000. "Being Black and Feeling Blue: The Mental Health Consequences of Racial Discrimination." Race & Society 2 (2): pp. 117–131.

Calders, T., and I. Žliobaitė. 2013. "Why Unbiased Computational Processes Can Lead to Discriminative Decision Procedures." In Discrimination and Privacy in the Information Society: Data Mining and Profiling in Large Databases, edited by Bart Custers, Toon Calders, Bart Schermer, and Tal Zarsky, pp. 43–57. Berlin, Heidelberg: Springer.

Castro, C. 2019. "What's Wrong with Machine Bias?" Ergo 6 (15): pp. 405–426.

Chouldechova, A. 2017. "Fair Prediction with Disparate Impact: A Study of Bias in Recidivism Prediction Instruments." Big Data 5 (2): pp. 153–163.

Corbett-Davies, S., and S. Goel. 2018. "The Measure and Mismeasure of Fairness: A Critical Review of Fair Machine Learning." ArXiv:1808.00023 [Cs]. http://arxiv.org/abs/1808.00023 [Accessed July 31, 2020].

Corbett-Davies, S., E. Pierson, A. Feller, S. Goel, and A. Huq. 2017. "Algorithmic Decision Making and the Cost of Fairness." In Proceedings of the 23rd Acm Sigkdd International Conference on Knowledge Discovery and Data Mining, pp. 797–806. New York: Association for Computer Machinery.

Crenshaw, K. 1989. "Demarginalizing the Intersection of Race and Sex: A Black Feminist Critique of Antidiscrimination Doctrine, Feminist Theory and Antiracist Politics." University of Chicago Legal Forum 1: pp. 139–167.

Custers, B., T. Calders, B. Schermer, and T. Zarsky (eds.) 2013. Discrimination and Privacy in the Information Society: Data Mining and Profiling in Large Databases. Berlin, Heidelberg: Springer.

Dieterich, W., C. Mendoza, and T. Brennan. 2016. COMPAS Risk Scales: Demonstrating Accuracy, Equity and Predictive Parity. Northpointe Inc. https://go.volarisgroup.com/rs/430-MBX-989/images/ProPublica_Commentary_Final_070616.pdf [Accessed July 31, 2020].

Dwork, C., M. Hardt, T. Pitassi, O. Reingold, and R. Zemel. 2012. "Fairness through Awareness." Proceedings of the 3rd Innovations in Theoretical Computer Science Conference, pp. 214–226. Cambridge, MA: Association for Computing Machinery.

Eidelson, B. 2015. Discrimination and Disrespect. Oxford: Oxford University Press.

Frase, R. S. 2014. "Recurring Policy Issues of Guidelines (and Non-Guidelines) Sentencing: Risk Assessments, Criminal History Enhancements, and the Enforcement of Release Conditions." Federal Sentencing Reporter 26 (3): pp. 145–157.

Garcia, J. 1996. "The Heart of Racism." Journal of Social Philosophy 27: pp. 5–45.

Gardner, J. 1996. "Discrimination as Injustice." Oxford Journal of Legal Studies 16: pp. 353–367.

Gardner, J. 2017. "Discrimination: The Good, the Bad, and the Wrongful." Proceedings of the Aristotelian Society 118: pp. 55–81.

Gardner, J. 1998. "On the Ground of Her Sex(uality)." Oxford Journal of Legal Studies 18: pp. 167–187.

Glasgow, J. 2009. "Racism as Disrespect." Ethics 120 (1): pp. 64–93.

Glasgow, J. 2015. "The Meaning and Wrongness of Discrimination." Criminal Justice Ethics 34: pp. 116–129.

Gosepath, S. 2007. "Equality." Stanford Encyclopedia of Philosophy, edited by Edward N. Zalta, (Accessed July 30, 2020) https://plato.stanford.edu/archives/sum2021/ entries/equality/.

Hacker, P. 2018. "Teaching Fairness to Artificial Intelligence: Existing and Novel Strategies against Algorithmic Discrimination under EU Law." Common Market Law Review 55 (4): pp. 1143–1186.

Halldenius, L. 2018. "Discrimination and Irrelevance." In The Routledge Handbook on the Ethics of Discrimination, edited by Kasper Lippert-Rasmussen, pp. 108–18. Abingdon: Routledge.

Hardt, M., E. Price, and N. Srebro. 2016. "Equality of Opportunity in Supervised Learning." In Advances in Neural Processing Systems 29, edited by Daniel D. Lee, Ulrike von Luxburg, Roman Garnett, Masashi Sugiyama, and Isabelle Guyon, pp. 3323–31. Red Hook, NY: Curran Associates.

Heinrichs, B. 2007. "What Is Discrimination and When Is It Morally Wrong?" Jahrbuch für Wissenschaft und Ethik 12 (1): pp. 97–114.

Hellman, D. 2018. "Discrimination and Social Meaning." In The Routledge Handbook on the Ethics of Discrimination, edited by Kasper Lippert-Rasmussen, pp. 97–107. Abingdon: Routledge.

Hellman, D. 2020. "Measuring Algorithmic Fairness." Virginia Law Review 106 (4): pp. 811–866.

Hellman, D. 2008. When Is Discrimination Wrong? Cambridge, MA: Harvard University Press.

Hosein, A. O. 2018. "Racial Profiling and a Reasonable Sense of Inferior Political Status." Journal of Political Philosophy 26: pp. e1–e20.

Huq, A. 2019. "Racial Equity in Algorithmic Criminal Justice." Duke Law Journal 68 (6): pp. 1043–1134.

Kennedy, R. 1997. Race, Crime and the Law. New York: Vintage Books.

Khaitan, T. 2015. "Indirect Discrimination in US and UK Law. OUP blog. https:// blog.oup.com/2015/07/indirect-discrimination-us-uk-law/ [Accessed October 2, 2020].

Khaitan, T. 2018. "Indirect Discrimination." In The Routledge Handbook on the Ethics of Discrimination, edited by Kasper Lippert-Rasmussen, pp. 30–41. Abingdon: Routledge.

Kleinberg, J., S. Mullainathan, and M. Raghavan. 2017. "Inherent Trade-Offs in the Fair Determination of Risk Scores." In 8th Innovations in Theoretical Computer Science Conference (ITCS 2017), edited by Christos H. Papadimitrou, pp. 43:1–43:23. Leibniz: LIPIcs.

Knight, C. 2018. "Discrimination and Equality of Opportunity." In The Routledge Handbook on the Ethics of Discrimination, edited by Kasper Lippert-Rasmussen, pp. 140–150. Abingdon: Routledge.

Kroll, J. A., S. Barocas, E. W. Felten, J. R. Reidenberg, D. G. Robinson, and H. Yu. 2017. "Accountable Algorithms." University of Pennsylvania Law Review 165 (3): pp. 633–706.

Kutz, C. 2000. Complicity. Cambridge: Cambridge University Press.

Lammy, D. 2017. The Lammy Review: An Independent Review into the Treatment of, and Outcomes for, Black, Asian and Minority Ethnic Individuals in the Criminal Justice System. https://assets.publishing.service.gov.uk/government/uploads/system/uploads/attachment_data/file/643001/lammy-review-final-report.pdf [Accessed July 29, 2020].

Lepri, B., N. Oliver, E. Letouzé, A. Pentland, and P. Vinck. 2018. "Fair, Transparent, and Accountable Algorithmic Decision-Making Processes: The Premise, the Proposed Solutions, and the Open Challenges." Philosophy and Technology 31 (4): pp. 611I–627.

Lever, A. 2017. "Racial Profiling and the Political Philosophy of Race." In The Oxford Handbook of Philosophy and Race, edited by Naomi Zack, pp. 425–435. Oxford: Oxford University Press.

Lim, D. 2019. "The Indirect Gender Discrimination of Skill-Selective Immigration Policies." Critical Review of International Social and Political Philosophy 22 (7): pp. 906–928.

Lippert-Rasmussen, K. 2014. Born Free and Equal? A Philosophical Inquiry into the Nature of Discrimination. Oxford: Oxford University Press.

Lippert-Rasmussen, K. 2008. "Discrimination and the Aim of Proportional Representation." Politics, Philosophy & Economics 7 (2): pp. 159–182.

Lippert-Rasmussen, K. 2011. "'We Are All Different': Statistical Discrimination and the Right to Be Treated as an Individual." Journal of Ethics 15 (1–2): pp. 47–59.

Lum, K., and W. Isaac. 2016. "To Predict and Serve?" Significance 13 (5): pp. 14–19.

Miller, D. 1999. Principles of Social Justice. London and Cambridge, MA: Harvard University Press.

Mogensen, A. 2019. "Racial Profiling and Cumulative Injustice." Philosophy and Phenomenological Research 98 (2): pp. 452–477.

Monahan, J. 2014. "The Inclusion of Biological Risk Factors in Violence Risk Assessments." In Bioprediction, Biomarkers, and Bad Behavior: Scientific, Legal and Ethical Implications, edited by Ilina Singh, Walter Sinnott-Armstrong, and Julian Savulescu, pp. 57–76. New York: Oxford University Press.

O'Neill, O. 2006. "Transparency and The Ethics of Communication." In Transparency: The Key to Better Governance?, edited by Christopher Hood and David Heald, pp. 75–89. Oxford: Oxford University Press.

Rawls, J. 1996. Political Liberalism. New York: Columbia University Press.

Royal Society. 2017. Machine Learning: The Power and Promise of Computers That Learn by Example, https://royalsociety.org/-/media/policy/projects/machine-learning/publications/machine-learning-report.pdf [Accessed July 30, 2020].

Scanlon, T. 2008. Moral Dimensions: Permissibility, Meaning, and Blame. Cambridge, MA: Belknap Press.

Segall, S. 2012. "What's So Bad about Discrimination?" Utilitas 24 (1): pp. 82–100.

Segev, R. 2018. "Discrimination and Law Enforcement." In The Routledge Handbook on the Ethics of Discrimination, edited by Kasper Lippert-Rasmussen, pp. 324–334. Abingdon: Routledge.

Shelby, T. 2002. "Is Racism in the 'Heart'?" Journal of Social Philosophy 33 (3): pp. 411–420.

Shin, P. 2018. "Discrimination and Race." In The Routledge Handbook on the Ethics of Discrimination, edited by Kasper Lippert-Rasmussen, pp. 196–206. Abingdon: Routledge.

Slobogin, C. 2012. "Risk Assessment and Risk Management in Juvenile Justice." Criminal Justice 27 (4): pp. 10–25.

Solanke, I. 2017. Discrimination as Stigma: A Theory of Anti-discrimination Law. Oxford: Hart Publishing.

Starr, Sonja B. 2014. "Evidence-Based Sentencing and the Scientific Rationalization of Discrimination." Stanford Law Review 66 (4): pp. 803–872.

Thomas, L. 1992. "Statistical Badness." Journal of Social Philosophy 23 (1): pp. 30–41.

Thomsen, F. K. 2011. "The Art of the Unseen—Three Challenges for Racial Profiling." The Journal of Ethics 15 (1): pp. 89–117.

Thomsen, F. K. 2018a. "Direct Discriminiation." In The Routledge Handbook on the Ethics of Discrimination, edited by Kasper Lippert-Rasmussen, pp. 19–29. Abingdon: Routledge.

Thomsen, F. K. 2018b. "Concept, Principle and Norm - Equality before the Law Reconsidered." Legal Theory 24 (2): pp. 103–134.

Walton, A. 1989. "Willie Horton and Me." The New York Times, August 20, http://www.nytimes.com/1989/08/20/magazine/willie-horton-and-me.html [Accessed July 30, 2020].

Yost, B. 2017. "What's Wrong with Differential Punishment?" Utilitas 29 (3): pp. 257–285.

Zack, N. 2005. "Race and Racial Discrimination." In The Oxford Handbook of Practical Ethics, edited by Hugh La Follette, pp. 245–271. Oxford: Oxford University Press.

Zehlike, M., P. Hacker, and E. Wiedermann. 2020. "Matching Code and Law: Achieving Algorithmic Fairness with Optimal Transport." Data Mining and Knowledge Discovery 34 (1): pp. 163–200.

Zimmermann, A., E. Di Rossi, and H. Kim. 2020. "Technology Can't Fix Algorithmic Injustice." Boston Review, January 9. http://bostonreview.net/science-nature-politics/annette-zimmermann-elena-di-rosa-hochan-kim-technology-cant-fix-algorithmic [Accessed January 9, 2020].

7

Enhancing the Integrity of the Sentencing Process through the Use of Artificial Intelligence

Mirko Bagaric and Dan Hunter

7.1 Introduction

There are few areas of society that science and technology have not infiltrated completely—except, perhaps, criminal sentencing. In this chapter we discuss why sentencing and criminal justice is so resistant to technological change, focusing specifically on the implications for artificial intelligence and machine learning research into predictions of offender recidivism. In the face of widespread concerns about the limitations of data-driven decision-making, we focus on limitations with human decision-making in criminal justice and ask how a combined human-computer decision process might improve outcomes for all.

Sentencing is the sharp end of the criminal law. Mistakes in sentencing law undermine the efficacy of the entire criminal justice system and threaten community safety. It is vital therefore that decisions in this area are as accurate and just as possible. There are numerous objectives of sentencing, and sometimes these conflict with each other. In most jurisdictions, important sentencing aims include community protection, general deterrence, specific deterrence, rehabilitation, and retribution. A key consideration that relates to several of these aims is the likelihood that an offender will reoffend. This is relevant to the specific deterrence, rehabilitation, and community protection.

As Berk and Hyatt (2015, 223) note:

Forecasting has been an integral part of the criminal justice system in the United States since its inception. Judges, as well as law enforcement and correctional personnel, have long used projections of relative and absolute

Mirko Bagaric and Dan Hunter, *Enhancing the Integrity of the Sentencing Process through the Use of Artificial Intelligence* In: *Sentencing and Artificial Intelligence*. Edited by: Jesper Ryberg and Julian V. Roberts, Oxford University Press.
© Oxford University Press 2022. DOI: 10.1093/oso/9780197539538.003.0007

risk to help inform their decisions. Assessing the likelihood of future crime is not a new idea, although it has enjoyed a recent resurgence: an increasing number of jurisdictions mandate the explicit consideration of risk at sentencing.

Hence, the penalty which will be imposed on an offender is considerably shaped by whether or not the offender is likely to reoffend. In relation to many sentencing decisions, this is arguably the cardinal factual inquiry given the importance of community protection in the sentencing calculus.

The empirical data establishes that courts are very poor in predicting which offenders are likely to reoffend and there is not even an established methodology for making such decisions. As a result, automated decision-making has several demonstrable advantages over human decision-making—it is quicker, more consistent, and in some cases more transparent than human thinking. These are all important rule-of-law attributes, and the possibility exists of the two forms of decision-making being integrated to provide for more just sentencing decisions.

Against these benefits, critics contend that automated decision-making in criminal justice is impossible or unjust for three main reasons: (1) the algorithms on which these systems are based are flawed; (2) machine learning systems rely on backward-looking data that inevitably encodes discrimination; and (3) machine learning systems are black boxes that cannot be interrogated. The question is whether these criticisms mean that AI and ML approaches can never be appropriate to sentencing; and this question needs to be answered within the context of human decision-making in sentencing—that is human judging—which has been shown to be replete with inappropriate heuristics, conscious and unconscious bias, and outright discrimination.

The considerations that influence the likelihood of reoffending are factually based and do not rely on subjective matters—such as demeanor or affect—and so they should, in theory, be capable of being captured by a data-driven algorithm. While the factors that influence criminal offending are numerous and complex, they are no less so than the considerations that impact life expectancy: No insurance company would permit life insurance premiums to be determined by human judgment, and so it is with sentencing. For the same reason, we suggest that no informed legal system should continue to allow recidivism risk to be determined solely by judges, and we argue that computers should be used in sentencing, bail, and parole decisions.

A number of criticisms of predictive algorithms have been made. The most damaging is that they are discriminatory in nature. The need to eliminate racism in the criminal justice system, including in sentencing, has been elevated considerably as a result of the brutal killing of George Floyd by white police officer Derek Chauvin in Minneapolis on May 25, 2020. The killing raised the Black Lives Matter movement to the forefront of the national psyche in the United States and led to worldwide demonstrations against racism. It has always been morally unacceptable to not redress racism in the criminal justice system; but it is now no longer socially and politically acceptable to not defeat this challenge. There is an urgent need to implement measures that will demonstrably ameliorate the disproportionate burden shouldered by minority groups in the criminal justice system. This only strengthens the argument for the use of data-driven decisions in sentencing. Charges that predictive algorithms discriminate against minority groups can be rebutted, especially if the reference point is human sentencing practice.

The question then is how do human judges determine the risk of recidivism? Incredibly, there is no protocol for this. The information they have is the details of the current offense and the offender's prior history, age, family, employment status, educational history, and appearance. How they use is this unchecked. It is hard to describe the number of objectionable aspects associated with the process. A starting point is that there is no guidance regarding which considerations that are assumed to influence reoffending that can be ignored by sentencing judges, and there is no guidance regarding which of these considerations should inform best practice. Sentencing—like most bail and parole determinations—is a largely impressionistic system that is almost certainly broken, from the perspective of the rule-of-law virtues of consistency and predictability. Indeed, this latter observation is established by the empirical data: human judges are as accurate in their recidivism predictions as their toss of a coin. They also commonly exhibit unconscious bias in their sentencing decision-making, and moreover, there is no mechanism to restrain this. As Marvin Frankel (1973, 29) notes:

> [S]weeping penalty statutes allow sentences to be "individualized" not so much in terms of defendants but mainly in terms of the wide spectrums of character, bias, neurosis, and daily vagary encountered among occupants of the trial bench.

Predictive algorithms based on machine learning systems have the potential to make far more effective and fair decisions than human judges. The weakness with current risk assessment algorithms is not the methodology underlying them, but rather the fact that the institution which is tasked to currently perform this activity has been so poor at identifying the factors which impact on whether offenders will recidivate. This means that the designers of risk assessment tools had little guidance regarding the integers that should inform the instruments. Despite this, trials of current risk assessment instruments already show they are more accurate than judges, and their accuracy will only get better through advanced machine learning techniques, since data can be constantly looped back into the model.

The only situation in which we would argue that algorithmic decision-making categorically should not displace human decision-making is if transpires that there are salient variables which relate to this prediction which are impressionistic and cannot be captured in data. Theoretical examples of this might include the demeanor of an accused, their behavior in court, or the way that they were dressed. However, it is difficult to imagine that salient variables of this kind exist, and the prospect is remote that we will see the emergence of impressionistic sentencing variables.

In this chapter, we examine (1) whether machine learning systems have a constructive role in determining whether offenders are likely to reoffend; (2) the implications of this for automated sentencing; and (3) how we can integrate both human and computational decision-making. In the next part of this chapter, section 7.2, we provide an overview of the current use of algorithms in sentencing hearings and note that they are, predictably, far more common in jurisdictions which have a formulaic approach to sentencing. In the process, we set out some of the main objections that have been made to this process. This is followed in section 7.3 by our assessment of the relative limitations of human and computational decision-making. We summarize our proposals in the concluding remarks in section 7.4.

7.2 Current Use of AI in Sentencing

Sentencing is a complex activity. There are number of different objectives, which sometimes conflict. Moreover, there is no clear hierarchy associated with these objectives and there a large number of considerations which can aggravate or mitigate the ultimate penalty. The complexity of the sentencing process militates against sentencing decisions become formularized, and this seems to have been a deterrent to the use of AI in the sentencing process. The shift from applying formulaic standards to utilizing algorithms is a logical progression; the shift from a largely unfettered discretion to computer-based decisions requires a profound step change. It is thus not surprising that in jurisdictions, such as Australia, where sentencing is mainly a discretionary, activity artificial intelligence plays no or little role in sentencing; whereas predictive systems have a more expansive role in sentencing systems like the United States where the sentencing process is more rule governed.

The sentencing methodology adopted in Australia is termed the "instinctive synthesis." Adam and Crockett JJ of the Full Court of the Supreme Court of Victoria coined this term in *R v. Williscroft* [1975] VR 292, stating:

> Now, ultimately, every sentence imposed represents the sentencing judge's instinctive synthesis of all the various aspects involved in the punitive process. (para. 300)

In utilizing the instinctive synthesis to reach a specific sanction, judges need to decide which sentencing considerations are relevant, attach a particular emphasis to them, and balance them against one another. Judges are prohibited from stipulating the precise mathematical weight that they have attached to any of the individual factors that have influenced their decisions. Courts are permitted to use the instinctive synthesis in all sentencing decision-making, including where sentences are governed by mandatory minimum terms (*Bahar v. The Queen* [2011] 45 WAR 100). As a result, Australian courts have been strongly resistant to any attempt to attenuate their discretion and thus algorithms have almost no role in sentencing in Australia.

This discretionary sentencing approach varies markedly to that adopted in many parts of America. Historically sentencing judges in the United States had a wide discretion regarding the appropriate choice of sanction (Gertner 2010). As noted by Judge Nancy Gertner (2010, 696):

> Consistent with [the] . . . view of judges as the sentencing experts, Congress took a back seat, prescribing a broad range of punishments for each offense, and intervening only occasionally to increase the maximum penalty for specific crimes in response to public demand. Judges had substantial

discretion to sentence, so long as it was within the statutory range. In effect, the breadth of the sentencing range left to the courts the task of "distinguishing between more or less serious crimes within the same category."

Approximately 50 years ago, there was a strong push toward attenuating the judicial sentencing discretion. In 1973, Judge Marvel Frankel (1973, 8) in an influential commentary asserted that this indeterminate system was "lawless." The push for prescriptive penalties in the United States coincided with the "tough on crime" political agenda that emerged in the 1960s and 1970s, which was a response to increases in the crime rate and skepticism about the capacity of the criminal justice system to rehabilitate offenders (Kim and Peterson 2014).

The move toward guideline (or mandatory) sentencing grew quickly and today all US jurisdictions to some degree have penalties of this nature (Tonry 2014, 516). Twenty US jurisdictions have *extensive* guideline sentencing systems. These guidelines assign fixed or presumptive penalties, with the two main determinants of penalty severity being the seriousness of the offense and the prior criminal history of the offender.

Fixed sentencing statutes in effect set out a formulaic approach to sentencing, which is in effect a sentencing algorithm, albeit one which judges must manually operate. In this climate, it is thus not surprising that there would be some receptivity toward computer-operated instruments.

Computational methods have been involved in sentencing in the United States in some respects since at least the 1980s. Recent approaches are able to model more sophisticated aspects of the sentencing process, and here the key focus has been on evaluating an offender's risk of reoffending. Risk and needs assessment tools are often referred to interchangeably with risk assessment tools; however, there are some significant functional differences between them. Risk assessments measure an offender's chances of reoffending and thereby endangering the public (McGarraugh 2012, 1091). The instruments seek to reduce an offender's risk of recidivism by determining which programs and other interventions would stop them reoffending (McGarraugh 2012, 1091). Risk and needs assessment tools rely on a technique called "structured professional judgment" (Slobogin 2012, 199). It differs from a strictly actuarial approach because the main goal of this type of instrument is to generate the information required to create a needs assessment and a risk management plan, whereas an actuarial approach predicts antisocial behavior (Slobogin 2012, 199). The main differences between them are the integers that they use and the weightings they apply to considerations viewed as relevant to the risk of future offending. These systems catalog "life facts" that can be used to determine an individual's propensity to commit crimes, which directly impacts the sentence a person may receive (Seo 2019, n.p.). An offender's criminal history is a constant, base determinant (Hamilton 2015, 89) and other key variables include an offender's criminal associates, pro-criminal attitudes, and antisocial personality (Hamilton 2015, 90).

One of the most sophisticated tools of this sort is the Post-Conviction Risk Assessment (PCRA), an instrument currently used for probation assessments in the US federal jurisdiction. It is one of the latest (fourth) generation predictive tools and it is more nuanced than many earlier predictive models. It scores not only static factors, such as prior criminal history, but also looks to dynamic variables, such as employment status and history, education, and family relationships (Hamilton 2015, 91–92). The score provided by this kind of risk and needs assessment system is not designed to only predict the offender's risk of reoffending, and considerations outside the instrument can be taken into account to reduce the individual's risk of recidivism.

Sentencing is an area where the use of risk assessment is controversial "because of the high stakes of criminal sentencing and because sentencing decisions are informed by many other goals beyond simply incapacitating those at high risk of reoffending . . ." (Stevenson and Doleac 2019, 7) Despite this, many states rely on risk and needs assessment tools when determining "an individual's likelihood of recidivism for bail, sentencing, and parole decisions" (Seo 2019, n.p.). And as the Brennan Center for Justice noted, "states are increasingly turning toward risk assessment tools to help decide how much time people should spend behind bars" (Austin et al. 2017, 46; Metz and Satariano 2020). The use of the tools has been sanctioned by the courts, despite concerns that the tools were flawed, and it is worth considering the approaches of the US courts to these tools (*Malenchik v. Indiana*, 928 N.E.2d 564 [Ind. 2010]; *State v. Loomis*, 371 Wis. 2d 235 [2016]).

The fact that the tools have withstood legal challenge has paved the way in the United States for increased use of the instruments. Predictive algorithms have been enshrined in the recently enacted FIRST STEP Act. Passed in December 2019, that statute aims to lower federal prison numbers (White House 2018). Pursuant to the Act, various offenses, including drug crimes, now attract more lenient sanctions; offenders' criminal history plays a greater role in the determination of their sentences and prisoners can be released early based on various criteria.

The legislation required the Attorney General to create a "Risk and Needs Assessment System," which evaluates prisoners' risk of reoffending and the programs that will assist them most to lower that risk (Sample 201, 2018). Pursuant to this legislation, the Department of Justice developed the "Prisoner Assessment Tool Targeting Estimated Risk and Needs"—or PATTERN—system. It is computationally driven, but incorporates the following key principles (Office of the Attorney General 2018, 26):

1. It utilizes a dynamic individualized assessment, which evaluates offenders' risks and needs by reference to factors that are susceptible to change, including their conduct while incarcerated, rather than solely immutable matters such as the nature of their offenses (Office of the Attorney General 2018, 26);

2. It is subject to periodic re-validation and updating (Office of the Attorney General 2018, 27–28);

3. The instrument which the system encodes is designed to be racially and ethnically neutral (and has been the subject of widespread consultation and modification to account for community concerns in this area) (Office of the Attorney General 2018, 28); and

4. It assesses the criminogenic profile of offenders in order that measures can be developed to lessen their risks of reoffending. (Office of the Attorney General 2018, 29)

The tool involves undertaking a risk and needs assessment of all prisoners; improving the needs assessment system; bringing the earned time credit system into operation; making the workflow automatic; and bringing into effect policies that incite prisoners to participate in programs that can reduce their risk of reoffending and thus maximize their chances of early release (Office of the Attorney General 2018, 71–72). After considerable consultation, the tool has been revised to contain 15 factors in total, 11 of which are dynamic and the remaining are static. These include factors focused on infractions while in prison, escape attempts, age, nature of offense, drug treatment, and so on (Office of the Attorney General 2020).

The Department of Justice has already commenced to implemented the FIRST STEP Act (Office of the Attorney General 2020). By early 2020, more than 3,100 prisoners who did not commit sexual or violent offenses have already been released pursuant to the Act (Department of Justice 2020). Additionally, 2,471 orders have been issued for sentence reduction, 124 requests for compassionate release have been approved, and 2,000 inmates are on home confinement (Department of Justice 2020). Moreover, 379 inmates have been approved to enroll in a pilot program that aims to transition "eligible elderly and terminally ill offenders" to home confinement (Department of Justice 2020).

7.3 Balancing Human and AI Limitations in Sentencing

As we saw in section 7.1, human decision-making in sentencing has been criticized as being unjust and, in some respects, structurally discriminatory. In section 7.2 we saw how early computational methods have been incorporated into some sentencing regimes—notably in the United States—to seek to improve the fairness and justice within the system. The question remains however: Given that both automated decision-making systems and human systems come with a host of problems, how might we build an integrated approach that uses the strengths of each, and ameliorates the limitations of both?

The criticisms of the use of artificial intelligence methods within sentencing are well known, and aired by many of the contributors to this book. Zerilli discusses the "CSI effect" where humans become too enamored of automated decision-making, and thereby cede all decision-making to the system. Thomsen, Ryberg, Chiao, and Ryberg and Petersen discuss concerns around transparency of systems built around large and inscrutable datasets; while Lippert-Rasmussen and Douglas and Davies examine issues that revolve around bias within those datasets. For their part, Schwarze and Roberts and Dagan and Baron argue that legal reasoning involves features that are more than binary and something may be lost if there is no sentencing hearing and these aspects are not codable or not found in the data alone.

Concerns about automated decision-making in sentencing are reflections of general ethical concerns about automated decision-making in society. Mittelstadt et al. give a useful six-element categorization of ethical AI concerns (2016): concerns about "inconclusive evidence" stem from the recognition that judgments are made on probabilistic assessment of data; "inscrutable evidence" focuses on the black box problem in current data-driven systems (Pasquale 2015); "misguided evidence" refers to the use of biased and/or inaccurate data in building the system; "unfair outcomes" stem from unguided actions of the algorithm; "transformative effects" focuses on

non-human perceptions of the world that come from the probabilistic assessment of risk; "traceability" focuses on the difficulty of ascribing responsibility mixed human-machine decision-making (Hood 2007; Wagner 2019).

All of the concerns expressed by the contributors in this book and others
outside are valid. But they generally operate within an assessment framework that presumes that human decision-making and the structural makeup
of the criminal justice system is fair, consistent, and just. As we document in
section 7.1 above, this is not the case. So, given that human decision-making
is nothing to write home about, how might we assess computational, data-
driven decision-making?

7.3.1 Advantages of AI

Algorithmic decision-making in sentencing has a number of clear benefits
over human decision-making. In purely pragmatic terms, algorithms are
fast, consistent, and tireless (Bolingford et al. 2020). In an environment
where resource constraints are a meaningful limit on just decision-making,
these attributes are significant.

Algorithms are also more transparent than human decision-making. This
is not to say that all aspects of machine learning systems are transparent—the
black box concerns of Pasquale and others are well-taken, and research is still
progressing on explanatory artificial intelligence (Adadi and Berrada 2018;
Miller 2019). But it is certainly the case that *all* algorithmic decision-making
is more transparent than *all* human decision-making: the reasoning process
by which humans make decisions is *always* opaque, since we have no idea
which group of synapses firing in the brain of a judge led to any given decision. All explanations of human decisions—in sentencing or otherwise—
are at best a reconstruction of lower-level operations in the brain, the details
of which we can only guess. Given the irreducible opaqueness of human
decision-making, algorithms decision-making can be readily made more
transparent and explainable.

Sentencing involves the deliberate infliction of sanctions on citizens, including the imposition of financial penalties; the deprivation of liberty; and,
in extreme cases, the death penalty. Sentencing decisions can have a major
impact on people's lives, and it is unjustifiable for courts to make inconsistent,
arbitrary, or opaque decisions, as such decisions would fundamentally violate
the rule of law (Raz 1979; Finnis 1980; Jowell 1985). The rule of law is both

a legal doctrine and normative concept of modern liberal democratic countries, which constitutes "an ideal towards which a legal order should move if it is . . . to secure certainty in human relations" (Walker 1988, 1). Although it is important that the law remains flexible and changes in response to shifting public opinion, there is a crucial "need for certainty and stability in the law so that people will be able to plan and organize their arrangements in accordance with it (Walker 1988, 42)." Consistent, predictable, and transparent sentencing decisions constitute a crucial safeguard of the rule of law. It is a cornerstone of our system of justice that like cases be treated alike (Hall 2005, 3), and "there is universal acceptance that consistency of approach should be an essential feature of sentencing decision-making" (Hall 2005, 31).

Of course, some sentencing or recidivism prediction systems are proprietary, and there is no legitimate basis for an acceptance of this in relation to sentencing. In some criminal justice areas, it is important to keep confidential the workings of an algorithmic system, for example, in predictive policing where perpetrators might be able exploit the system if known. But the sentencing system is a backward-looking field and has a lesser chance to game the system by identifying the relevant algorithm or data (apart from factors which are informed by answers given defendants). The general acceptance of the commercially locked black box of some current risk assessment instruments is not a necessary feature of automated decision-making systems in sentencing and should be resisted.

The final advantage of artificial intelligence-based systems is they are more accurate in predicting certain types of future behavior. This is particularly notable in recidivism prediction. Although human decision-making in sentencing could theoretically be better than a computational alternative, the problem is that humans are susceptible to numerous biases and heuristics which—as we discussed in section 7.1 above—means that their recidivism assessments tend to be systematically skewed and unjust. Of course, this is not true for all types of assessment, and in areas such as witness credibility humans will beat computers for a long time. That sort of assessment depends on a range of considerations, including logical coherence of the statement, or assessment of witness affect, body language, and demeanor—the assessment of which computers are unlikely ever to be as capable as humans.

The likelihood that a person will reoffend is not, however, one that involves impressionistic considerations (and certainly none have been plausibly articulated). The factors that inform recidivism risk are all binary, in that they do not require an assessment of impressionistic considerations such as credibility. Certainly, the current practices which are used to determine recidivism risks do not incorporate offender credibility into the decision-making process, and in most sentencing hearings offenders do not give evidence. The considerations that effect recidivism risk are of the same nature as those which impact on an individual's life expectancy or the likelihood that they will suffer a specific illness. Computers are much better at determining these sorts of factors than humans. There is no reason in principle that recidivism risk is any different. For example, a study by Aleš Završnik involving 1.36 million pretrial detention cases showed that "a computer could predict whether a suspect would flee or re-offend better than a human judge" (2019, 3), though there are debates within scholarly circles as to what constitutes "success" (2019, 2) and fairness (Hellman 2020, 2) in the context of using AI in the criminal justice system.

The overall conclusion of all of the studies is clear: although risk assessment and risk and needs assessment tools are far from perfect, the best instruments, when administered by well-trained staff, can predict r-offending with 70% accuracy (Latessa and Lovins 2010, 212). Risk assessment and risk and needs assessment tools are generally more accurate than unstructured court judgments and, moreover, the rate of recidivism even among offenders who were deemed to have a high risk of reoffending was reduced when they participated in treatment programs recommended by risk and needs assessments (James 2015, 8).

It seems then that case for the measured application of algorithmic decision-making in sentencing—especially in recidivism assessment—is clear. However, there are two remaining concerns that can undermine the desirability of using artificial intelligence in this area. The first relates to bias, and the second relates to human aversion to algorithmic decision-making. We consider each of these issues in the sections following.

7.3.2 Overcoming Bias

To prevent the recreation of existing biases, predictive instruments must be developed carefully with a focus on preventing the operation of factors that lead to indirect discrimination, which will minimize the potential for race and other immutable factors to influence the outcomes of risk assessment algorithms. The key to achieving this is to understand fully the types of considerations that can act as proxies for the coding of inappropriate traits and to exclude them from the design of the algorithm (Bagaric, Hunter , and Stobbs 2020). This objective is not readily achievable.

Although algorithms are designed to discriminate or discern information, they are not necessarily in tune with what is socially acceptable (Edwards and Veale 2017, 28). Things that would normally be considered protected characteristics, such as gender, race, pregnancy status, religion, sexuality, and disability, all play a part in human decision-making processes. This suggests that algorithms trained using "past biased data" are likely to recreate the same biases in their decision-making processes, further exacerbating discrimination and unfairness (Edwards and Veale 2017, 28). Julia Dressel and Hany Farid found that one of the most widely used risk assessments systems, COMPAS (an acronym for "Correctional Offender Management Profiling for Alternative Sanctions") had an inherent bias which resulted in it incorrectly categorizing a number of Black defendants as high risk (Lapowsky 2018). The bias confirms that certain data may "act as proxies" for racial data even when race is not specifically considered as a data point.

This conclusion is disputed by the private company that created COMPAS who have argued that "the overall predictive accuracy of the COMPAS is similar across racial groups, making the algorithm itself ostensibly unbiased, even where *outcomes* based on the tool—such as who gets detained pretrial— differ systematically by race" (Picard et al. 2019, 3).

In an effort to determine the extent to which recidivism algorithms discriminate against certain racial groups, the Center for Court Innovation conducted a study "using a sample of 175,000 anonymized New York City defendants and an assessment tool created solely for the purpose of exploring questions related to risk prediction and pretrial outcomes" (Picard et al. 2019, 4). The analysis suggested that the concerns surrounding COMPAS may apply to "other risk assessment tools and jurisdictions," as the Center for Court Innovation's risk assessment tool was also "more likely to misclassify Black defendants as high-risk when compared to Hispanic or White defendants" (Picard et al. 2019, 4). The authors found, however, that their risk assessment tool was able to perform well in making predictions, regardless of race or ethnicity, concluding that "re-arrest rates increased progressively, in near-lockstep, as risk categories move from minimal to high" (Picard et al. 2019, 6).

Despite racial disparities, the Center for Court Innovation did not argue that pretrial risk assessment tools should be abandoned (Picard et al. 2019, 13). Instead, the Center argued that taking on a "strategy of reserving pretrial detention only for defendants facing serious, violent charges and using risk based decision-making only with those charges" will help reduce "both un-necessary detention and . . . racial disparities" (Picard et al. 2019, 14).

We agree with Christopher Slobogin that "enhancing the punishment of an offender because of gender, age, or any other immutable characteristic strikes some as grossly unfair" (2012, 203–205). If immutable traits are to be factored into the sentencing calculus, there must be an examination of how they operate and a sound justification for how the trait in question should properly impact sentencing outcomes. This, too, has been noted by Slobogin (2012, 203–205):

> The Supreme Court, however, does not believe that risk assessment is an-tithetical to criminal justice. . . . If sentences can be enhanced in response to risk, then neither society's nor the offender's interests are advanced by prohibiting consideration of factors that might aggravate or mitigate that risk simply because they consist of immutable characteristics. In any event, risk-based sentences are ultimately based on a prediction of what a person will do, not what he is; immutable risk factors are merely evidence of future conduct, in the same way that various pieces of circumstantial evidence are not blameworthy in themselves.

As noted by Sam Corbett-Davies, we need to distinguish between poorly designed algorithms and well-designed algorithms, the latter of which "can mitigate pernicious problems with unaided human decisions" (Corbett-Davies, Goel, and González-Bailón 2017). Algorithms are not perfect, but "[i]t is misleading and counterproductive to blame the algorithm for uncovering real statistical patterns" (Corbett-Davies, Goel, and González-Bailón 2017, n.p.). Because algorithms are not perfect, Corbett-Davies noted that policymakers must be aware of how statistical judgments may become corrupted (Corbett-Davies, Goel, and González-Bailón 2017). Criticisms of algorithms cannot just compare them to "some perfect ideal, but also against the very imperfect status quo" (Neufield 2017, n.p.). Accordingly, "[p]ublic officials have a social responsibility to pursue the opportunities that algorithms present, but to do so thoughtfully and rigorously" (Neufield 2017, n.p.). As part of this effort, public officials must know how algorithms work and must expand research to improve accuracy and fairness (Neufield 2017). Algorithms can help reform the criminal justice system, but they "must be carefully applied and regularly tested to confirm that they perform as in-tended" (Corbett-Davies, Goel, and González-Bailón 2017, n.p.).

In terms of evaluating the desirability of incorporating algorithms into sentencing, it is important to contrast human with computer decision-making. To this end, subconscious bias in sentencing is rife. African Americans are imprisoned at more than five times the rate at which white Americans are imprisoned (West, Sabol, and Greenman 2010). Moreover, according to a particularly wide-ranging study that surveyed over 77,000 offenders who received sentences, Black defendants are sentenced to prison terms that are 12% longer than prison terms issued to White offenders who have committed the same crimes and have identical criminal histories (Everett and Wojtkiewicz 2002; Abrams, Bertrand, and Mullainathan 2012). Likewise, a study undertaken for the United States Bureau of Justice Statistics and the United States Department of Justice Working Group on Racial Disparity found that, in the federal jurisdiction between 2005 and 2012, judges imposed prison sentences on Black men that were approximately 5% to 10% longer than those imposed on white offenders for similar offenses (Rhodes et al. 2015). During that period, courts had considerable discretion regarding sentencing because, the United States Supreme Court held in *United States v. Booker* that the federal Sentencing Guidelines were advisory rather than mandatory (Rhodes et al. 2015, 23). While the report for this study notes that it is "difficult to attribute racial disparity to skin color alone" (Rhodes et al. 2015, 67). it also comments:

> We are concerned that racial disparity has increased over time since Booker. Perhaps judges, who feel increasingly emancipated from their guidelines restrictions, are improving justice administration by incorporating relevant but previously ignored factors into their sentencing calculus, even if this improvement disadvantages black males as a class. But in a society that sees intentional and unintentional racial bias in many areas of social and economic activity, these trends are a warning sign. It is further distressing that judges disagree about the relative sentences for white and black males because those disagreements cannot be so easily explained by sentencing-relevant factors that vary systematically between black and white males . . . We take the random effect as strong evidence of disparity in the imposition of sentences for white and black males. (Rhodes et al. 2015, 68)

Other studies have also found that heavier penalties have been imposed on Black offenders who harmed White victims than on offenders who harmed

Black victims, which the authors concluded was attributable to the notion that because "the judges were also white . . . their in-group or worldview was more threatened by criminal conduct against persons from their in-group" (Sporer and Goodman-Delahunty 2009, 390).

Empirical studies have uncovered that offenders from minority groups—especially African Americans—often receive more severe sentences than white offenders who have committed comparable crimes (Ochi 1985). Researchers have found that racial bias has contributed to this disparity, thereby undermining the rule of law, a critical component of which is "the rules of natural justice," including "the requirement of an unbiased tribunal" (Walker 1988).

By contrast, data-driven algorithmic decision-making can methodically eliminate bias in recidivism predictive tools. This is an express object of the US Department of Justice in relation to the PATTERN tool, and although algorithms like PATTERN are not perfect from the perspective of discriminating against African Americans, they discriminate against African Americans far less than judges. Since it is possible to run regressions over the data used in these algorithms, the systems can be trained to weed out bias. This is considerable improvement on human decision-making, where it has been demonstrated that there is little that can be done to negate subconscious bias.

The key point here is not to suggest that algorithmic systems are perfect. Rather, it is to recognize that we can build automated decision-making that can control for discriminatory elements. By contrast, little is being—or can be—done to negate judicial bias.

7.2.3 Overcoming Algorithmic Aversion

Part of the reason why computationally based sentencing is troubling lies in a lack of confidence in the process, and to an issue sometimes labeled "algorithmic aversion" (Bagaric, Hunter, and Stobbs 2019).

Although algorithms in a wide range of areas have now been around for some time, most studies have concentrated on consumer algorithms, marketing algorithms, and social media algorithms, which are likely to affect choice, governance, and social behaviors. Developments in technology have allowed for further growth of algorithms in all areas of human life. Tensions exist and continue to develop around the ethics, transparency, and fairness of algorithmic decision-making, specifically around decisions predominately or at least historically made by humans. One reason for distrust of algorithms is widespread confusion regarding their functionalities and in particular the manner in which computer systems are capable of self-learning. This leads to fears that AI will trump human sovereignty.

Numerous studies have been undertaken which consider these tensions, in particular the perceived lack of trust and lack of control around algorithmic decisions (Dietvorst 2016; Dietvorst, Simmons, and Massey 2018). Indeed, researchers have gone as far as to label this lack of control and bias in favoring human forecasting and outcome predicting as "algorithmic aversion" (Dietvorst, Simmons, and Massey 2015). Essentially, algorithmic aversion, as coined by Dietvorst in his studies in this field, refers to the phenomenon of a positive bias toward human-based decision-making, even when an algorithm has proven more competent than its human counterpart (Dietvorst, Simmons, and Massey 2015, 114). One theme seen throughout various studies in human-automation trust research is that humans expect algorithmic perfection—meaning zero errors—while permitting humans to be imperfect and to make mistakes and still favoring human decision-making (Prahl and Van Swol 2017; Goodwin, Gönül, and Önkal 2013). In fact, studies have shown that people prefer flawed human forecasts to flawless algorithmic forecasts (Diab et al. 2011; Dietvorst, Simmons, and Massey 2015; Eastwood, Snook, and Luther 2012). The reason why humans are so averse to trusting algorithms in making correct predictions and decisions is based on several themes that have been deduced by these studies. The main themes around aversion to algorithmic-based decisions and judgments falls into the broad categories of trust/control/transparency that underpin the basics of human nature and social norms.

However, algorithmic aversion is not insurmountable. It has been shown that people are much more inclined to trust and maintain confidence in an algorithm when they have, or believe they have, some level of control over the outcome (Dietvorst 2016; Dietvorst, Simmons, and Massey 2015, 2018; Prahl and Van Swol 2017). They are also more likely to trust and use an algorithm when they have seen how it works and how well it determines correct outcomes (Dietvorst 2016; Dietvorst, Simmons, and Massey 2018). Another avenue for building control and trust is the opacity and transparency of algorithmic decision-making processes. Legislation such as Europe's General Data Protection Regulation ("GDPR") regulates the right to an explanation for a decision made by an algorithm. Although new, and as some scholars note "restrictive, unclear and paradoxical" (Edwards and Veale 2017, 18) this is a step in the right direction for increasing trust in algorithmic decisions. In terms of public decision-making, this is similar to an explanation of rights made under the Freedom of Information Act, where transparency is seen "as one of the bastions of democracy, liberal government, accountability and restrain on arbitrary or self-interested exercises of power" (Edwards and Veale 2017, 39). However, as Edwards and Veale note, "the apparatus of accountability of private decision-making" is less than transparent due to commercial and trade secrets and protection of IP rights (2017, 39). Transparency and accountability are important in the use of algorithmic decision-making especially where it may have an adverse effect on an individual. Edwards and Veale state that transparency rights "remain intimately linked to the ideal of effective control of algorithmic decision-making" (2017, 41). Furthermore, social values such as "human dignity," "information accountability," and "autonomy and respect" all play a part in how society views decision-making processes.

In order to overcome algorithmic aversion in the sentencing domain researchers need to have access to the largest possible datasets and have access to the outcomes from existing widely used risk and needs assessment tools in order that they can evaluate the variables which are most relevant to accurately predicting recidivism. These can be used as a starting point in developing more accurate algorithms, which are nuanced to the particular offender and offense profiles. This type of approach has been successfully applied in a manual manner in the New Zealand Department of Corrections study on the risk of imprisonment and risk of reconviction (Bakker, O'Malley, and Riley 1999). In that study, the researchers used a very large dataset collected by the NZ Department of Corrections, detailing the criminal lives of 133,000 offenders. They were able to demonstrate a statistical model that predicted the probabilities of offenders reoffending and their likelihood of going to prison for the offense. This kind of dataset and model can be easily used by machine learning systems to generate meaningful outputs that can provide immediate guidance in sentencing decisions.

A key component of a fair offense predictive model is transparency, which we discussed earlier in this chapter. As we have seen, commercial interests often preclude the dissemination of the coding used to develop and run algorithms. In the context of the criminal justice system, however, commerciality cannot be used a basis for limiting full transparency. The criminal justice system is the forum where society, through its courts, acts in its most coercive manner against individuals. It is a public and democratic demonstration and utilization of power and results in the deliberate infliction of suffering against offenders. The commercial interests of individuals or corporations cannot undercut the public nature of the criminal justice system. The integrity of the system commands total transparency. Thus, algorithms which are used to determine future offending should be developed by public institutions. Alternatively, if they are developed by the private sector and adopted by the criminal justice system, then the government must purchase all legal and commercial interests in the programs in order that their workings can be made public. Moreover, the benefit of greater transparency is that it will facilitate the testing of the algorithms and provide scope for their continual evaluation, refinement, and improvement.

The need for transparency and validation of risk and needs assessment tools is well recognized and in relation to some tools, steps are being taken to ensure that this occurs. Thus, there is still work to be done to make to achieve total transparency regarding the workings of predictive algorithms. But considerable progress is unquestionably being made. By contrast, little progress is occurring in changing the structural and psychological problems with human (judicial) recidivism predictions.

7.4 Conclusion

The likelihood that an offender will reoffend is an important consideration regarding three sentencing objectives: specific deterrence, rehabilitation, and community protection. Despite the seminal role of this factor, the courts and lawmakers have not set out in detail the process by which this should be determined. Thus, courts are inaccurate in making these decisions.

It is thus, not surprising that in at least some jurisdictions algorithmic decision-making is being used to determine the risk of recidivism. This technology is still at an early stage and its use is controversial, especially because some commentators have argued that programs discriminate against certain offenders. Despite this, artificial intelligence promises to ameliorate many of the limitations in human decision-making in sentencing.

The factors that culminate in people committing crime are not random. They are numerous and complex but identifiable in the same way as life expectancy. No insurance company would use human judgment to determine life insurance premiums and no court should only use judges to determine recidivism risk.

The real question is not whether artificial intelligence should or will replace judges, but rather what the design features of an optimal sentencing system that involves both humans and machines. The key to securing greater receptivity and efficacy of artificial intelligence in all areas of the criminal justice is ensuring greater transparency regarding the design of the algorithms and explaining their operation to users and the public. But even then, the aversion that we all have to inexplicable machine decisions will mean a long and difficult journey for those seeking the adoption of automated decision-making in sentencing.

References

Abrams, D. S., M. Bertrand, and S. Mullainathan. 2012. "Do Judges Vary in Their Treatment of Race?" The Journal of Legal Studies 41: 347–383.

Adadi, A., and M. Berrada. 2018. "Peeking Inside the Black-Box: A Survey on Explainable Artificial Intelligence (XAI)." IEEE Access 6: 52138–52160.

Austin, J., L.-B. Eisen, J. Cullen, J. Frank, I. Chattiar, and C. W. Brooks. 2017. "How Many Americans Are Unnecessarily Incarcerated?" Federal Sentencing Reporter 29: 140–174.

Bagaric, M., D. Hunter, and N. Stobbs. 2019. "Erasing the Bias against Using Artificial Intelligence to Predict Future Criminality: Algorithms Are Color Blind and Never Tire." University of Cincinnati Law Review 88: 1037–1081.

Bagaric, M., D. Hunter, and N. Stobbs. 2020. "Framework for the Efficient and Ethical Yse of Artificial Intelligence in the Criminal Justice System." Florida State University Law Review: 47: 749–800.

Bakker, L., J. O'Malley, and D. Riley. 1999". Risk of Reconviction: Statistical Models Which Predict Four Types of Re-offending," viewed September 6, 2020, https://www.corrections.govt.nz/__data/assets/pdf_file/0020/10667/roc.pdf

Berk, R., and J. Hyatt. 2015. "Machine Learning Forecasts of Risk to Inform Sentencing Decisions." Federal Sentencing Reporter 27: 222–228.

Bolingford, I., M. Bagaric, M. Bull, D. Hunter, and N. Stobbs. 2020. "Is Australia Ready for AI on the Bench?" Journal of Judicial Administration 30: 3–18.

Corbett-Davies, S., S. Goel, and S. Gonzales-Bailon. 2017. "Even Imperfect Algorithms Can Improve the Criminal Justice System." New York Times, viewed September 6, 2020, https://www.nytimes.com/2017/12/20/upshot/algorithms-bail-criminal-justice-system.html.

Department of Justice. 2020. "Department of Justice Announces Enhancements to the Risk Assessment System and Updates on First Step Act Implementation," viewed September 5, 2020, https://www.justice.gov/opa/pr/department-justice-announces-enhancements-risk-assessment-system-and-updates-first-step-act.

Diab, D. L., S. Y. Pui, M. Yankelevich, and S. Highhouse. 2011. "Lay Perceptions of Selection Decision Aids in US and Non-US Samples." International Journal of Selection and Assessment 19: 209–216.

Dietvorst, B. 2016. "People Reject (Superior) Algorithms Because They Compare Them to Counter-Normative Reference Points." Available at: SSRN 2881503.

Dietvorst, B. J., J. P. Simmons, and C. Massey, C. 2015. "Algorithm Aversion: People Erroneously Avoid Algorithms after Seeing Them Err." Journal of Experimental Psychology: General 144: 114.

Dietvorst, B. J., J. P. Simmons, and C. Massey. 2018. "Overcoming Algorithm Aversion: People Will Use Imperfect Algorithms if They Can (Even Slightly) Modify Them." Management Science 64: 1155–1170.

Eastwood, J., B. Snook, and K. Luther. 2012. "What People Want from Their Professionals: Attitudes toward Decision-Making Strategies." Journal of Behavioral Decision Making 25: 458–468.

Edwards, L., and M. Veale. 2017. "'Slave to the Algorithm: Why a Right to an Explanation Is Probably Not the Remedy You Are Looking For." Duke Law & Technology Review 16: 18.

Everett, R. S., and R. A. Wojtkiewicz. 2002. "Difference, Disparity, and Race/Ethnic Bias in Federal Sentencing." Journal of Quantitative Criminology 18: 189–211.

Finnis, J. 1980. Natural Law and Natural Rights. Oxford: Clarendon Press.

Frankel, M. E. 1973. Criminal Sentences: Law without Order. New York: Hill & Wang.

Gertner, J. N. 2010. "A Short History of American Sentencing: Too Little Law, Too Much Law, or Just Right." The Journal of Criminal Law and Criminology (1973–): 100: 691–708.

Goodwin, P., M. S. Gönül, and D. Önkal. 2013. "Antecedents and Effects of Trust in Forecasting Advice." International Journal of Forecasting 29: 354–366.

Hall, M. J. J., D. Calabro, T. Soudin, and A. Stranier 2005. "Supporting Discretionary Decision-Making with Information Technology: A Case Study in the Criminal Sentencing Jurisdiction." University of Ottawa Law and Technology Journal 1: 1–36.

Hamilton, M. 2015. "Back to the Future: The Influence of Criminal History on Risk Assessments." Berkeley Journal of Criminal Law 20: 75.

Hellman, D. 2020. "Measuring Algorithmic Fairness." Virginia Law Review 106: 811 (In Press).

Hood, C. 2007. "What Happens When Transparency Meets Blame-Avoidance." Public Management Review 9: 191–210.

James, N. 2015. Risk and Needs Assessment in the Criminal Justice System. Washington, DC: Congressional Research Service.

Jowell, J. L. 1985. "The Rule of Law Today." In The Changing Constitution, edited by J. Jowell and D. Olivier, 2nd ed, pp. 3–20. Oxford: Clarendon Press.

Kim, K., and B. Peterson. 2014. Aging Behind Bars: Trends and Implications of Graying Prisoners in the Federal Prison System. Washington, DC: Urban Institute.

Lapowsky, I. 2018. "Crime-Predicting Algorithms May Not Fare Much Better Than Untrained Humans," viewed September 6, 2020, https://www.wired.com/story/crime-predicting-algorithms-may-not-outperform-untrained-humans/.

Latessa, E. J., and B. Lovins. 2010. "The Role of Offender Risk Assessment: A Policy Maker Guide." Victims and Offenders 5: 203–219.

McGarraugh, P. 2012. "Up or Out: Why Sufficiently Reliable Statistical Risk Assessment Is Appropriate at Sentencing and Inappropriate at Parole." Minnesota Law Review 97: 1079.

Metz, C., and A. Satariano. 2020. "An Algorithm That Grants Freedom, or Takes It Away," viewed September 5, 2020, https://www.nytimes.com/2020/02/06/technology/predictive-algorithms-crime.html.

Miller, T. 2019. "Explanation in Artificial Intelligence: Insights from the Social Sciences." Artificial Intelligence 267: 1–38.

Mittelstadt, B. D., M. P. Allo, M. Taddeo, S. Watcher, and L. Floridi. 2016. "The Ethics of Algorithms: Mapping the Debate." Big Data & Society 3: 2053951716679679.

Ochi, R. M. 1985. "Racial Discrimination in Criminal Sentencing." Judges' Journal 24: 6.

Office of The Attorney General. 2018. "The FIRST STEP Act of 2018: Risk and Needs Assessment System," viewed September 5, 2020, https://nij.ojp.gov/sites/g/files/xyckuh171/files/media/document/the-first-step-act-of-2018-risk-and-needs-assessment-system_1.pdf.

Office of The Attorney General. 2020. "The FIRST STEP Act of 2018: Risk and Needs Assessment System UPDATE," viewed September 5, 2020, https://www.bop.gov/inmates/fsa/docs/the-first-step-act-of-2018-risk-and-needs-assessment-system-updated.pdf.

Pasquale, F. 2015. The Black Box Society. Cambridge, MA: Harvard University Press.

Picard, S., M. Watkins, M. Rempel, and A. Kerodal. 2019. Beyond the Algorithm: Pretrial Reform, Risk Assessment, and Racial Fairness. New York: Center for Court Innovation.

Prahl, A., & L. Van Swol. 2017. "Understanding Algorithm Aversion: When Is Advice from Automation Discounted?" Journal of Forecasting 36: 691–702.

Raz, J. 1979. The Rule of Law and Its Virtues. Reprinted in His Authority of Law. Oxford: Clarendon Press.

Rhodes, W., R. Kling, J. Luallen, and C. Dyous. 2015. "Federal Sentencing Disparity: 2005–2012, viewed 6 September 6, 2020, https://www.bjs.gov/content/pub/pdf/fsd0512.pdf.

Sample, B. 2018. The First Step Act Bill Summary Explained: A Comprehensive Analysis, viewed September 5, 2020, https://sentencing.net/legislation/the-first-step-act-2018-summary.

Seo, S. 2019. "What Cars Can Teach Us about New Policing Technologies," viewed September 5, 2020, https://www.nybooks.com/daily/2019/10/12/what-cars-can-teach-us-about-new-policing-technologies/.

Slobogin, C. 2012. "Risk Assessment." In The Oxford Handbook of Sentencing and Corrections, edited by Joan Petersilia and Kevin R. Reitz, pp. 196–214. Oxford: Oxford University Press.

Sporer, S. L., and J. Goodman-Delahunty. 2009. "Disparities in Sentencing Decisions." Social Psychology of Punishment of Crime, 379–401.

Stevenson, M. T., and J. L. Doleac. 2019. "Algorithmic Risk Assessment in the Hands of Humans." Available at SSRN, https://papers.ssrn.com/sol3/papers.cfm?abstract_id=3489440

Tonry, M. 2014. "Remodeling American Sentencing: A Ten-Step Blueprint for Moving Past Mass Incarceration." Criminology & Public Policy 13: 503–533.

Wagner, B. 2019. "Liable, but Not in Control? Ensuring Meaningful Human Agency in Automated Decision-Making Systems." Policy & Internet 11: 104–122.

Walker, G. D. Q. 1988. The Rule of Law: Foundation of Constitutional Democracy. Melbourne: Melbourne University Press.

West, H. C., W. J. Sabol, and S. J. Greenman. 2010, "Prisoners in 2009," viewed September 6, 2020, https://bjs.gov/content/pub/pdf/p09.pdf.

White House. 2018. "President Donald J Trump Secures Landmark Legislation to Make Our Federal Justice System Fairer and Our Communities Safer," viewed September 5, 2020, https://www.whitehouse.gov/briefings-statements/president-donald-j-trump-secures-landmark-legislation-to-make-our-federal-justice-system-fairer-and-our-communities-safer/.

Zavsnik, A. 2019. "Algorithmic Justice: Algorithms and Big Data in Criminal Justice Settings." European Journal of Criminology: 1477370819876762.

Cases

Bahar v. The Queen (2011) 45 WAR 100.
R v. Williscroft [1975] VR 292
Malenchik v. Indiana 928 N.E.2d 564 (Ind. 2010)
State v. Loomis, 371 Wis. 2d 235 (2016)

8

The Compassionate Computer

Algorithms, Sentencing, and Mercy

Netanel Dagan and Shmuel Baron

The future has arrived. Machine-based legal decision-making seems even more plausible than ever, and even desirable, by policymakers and scholars.[1] Estonia, for example, planned to design a "robot judge" that could adjudicate small contract disputes. In New York, a "chatbot"[2] has begun appealing parking fines, collectively saving people millions in fines (Re and Solow-Niederman 2019). Criminal sentencing is no exception to this movement. Algorithms (or similar computerized technologies) already play a significant role in making sentencing decisions, mainly through the widespread use of recidivism risk assessment tools (Rizer and Watney 2018) and other evidence-based numerical instruments (Bagaric and Wolf 2017). At least 20 US states use risk assessment algorithms in their bail, sentencing, or parole proceedings, with the aim of fostering accuracy, uniformity, consistency, rationality, objective. and cost-effective decision-making (Bagaric and Wolf 2017; Roth 2015; Starr 2014; see Ryberg and Roberts, this volume).

The growing attempts to apply computerized algorithms (and similar technologies) at sentencing focus on two primary rationales: crime prevention (e.g., deterrence, rehabilitation, or reducing risk) (Rizer and Watney 2018; Roth 2015), and, so far, to a lesser extent, on retributive-based proportionality (Chiao 2018)—the notion that the severity of punishment should be commensurate with the seriousness of the crime (Ashworth 2015; von Hirsch 2017). However, the theory and practice of sentencing are not just a matter of implementing retributive justice or promoting crime prevention. Other, "softer" considerations (Bierschbach 2012, 1785)—such as equity, benevolence, compassion, and other types of mercy—are an important part of modern criminal justice (Jacobson and Hough 2007; Robinson 2012; Robinson et al 2012).

Netanel Dagan and Shmuel Baron, *The Compassionate Computer* In: *Sentencing and Artificial Intelligence*. Edited by: Jesper Ryberg and Julian V. Roberts, Oxford University Press. © Oxford University Press 2022. DOI: 10.1093/oso/9780197539538.003.0008

Many scholars refer to mercy as a virtuous human characteristic (Smart 1968). People incapable of empathy or compassion are often categorized as suffering from mental illness and even considered psychopaths (see Seppälä et al. 2017). Indeed, whether for promoting individualized equity, more inclusive justice, or as a parsimonious penal policy, being a "safety valve" against overly harsh sentencing—mercy is part of everyday sentencing (Easton and Piper 2012; Ashworth 2015) and parole (e.g., compassionate release; see American Law Institute 2011). Empirical research also demonstrates that the effects of personal mitigation on sentencing decision-making can be significant (Jacobson and Hough 2007; Robinson et al. 2012). Further, as studies suggest, public opinion supports, to some extent, the use of mercy: for example, in cases in which the offender showed true remorse, acknowledged guilt, offered sincere apology, or where the sentence would impose additional hardship on offenders or their families (Robinson 2012).

The "mercy challenge" for algorithmic-based sentencing

Mercy-based considerations present a puzzle for algorithmic sentencing. If "by its nature, mercy may be something that is necessarily unexpected and unpredictable" (Robinson 2012, 118) how can it be integrated within an algorithmic sentencing framework? After all, is there any greater contradiction between mechanical, automated, and artificial sentencing decision-making, blamed for "deconstruction of subjectivity" (Aas 2005, 110), and mercy—"one of the original passions of *human* nature"? (Crisp 2008, 240; emphasis added). Allegedly then, algorithms cannot feel (and therefore exercise) mercy. Indeed, empirical research confirms that some people are often averse to machines making moral decisions since machines are "lacking in emotional experience and compassion" (Bigman and Gray 2018, 25; Bigman et al. 2019). A recent survey found that one of the primary concerns with algorithms, even among technology and policy experts, is that they "tend to dehumanize the decision-making process" and the decisions "are no longer considered to be 'real, thinking, feeling, changing beings' as they are merely a piece of data for an algorithm to manipulate" (Simmons 2018, 1094).

It should not come as a surprise therefore that sentencing scholarship has neglected the possibilities of algorithmic decision-making for mercy considerations. The common view usually offers a pessimistic, and more often, critical view regarding the use of algorithms for incorporating mercy into sentencing. Turkel (in Aas 2005, 158), for example, argued that: "[j]udges have to have compassion for the particular circumstances of the people before them. Computers could never develop this quality."

In a similar vein, several scholars have argued that "no algorithm will ever tell a judge how to temper justice with mercy" since sentencing is a "moment of freedom when one has a creative epiphany" and, the argument goes, is radically inconsistent with an objective model that programmed to predict the subjective (Lipshaw 2006, 330). Others have argued that assessments of the severity of the crime and the blameworthiness of the offender require qualities like empathy and compassion. However, it is currently impossible to convert such human values to an algorithm. For such scholars, moral ethics are too complex to transfer to an algorithm. Furthermore, algorithms lack common sense and world knowledge. They cannot, for example, understand what constitutes harm in the real world (van Wingerden and Plesničar, this volume). Several other scholars accuse algorithmic decision-making as being blind to the nuanced quality of exercising mercy:

> predictive algorithms cannot show mercy; they are like an automated vacuum cleaner that sucks up the dust and the crickets without caring or even realizing the difference. (Simmons 2018, 1095; see also Bierschbach and Bibas 2017; van Wingerden and Plesničar, this volume).

This view, also shared by some policymakers, often represents sentencing as an "art not a science" (Tata, 2000, 299). As American Judge Noel L. Hillman (2019) argued regarding remorse—a common ground of mercy:

> . . . judges make credibility determinations about statements of contrition and remorse . . . These critical components of the sentencing process, which cannot be reduced to a precise formula, mean that sentencing should not be merely the function of an algorithm or electrons coursing through integrated circuits. It is a uniquely human and dynamic endeavor.[3]

These concerns may lead those who support mercy-based considerations in sentencing to reject algorithmic sentencing completely, arguing that sentencing should remain a human task (Henderson 2018).

8.1   Overview

In this chapter we challenge the position that mercy and algorithmic sentencing can never be integrated and offer a preliminary framework for reconciling the two. We argue that as long as one accepts algorithmic sentencing, the importance of exercising mercy, by itself, is not a reason to reject algorithmic sentencing. In section 8.2, we set the stage and provide preliminary observations. In section 8.3, we distinguish between different types of algorithms and different conceptions of mercy. In section 8.4, we present our main argument that mercy considerations can, to some extent at least, be incorporated via algorithmic sentencing. Our argument is that as long as mercy can be reduced to retributive-related considerations, there is no impediment to incorporating it through deductive algorithms. If mercy involves a departure from retributive assessment on grounds of leniency, it may be decided by an inductive inferencing system. That will be useful, we argue, not only for theories that require equal exercise of pure mercy in similar cases, but also for those theories that allow for different exercise of mercy in similar cases. In section 8.5, we respond to some objections to our analysis.

8.2   Some Preliminaries

This part clarifies the question and focuses the rest of the discussion. The purpose is not to defend any substantive positions or to engage with their supporting scholarship. Our question is about the ability, if any, to integrate mercy with algorithmic sentencing. We will examine whether, at the theoretical level, mercy considerations can be applied within an algorithmic sentencing framework cursively.

The two issues we deal with here—mercy and algorithms—are at the heart of controversy in sentencing scholarship. The moral value of mercy and its feasibility in a legitimate, just, and fair criminal justice system are complicated and well-debated. The positions vary greatly between philosophers, penal theorists, and sentencing scholars (e.g., Bottoms 1998; Duff 2011; Markel 2003). Empirical evidence also reveals disagreement among community members, and presumably among judges, regarding the factors that might justify the exercise of mercy (Robinson 2012; Robinson et al 2012).

Some have argued that mercy should not be considered at sentencing, claiming that if mercy is part of justice, there is no point in treating it as distinct, while if mercy expresses deviation from justice it cannot be justified (Murphy and Hampton 1988; *c.f.* Johnson 1991). Many theorists argue that mercy-based mitigation would diminish the seriousness of the crime and the harm inflicted, and therefore we should eliminate it completely from the range of mitigating factors (Markel 2003; Robinson 2012; von Hirsch 2017). Other scholars have defended various versions of mercy. They argue that there is justification (and in some cases even a duty) to apply mercy at sentencing (Bottoms 1998; Fox 1999; Nussbaum 1993). The controversy regarding the exercise of mercy plays out among policymakers (Ashworth 2015; Fox 1999).

As with mercy, a widespread dispute has emerged about the feasibility of algorithmic sentencing. The alleged advantages of algorithmic sentencing include promoting consistency, fairness, accuracy, and cost-effective sentencing. Alongside these virtues, though, serious doubts have been raised as to whether algorithmic sentencing is complex enough to weigh all the necessary factors in sentencing, especially as to components that derive from human intuitions and experiences (Brennan-Marquez and Henderson 2019). That is particularly true, the argument goes, when balancing conflicting sentencing purposes, when the same facts may produce different outcomes, depending on the theory applied (Stevenson and Slobogin 2018). Others have posed questions about the moral costs that would accompany algorithmic sentencing. These include a lack of transparency, implicit biases, decreasing public trust, and perceptions of legitimacy in the criminal justice system (Rizer and Watney 2018; Roth 2015; Simmons 2018), and dehumanization of the sentencing process (Aas 2005).

In this chapter, we remain neutral with respect to the use of algorithms and the consideration of mercy at sentencing. Moreover, our argument does not rely on the position that mercy factors should be considered in sentencing or on the desirability of algorithmic sentencing. Our aim here is rather modest. We will argue that as far as it is possible and appropriate *in all other respects* to use algorithms in sentencing, mercy considerations should not restrict us from doing so. In other words, if one rejects algorithmic sentencing, it should not be because of the inability to integrate it with mercy. Therefore, other things being equal, those who support mercy should be willing, in principle, to consider the use of algorithmic sentencing.

Furthermore, as we shall see, different theorists have proposed different accounts of mercy. In this chapter we do not argue for one theory or another. We leave the true theory of mercy to others to resolve. The argument that we seek to promote here should accommodate as wide a range of mercy theories as possible. In addition, even though our argument may be applied to other "soft" (and maybe different) concepts such as benevolence, compassion, kindness, and grace, we will restrict ourselves to the concept of mercy alone. Further, while our analysis may also fit other mercy-relevant mechanisms (e.g., pardon, clemency, or other royal or presidential forms of prerogative mercy) that may be granted for political, administrative, or correctional expediency, we focus here on mercy at sentencing.

Finally, the chapter does not discuss guidelines for implementing mercy in algorithmic sentencing and the technical details of the favorable computer science methods for designing algorithmic sentencing in general or mercy in particular. We do not propose any "magic numbers" regarding the exact weight that should be given to mercy within the sentencing framework. Our argument merely highlights the possibilities of reconciling mercy and algorithmic sentencing.

8.3 Different Algorithms, Different Mercies

In this section we clarify the different main concepts of sentencing algorithms (deductive and inductive) and mercy (justice and pure).

8.3.1 Deductive versus Inductive Algorithms

It is important to distinguish between different types of algorithmic sentencing. Algorithms can operate in more than one operating mode. We will differentiate between two types of algorithms: the deductive rule-based system and the inductive inferencing system. The general idea behind every sentencing algorithm is to create a function which adjusts the appropriate sentence according to its input.

8.3.1.1 Deductive Algorithms

What we call a deductive algorithm is an algorithm that attempts to mimic human reasoning (or more correctly, the reasoning process human beings ought to follow) when determining sentencing. This is accomplished by accurate mapping of all sentencing factors, and the weight that should be assigned to each of these considerations. The algorithm planner encodes the relevant substantive sentencing principles into the algorithm and designs the software to weigh all of these considerations properly. After doing so, the relevant considerations can be entered into the system by the sentencing judge, and the system will provide the appropriate sentence (Hutton 1995; Stobbs et al. 2017). The function can be constructed in accordance with the sentencing theory preferred by the function planner (legislature, sentencing council, or sentencing court, for instance), and it can also take into account (but not be limited to) any particular penal policy and practice. Bagaric and Wolf (2017, 689) have offered such a deductive-based algorithm for every sentencing purpose, including retributive proportionality, while providing:

A constant, unvarying suite of factors that inform penalty, including aggravating and mitigating considerations that increase or decrease penalties respectively, and specifications of the weight to attach to each of those factors in certain circumstances should be built into the computer algorithm. Underpinning those factors and their impact on penalties would be clearly articulated objectives that the sentences are designed to achieve, namely, rehabilitation, community protection (and incapacitation where serious sexual and violent offenses have been committed), and punishment that is commensurate with the seriousness of an offense.[4]

In this manner, a deductive algorithm functions basically as a computerized version of a sentencing guideline. Such a mandatory sentencing system was common through the 1990s in the US' federal system for serious violent and drug offenses; it applied strict guidelines for its grid system (Donohue 2019). This system was automated through a computer program in a later stage (Rizer and Watney 2018).

8.3.1.2 Inductive Algorithms
The inductive algorithm works in a completely different way; it does not purport to mimic human reasoning. Instead, an inductive algorithm predicts, based upon a large number of cases or case-factors input in a given jurisdiction, the sentence that would have been imposed on an offender under similar circumstances and by a judge in the same jurisdiction. If we have a sufficiently rich database containing a very large number of sentencing decisions and a full characterization of these decisions (such as the circumstances of every event, the specific properties of the case, etc.), a machine learning-based algorithm can find relevant correlations and through them be able to predict

reliably what would be the output (for instance, number of prison years) that reflects all input (a set of case factors) (Chiao 2018, 245).

In addition, such an inductive algorithm will be able to reveal which factual changes affect sentencing. That is, which characteristics of a case result in a mitigated or aggravated sentence? (Chiao 2018). In this way, an inductive algorithm does not decide what constitutes the appropriate punishment according to the substantial considerations and their weight. It does not make the moral calculation that judges make when they decide an appropriate sentence. All the inductive algorithm does is to find correlations case factors and sentences and sets out these correlations in an organized array. Chiao (2018, 247) illustrates this point via an analogy:

> Algorithms have been devised to predict peoples' taste in music or films. This does not imply either that people develop a sense of taste in music or film by applying general rules of the kind observed by the algorithm, nor that the algorithm must model the way in which people do develop their tastes in order to successfully predict their taste in music or films. The sentencing algorithm stands to proportionality judgments in the way that a music or film-recommending algorithm stands to taste. Its criterion of success is how well it predicts the latter, not how well it applies it.

To sum up, the difference between the two types of algorithms is that whereas a deductive algorithm takes all relevant factors into account and devises the appropriate sentence according to preprogramed principles, inductive algorithm draws upon previous sentencing decisions to predict, with greater accuracy than humans, what the sentence would be, based upon these previous judgments. The differences between deductive and inductive algorithms will serve us later in this chapter.[5]

8.3.2 Justice Mercy versus Pure Mercy

As we can qualify different types of algorithms, we can also qualify different types of mercies (Bottoms 1998). Many theorists who support mercy at sentencing draw upon different concepts of mercy (Duff 2011). At the outset, we will distinguish between two broad concepts of mercy theories: *Justice mercy* and *Pure mercy*.

One set of theories perceives mercy as part justice. We refer to these as *justice mercy* theories. According to justice mercy theorists, mercy is not intended to mitigate the sentence in a way that deviates from the just punishment. On the contrary, mercy considerations must be considered in order to ensure just and proportionate punishment. According to the second group of theories (which we will call *pure mercy* theories), the role of mercy is to allow, in appropriate cases, deviation from justice and proportionality in order to achieve a more appropriate sentence.

8.3.2.1 Conceptualizing Justice Mercy

Justice mercy theorists try to reconcile mercy with retributive-based proportionality. As we noted, such theorists often present mercy not as opposing or competing with, but rather as complementing justice. One central justice mercy theory considers mercy to be synonymous with equity. Mercy is in fact the requirement for a more careful moral assessment of the offender and must be sensitive to his or her specific circumstances (Brett 1992; Nussbaum 1993). This idea goes all the way back to Aristotle, who wrote that the law is a general phenomenon and therefore cannot take into account all the special circumstances of every specific case (see Nussbaum 1993). Automatic application of the law is therefore unjust. The merciful person, Aristotle argued, treats others in a less rigid way and readily pays attention to all relevant circumstances. According to this interpretation, it is easy to see mercy as: "being a kind of justice and not a distinct trait of character" (Aristotle, 1138a3, in Nussbaum 1993, 94).

Sensitivity to the specific circumstances leads to mitigation because, in many cases, life conditions force humans to breach their moral obligations. Therefore, a careful scrutiny of the circumstances that led a person to commit an offense would lead to his improved moral evaluation, and thus to a more lenient—and just—punishment (Nussbaum 1993). Mercy (or *Epieikeia* as Aristotle called it) "is a gentle art of particular perception, a temper of mind that refuses to demand retribution without understanding the whole story" (Nussbaum 1993, 92).

This understanding of mercy as sensitivity toward the moral assessment of all circumstances has brought many writers to identify mercy with equity and with other general principles of fairness. Mercy, like equity, is a principle that developed to mitigate the harsh provisions of the law, and to allow such discretion to fit the general law into the circumstances of each case (Posner

2009). Other theorists have gone even further, arguing that since moral evaluation is required to take into account the specific circumstances of each
case, there is no justification for treating mercy as a distinct and independent
concept. According to this view, mercy, if ever justified, is redundant because
it is already part of the framework of justice (Murphy and Hampton 1988).[6]

8.4.2 Conceptualizing Pure Mercy

According to pure mercy theorists, mercy's role is to allow appropriate cases
to depart from the proportionate-retributive and just sentencing. This concept sees mercy as an autonomous moral virtue that is "not reducible to any
other virtue, especially justice; that it tempers or 'seasons' justice; and that is
not owed to the individual as a matter of right or desert" (Bottoms 1998, 67).
Fox (1999, 13) states it as the following:

> The true privilege of mercy is to be found in the residual discretion vested
> in each sentencer which allows a *downward departure from the principle of
> proportionality outside the principles of mitigation*. It can be utilised in excep-
> tional circumstances to allow weight to be given to factors which are ordi-
> narily not regarded as relevant mitigating considerations. It allows sentencers
> to give effect to significant, but as yet unaccepted, circumstances which, in
> their opinion, warrant leniency (emphasis added; also see Smart (1968)).

Pure mercy treats the avoidance of suffering as a virtue in itself (Smart 1968),
echoes a quasi-religious conception of divine pity regarding the sinner
(Fox 1999), or reflects appropriate interpersonal connections that promote
enriching and enduring relationships (Robinson 2012). The character of
the merciful person is often perceived as human, kind, generous, graceful,
and compassionate (Fox 1999; Robinson 2012). Therefore, mercy is conceptualized not as a moral obligation but rather as an act of grace, love, and
compassion.

An important difference between various theories of pure mercy is
whether similar cases should be treated alike when considering mercy (see
Bottoms 1998 for discussion). Some scholars have argued that applying
mercy does not mean giving up on equality altogether (Smart 1968; Fox
1999). The emotional dimension of mercy, they argued, does not mean that
mercy is a "black box" that lacks any guidelines or constraints and that it

can be exercised in an arbitrary fashion. Fox (1999, 26) explained that when exercising mercy: "The discretion must be exercised in a considered manner, not arbitrarily. In accordance with general principles,"

Other scholars, while acknowledging the difficulty of doing so, have argued that considering mercy may mean a departure from equality in some cases (see Dolinko 2006; Garvey 2004). Different theorists offer different arguments to justify such position. One argument envisions mercy as an "imperfect obligation" that, unlike a "perfect obligation," does not have to be satisfied whenever it arises, but rather can be considered in only some of the cases (see Garvey 2004, 1330). A second argument suggests that our notions of what is considered as deserved punishment have no single clear-cut answer. Therefore, the sentencing judge, in different cases, can arrive at different conclusions regarding whether and to what extent mercy should be applied, and both sentences can still be considered appropriate (Dolinko 2006, 359).

8.4 Applying Mercy to Algorithmic Sentencing

After clarifying the different concepts of sentencing algorithms (deductive and inductive) and mercy (justice and pure), we now explore the policy options under which algorithms could be used for different kinds of mercy-based discretion. These possibilities will support our conclusion that mercy can be implemented through an algorithmic system.

8.4.1 Justice Mercy and Algorithmic Sentencing

Justice mercy, as we saw, endeavors to consider the specific circumstances of the case. These factors may have led the offender to commit the offense or may explain any additional suffering of the offender. The goal of justice mercy is not to depart from the deserved sentence, but rather to provide a more precise and fair method for determining the proportionate punishment.

In this respect, a closer examination of sentencing practices shows that mercy and proportionality in many cases are framed as partly or fully overlapping concepts. Policy makers often use mercy not for the "avoidance of proportionality" (Jacobson and Hough 2007, 40) but for promoting proportionality and justice (see Ashworth 2015; Robinson 2012).

As for sentencing, one common source of mitigation is an extra punitive "penal impact" due to an especially harsh subjective (e.g., special vulnerability) or objective (e.g., serving prison time in solitary confinement) impact of the punishment (Hayes 2016; Easton and Piper 2012; Kolber 2009; *c.f.* von Hirsch 2017). Penal impact-based mitigation may be based on mercy and proportionality grounds. The sentencing guidelines in England and Wales (2019), for example, allow mitigation to reflect "physical disability or a serious medical condition." Such mitigation, the guidelines' explanatory notes elaborate, may be given: ". . . either on the ground of the greater impact which imprisonment will have on the offender, *or as a matter of generally expressed mercy in the individual circumstances of the case*" (Sentencing Council 2019; emphasis added). Another example of mercy is based on the rationale of avoiding "crushing" the offender in case of multiple offenses' sentencing, which may carry lengthy custodial sentences; granting mercy on this basis also serves a proportionality rationale (Ashworth 2015; Bottoms 1998; Fox 1999).[7]

Framing justice mercy as a form of impact-based mitigation holds significant implications for algorithmizing mercy. If mercy considerations provide nothing over and above retributive considerations, why should mercy not be calculated by algorithms? If the role of mercy at sentencing is to take into account the offender's perspective by weighing anticipated extra penal suffering (the offender's or their family's) as a relevant sentencing factor, there should be no prohibition against using and this (along with other relevant factors) using through an algorithm. As long as deductive algorithms can calculate many moral and factual considerations so that the algorithm will produce a sentence (e.g., Bagaric and Wolf 2017), it should be possible to add mercy considerations to this equation. Such algorithmic calculation is likely to be done in a more systematic, equal, and consistent manner and would ensure that all the relevant data will be considered. That also helps to avoid "drifting into the blancmange of mercy" (Ashworth 2015, 197) while framing mitigation within a clear penal framework of retributive-based proportionality.

That also may enhance the moral credibility of criminal law and more accurately track community notions of the appropriate sentences. In that case, as Robinson (2012, 122) explained, "the more specific the articulation of the criteria of mercy, the more reliable and predicable its application and the better the system's reputation in the community for getting it right." Furthermore, if one is skeptical regarding the ability of a deductive algorithm to engage in complicated considerations and to apply proportionality to actual cases (Chiao 2018), the sentence still can be imposed via inductive algorithm.

8.4.2 Pure Mercy and Algorithmic Sentencing

If one accepts that it is possible to map in advance all pure mercy-relevant considerations, a deductive algorithm can be used to do so as in the case of justice mercy. There is an option for such a mapping of the mercy considerations since many of the paradigmatic cases of mercy are repeated occasionally. A repentant offender showing sincere remorse and apology for victims or the offender's especially disadvantageous social background are common examples (Robinson 2012; Robinson et al. 2012). If these factors (and perhaps some others) exhaust all the pure mercy-relevant factors, it may be possible to consider them by a deductive algorithm, along with other considerations.

Pure mercy presents a greater challenge for algorithmic sentencing. As deviating from proportionality and being discretionary based, pure mercy opens the door for considering a wide, and perhaps unmappable and unidentifiable, range of factors. This aspect of mercy-based discretion has implications for how the various factors are evaluated. The way in which judges apply pure mercy may be more intuitive and capricious than the way they apply justice mercy (Smart 1968; Robinson 2012). As such, pure mercy considerations are inherently less predictable. A judge who exercises pure mercy on behalf of an offender usually does not, and cannot, anticipate in advance that she will feel merciful toward this particular offender. Certainly, she does not know *in advance* which circumstances would justify a merciful reaction toward the offender. Therefore, a deductive algorithm is a poor fit with respect to pure mercy discretion.

Nevertheless, an inductive algorithm may still be used. In this context, the theoretical controversy among pure mercy theorists regarding equality seems relevant. For those theorists who claim that even when exercising mercy, like cases should be treated alike, inductive algorithms may include pure mercy. If equality matters, it means that when a judge imposes a lenient sentence for a mercy reason, she would have to pass lenient sentences whenever this same reason applies (Harrison, in Bottom 1998, 69; see also Robinson 2012; Chiao 2018). If two offenders are identical in all relevant aspects, then even pure mercy should recommend the same mercy-based leniency for them both.

Hence, if a sufficient number of mercy-based cases and their characteristics are entered into an algorithm, the algorithm would be able to find relevant correlations. Put differently, if inductive algorithms can find correlations that reliably predict the way judges apply traditional sentencing considerations—given that like cases should be treated alike—there is no reason why they should not find similar correlations regarding judges' applications of mercy. After all, a consideration that justified the exercise of pure mercy in one case should justify the exercise of pure mercy in all other similar cases. Considering that "dispensation of 'mercy' is an important aspect of sentencing practice" (Ashworth 2015, 196–202; Jacobson and Hough 2007), it seems possible to build a sufficiently rich database for a detailed characterization of these mercy-based decisions.

The challenge of exercising pure mercy becomes even greater according to scholars who support an imposition of different sentences for similar cases (see Dolinko 2006; Garvey 2004). If a mercy-based mitigation is made in a purely discretionary and ad hoc way, there is no guarantee that a similar offender will receive the same level of mitigation. Accordingly, it seems impossible to reliably predict the judge's decision in exercising mercy in accordance with past cases. Therefore, no algorithm-based sentencing framework is possible according to such pure mercy theorists.

Nevertheless, it is possible to overcome this challenge as well, at least to some extent. Exercising mercy by inductive algorithms can be justified even according to these pure mercy theorists. These scholars, who accept that in some cases it is justifiable to deviate from parity, do not think that exercising mercy is totally arbitrary and capricious. Even if it is possible (and appropriate) that mercy will be exercised in one case and not in another (similar) case, this does not mean that there are no rules to guide the exercise of mercy. All pure mercy theorists agree, for example, that it is impossible to justify differentiation in mercy-implementation on the basis of invidious racial or ethnic-based discrimination. As Garvey (2004, 1331–1332) put it:

> . . . mercy's association with caprice should not be confused with invidious discrimination. The reasons mercy legitimately countenances are those rightly tending to evoke our sympathy and compassion. We can disagree about what those reasons are, but in no event should they include a person's race, creed, or ethnicity. A mercy-giver could, if he wanted, flip a coin to decide who among those eligible for mercy will receive it. Mercy can tolerate such caprice. But it should not be understood to tolerate invidious discrimination. (see also Dolinko 2006, 358–359)

Thus, pure mercy scholars agree that there are considerations that may, or may not the exercise of mercy. Although they accept that due to the "soft" and emotional nature of pure mercy it is allowed to exercise mercy unequally, they insist that in any case in which mercy is considered, it will be considered only on the basis of relevant considerations (even if these relevant consider-ations will not be considered in every single case). Their contention is that it is better for mercy to be considered *in some cases* than not to be considered at all. As long as the exercise of mercy is performed at least in some cases, the system is working properly (Garvey 2004).

In light of the what has been discussed, it seems that inductive algorithms can generate mercy-based discretion. Although there is no guarantee that judgments given in the past will be given in the future in the same way, it will nevertheless be possible to find correlations between circumstances and mitigation of sentences at least *in certain cases*. That is, a sufficiently large set of sentences will make it possible to build a database and discern certain factual characteristics that have occasionally—even if not always—occurred in parallel with mercy-based mitigation. According to these correlations, an inductive algorithm will assess what facts should justify mercy-based mit-igation generally. Once a particular circumstance is entered, the algorithm should identify the cases in which that (or most similar) circumstance was included and select (randomly) from that group one of the sentences as an output. In that manner, the inductive algorithm will be able to predict the *probability* of a particular circumstance to justify a mercy-based mitigation. Thus, even though an inductive algorithm will not guarantee that mercy will be exercised whenever it is justified, it will ensure that mercy will be exercised in a certain percentage of those cases. Algorithmic-based sentencing may be possible then, at least to some extent, even to pure mercy theorists who allow deviations from the requirement of parity.

8.5 Responding to (Some) Objections

In this section we address two objections to our analysis. First, some may assert that the importance of mercy is not exhausted by mitigating the sentence. Instead, the virtue of mercy is that the judge will go through the mental-moral process of *feeling* mercy. If we wish mercy to be part of our community values, the argument goes, it is important that human judges *ex-perience* mercy-related emotions, regardless of the merciful *results*. Hence, even if algorithms can achieve perfectly merciful results, they cannot cause the decision maker to feel mercy and therefore they cannot exercise mercy in the appropriate way.

Even conceptualizing mercy in this way permits algorithm-based sentencing. Exercising mercy through an algorithm does not prevent the judge from *feeling* mercy toward the offender. Mercy-based algorithms should generate mercy-based sentencing results; judges are still free to feel merciful alongside these results. Indeed, in this case the mitigation is not causally connected to the judge's merciful feelings. Nevertheless, even under our analysis both components of exercising mercy are still present. Whether the importance of mercy lies in the offender's desire for leniency or society's interest in promoting benevolent feelings of judges, this solution answers both needs. After all, the offender will benefit and the judge will feel merciful. Therefore, insisting on a causal link between the mercy-based mitigation and the judge's merciful feelings should not be overemphasized.

Another possible objection is that mercy considerations are dynamic and may change with the passage of time. Therefore, if mercy considerations are to reflect the evolving attitudes of society, we must allow judges to implement them. Mimicking what judges think *today*, the argument continues, does not tell us what the view will be *tomorrow*. We have no guarantee that mercy-based algorithms, even if are successful today, will remain successful tomorrow. In response to such argument, we recognize that, indeed, the problem of changing societal penal attitudes over time is complex and controversial for both penal theory and policy (Roberts 2020). We offer no magic solutions. However, it is important to see that this problem is not unique to mercy but is relevant for retributive and utilitarian sentencing in general: societal attitudes toward the seriousness of crime and punishment may change over time (Roberts 2020).

Moreover, we expect that the mercy-based algorithm may be synchronized with judicial and public opinion with the passage of a reasonable period of time, in order to accurately societal attitudes. To achieve such synchronization, "second look" mechanisms or parole boards that review the case periodically may exercise an updated understanding of mercy (see American Law Institute 2011).

8.6 Conclusion

This chapter has offered a preliminary exploration of using algorithms for mercy-based sentencing. Our main argument is that if a policymaker accepts the plausibility of algorithmic sentencing in other respects, and the need for the exercise of mercy in sentencing in general (we remain neutral regarding these well-debated and complex questions)—the need to exercise mercy, *by itself*, should not be count as a reason to reject algorithmic sentencing.

When exercising mercy through algorithms, we have offered a clarification and distinction between different algorithms and mercies. A modest proposal was suggested for two main concepts of mercy:

(a) *Justice Mercy*—We suggest that as long as justice mercy factors can be reduced to a proportionality-related calculus (e.g., extra penal suffering and so forth), justice mercy can be exercised through a *deductive algorithm.*

(b) *Pure mercy*—Pure mercy, being unpredictable, and deviating from justice, presents a greater challenge for algorithmic sentencing. However, we suggest that even pure mercy can be exercised in sentencing through an *inductive algorithm* that finds correlations between factors and sentences and sets out these correlations in an organized array. That will be helpful, we argue, not only for theorists who require equal exercise of pure mercy, but also, at least to some extent, for those who allow deviation from equality in exercising mercy in similar cases (e.g., by calculating the probability that a particular case would entail a mercy-based mitigation).

Finally, in a recent lecture, a British Supreme Court Justice, Lord Phillip Sales, called for an expert commission that could help ensure that automated decision-making processes have "equity and mercy." Lord Sales argued that "AI may get to the stage where it will understand the rules of equity and how to recognise hard cases, but we are not there yet" (Cross 2019). Lord Sales's call is important and timely. Scholars should attempt to reconcile algorithmic sentencing and "softer," "extra-legal," or "personal" sentencing considerations both by sentencing and computer science scholars, in regard to the theoretical, normative, policy, and empirical aspects of the problem.

Notes

1. The authors thank Alon Harel, Ruth Kannai, Noam Kolt, Asaf Nurick, and Julian Roberts for their helpful comments.
2. A "chatbot" is a software application used to conduct an online chat conversation, usually via text, in lieu of providing direct contact with a live human agent.
3. Others warn that algorithmic-based sentencing may lead to an inadvertent "value distortion" (Roth 2015, 1282)—a pressure for societal change that encourages relying on

relatively cheap and comparatively consistent technologies—at the expense of potentially subtle human decision-making such as mercy, empathy, and sensitivity to human rights (Re and Solow-Niederman 2019).

4. Another kind of a desert-based algorithm was proposed by Schild and Kannai (2005) for evaluating the offender's criminal record. This system "applies logical deduction to the rules" (Schild and Kannai 2005, 392). The database was created primarily by eliciting knowledge from legal, academic experts and the current legal policy. The judge can introduce his own preferences and thereby apply different sentencing principles.

5. Another type of algorithm, which we do not need to discuss here, takes a mixed form. These algorithms work as an inductive algorithm as they collect data and find correlations. However, after the database is collected, the algorithm builds a tree of operations for itself and produces the output according to the deductive inference learned from it. We treat mixed algorithms as inductive algorithms.

6. Another suggestion, still in the group of justice mercy theories, understands the concept of mercy as referring to a judge's particular state of mind that considers the punishment from the offender's point of view. As Muller (1993, 329) wrote: "In a sentencer's process of selecting a sentence from within a range of authorized punishments, mercy is a frame of mind induced by the imaginative effort to see both the impact of the possible sentences and the nature of the criminal conduct from the defendant's perspective."

7. Penal impact-discretion extends beyond the sentencing stage. During the post-sentencing phase, "compassionate release" mechanisms may be framed as serving penal-impact considerations. These provisions, existing in many jurisdictions, offer early release from prison for "extraordinary and compelling reasons" such as a prisoner's terminal illness (American Law Institute 2011). In Canada, for example, among risk related reasons, parole may be granted prisoners "for whom continued confinement would constitute an excessive hardship that was not reasonably foreseeable at the time the offender was sentenced" (Corrections and Conditional Release Act, 1992, s. 121(c)).

References

Aas Franko, K. 2005. Sentencing in the Age of Information: From Faust to Macintosh. London: Glasshouse Press.

American Law Institute. 2011. "Model Penal Code: Sentencing (Tentative Draft No. 2) (March 25, 2011)." Philadelphia: American Law Institute.

Ashworth, A. 2015. Sentencing and Criminal Justice. Cambridge: Cambridge University Press.

Bagaric, M., and G. Wolf. 2017. "Sentencing by Computer: Enhancing Sentencing Transparency and Predictability and (Possibly) Bridging the Gap between Sentencing Knowledge and Practice." George Mason Law Review 25: pp. 653–710.

Bierschbach, R. A. 2012. "Proportionality and Parole." University of Pennsylvania Law Review 160 (6): pp. 1745–1788.

Bierschbach, R., and S. Bibas. 2017. "Rationing Criminal Justice." Michigan Law Review 116: pp. 187–246.

Bigman, Y. E., A. Waytz, R. Alterovitz, and K. Gray. 2019. "Holding Robots Responsible: The Elements of Machine Morality." Trends in Cognitive Sciences 23 (5): pp. 365–368.

Bigman, Y. E., and K. Gray. 2018. "People Are Averse to Machines Making Moral Decisions." Cognition 181: pp. 21–34.

Bottoms, A. E. 1998. "Five Puzzles in von Hirsch's Theory of Punishment." In Fundamentals of Sentencing Theory: Essays in Honour of Andrew von Hirsch, edited by Andrew Ashworth and Martin Wasik, pp. 53–100. Oxford: Clarendon Press.

Brennan-Marquez, K., and S. E. Henderson. 2019. "Artificial Intelligence and Role-Reversible Judgment." Journal of Criminal Law & Criminology 109: pp. 137–164.

Brett, N. 1992. "Mercy and Criminal Justice: A Plea for Mercy." Canadian Journal of Law and Jurisprudence 5: pp. 81–94.

Chiao, V. 2018. "Predicting Proportionality: The Case for Algorithmic Sentencing." Criminal Justice Ethics 37 (3): pp. 238–261.

Corrections and Conditional Release Act, S.C. 1992, c. 20 (Canada).

Crisp, R. 2008. "Compassion and Beyond." Ethical Theory and Moral Practice 11 (3): pp. 233–246.

Cross, M. 2019. "SC Judge Calls for 'Expert Commission' on Algorithms." The Law Society Gazette, https://www.lawgazette.co.uk/law/sc-judge-calls-for-expert-commission-on-algorithms/5102154.article.

Dolinko, D. 2006. "Some Naïve Thoughts about Justice and Mercy." Ohio State Journal of Criminal Law 4: pp. 349–360.

Donohue, M. E. 2019. "A Replacement for Justitia's Scales? Machine Learning's Role in Sentencing." Harvard Journal of Law & Technology 32 (2): pp. 657–678.

Duff, R. A. 2011. "Mercy." In The Oxford Handbook of Philosophy of Criminal Law, edited by John Deigh and David Dolinko, pp. 467–492. Oxford: Oxford University Press.

Easton, S., and C. Piper. 2012. Sentencing and Punishment: The Quest for Justice. Oxford: Oxford University Press.

Fox, R. G. 1999. "When Justice Sheds a Tear: The Place of Mercy in Sentencing." Monash University Law Review 25: pp. 1–28.

Garvey, S. P. 2004. "Is It Wrong to Commute Death Row-Retribution, Atonement, and Mercy." North Carolina Law Review 82: pp. 1319–1344.

Hayes, D. J. 2016. "Penal Impact: Towards a More Intersubjective Measurement of Penal Severity." Oxford Journal of Legal Studies 36 (4): pp. 724–750.

Henderson, S. E. 2018. "A Few Criminal Justice Big Data Rules." Ohio State Journal of Criminal Law 15: pp. 527–542.

Hillman, N. L. 2019. "The Use of Artificial Intelligence in Gauging the Risk of Recidivism." Judges' Journal 58 (1). https://bit.ly/369bGHK.

Hutton, N. 1995. "Sentencing, Rationality, and Computer Technology." Journal of Law and Society 22 (4): pp. 549–570.

Jacobson, J., and M. Hough. 2007. Mitigation: The Role of Personal Factors in Sentencing. London: Prison Reform Trust.

Johnson, C. A. H. 1991. "Entitled to Clemency: Mercy in the Criminal Law." Law and Philosophy 10 (1): pp. 109–118.

Kolber, A. J. 2009. "The Subjective Experience of Punishment." Columbia Law Review 109: pp. 182–236.

Lipshaw, J. M. 2006. "Duty and Consequence: A Non-Conflating Theory of Promise and Contract." Cumberland Law Review 36 (2): pp. 321–341.

Markel, D. 2003. "Against Mercy." Minnesota Law Review 88: pp. 1421–1480.

Muller, E. L. 1993. "The Virtue of Mercy in Criminal Sentencing." Seton Hall Law Review 24: pp. 288–346.

Murphy, J. G., and J. Hampton. 1988. "Mercy and Legal Justice." In *Forgiveness and Mercy*, edited by Jeffrie G. Murphy and Jean Hampton, pp. 162–186. Cambridge: Cambridge University Press.

Nussbaum, M. C. 1993. "Equity and Mercy." Philosophy & Public Affairs 22: pp. 83–125.

Posner, Richard A. 2009. Law and Literature. Cambridge, MA: Harvard University Press.

Re, R. M., and A. Solow-Niederman. 2019. "Developing Artificially Intelligent Justice." Stanford Technology Law Review 22: pp. 242–289.

Rizer, A., and C. Watney. 2018. "Artificial Intelligence Can Make Our Jail System More Efficient, Equitable and Just." Texas Review of Law & Politics 23 (1): pp. 181–227.

Roberts, J. V. 2020. "The Time of Punishment." In Of One-Eyed and Toothless Miscreants: Making the Punishment Fit the Crime?, edited by Michael Tonry, pp. 149–182. Oxford: Oxford University Press.

Robinson, P. H. 2012. "Mercy, Crime Control, and Moral Credibility". In Merciful Judgments and Contemporary Society: Legal Problems, Legal Possibilities, edited by Austin Sarat, pp. 99–123. Cambridge: Cambridge University Press.

Robinson, P. H., S. E. Jackowitz, and D. M. Bartels. 2012. "Extralegal Punishment Factors: A Study of Forgiveness, Hardship, Good Deeds, Apology, Remorse, and Other Such Discretionary Factors in Assessing Criminal Punishment." Vanderbilt Law Review 65 (3): pp. 737–829.

Roth, A. 2015. "Trial by Machine." Georgetown Law Journal 104: pp. 1245–1305.

Ryberg J., and Roberts. J. V. 2022. "Sentencing and Artificial Intelligence: Setting the Stage." In Sentencing and Artificial Intelligence, edited by J. Ryberg and J. V. Roberts, pp. 1–12. Oxford: Oxford University Press.

Schild, U. J., and R. Kannai. 2005. "Intelligent Computer Evaluation of Offender's Previous Record." Artificial Intelligence and Law 13 (3): pp. 373–405.

Sentencing Council for England and Wales. 2019. "General Guideline: Overarching Principles." https://www.sentencingcouncil.org.uk/overarching-guides/magistrates-court/item/general-guideline-overarching-principles/ (last accessed July 22, 2020).

Seppälä, E. M. et al. (eds.). 2017. The Oxford Handbook of Compassion Science. Oxford: Oxford University Press.

Simmons, R. 2018. "Big Data, Machine Judges, and the Legitimacy of the Criminal Justice System." University of California Davis Law Review 52: pp. 1067–1118.

Smart, A. (1968). "Mercy." Philosophy 43: pp. 345–359.

Starr, S. 2014. "Evidence-Based Sentencing and the Scientific Rationalization of Discrimination." Stanford Law Review 66: pp. 803–872.

Stevenson, M. T., and C. Slobogin. 2018. "Algorithmic Risk Assessments and the Double-Edged Sword of Youth." Behavioral Sciences & Law 36 (5): pp. 638–656.

Stobbs, N., M. Bagaric, and D. Hunter. 2017. "Can Sentencing Be Enhanced by the Use of Artificial Intelligence?" Criminal Law Journal 41(5): pp. 261–277.

Tata, C. 2000. "Resolute Ambivalence: Why Judiciaries Do Not Institutionalize Their Decision Support Systems. International Review of Law, Computers & Technology 14 (3): pp. 297–316.

van Wingerden, S., and M. Plesničar. (This volume). "AI and Sentencing: Man Against the Machine." 232–253

von Hirsch, A. 2017. Deserved Criminal Sentences. Portland, OR: Bloomsbury Publishing.

9

Algorithmic Sentencing

Drawing Lessons from Human Factors Research

John Zerilli

The use of forecasting techniques in sentencing makes most sense on a variety of consequentialist assumptions about the aims of punishment. If the purpose of punishment is to prevent crime—the most obvious consequentialist justification for state-inflicted suffering—then an accurate assessment of an offender's likelihood of reoffending will be necessary for establishing whether (and if so to what extent) the offender should be incapacitated (e.g., by a term of imprisonment). Likewise, efforts to deter or rehabilitate an offender presumably stand to benefit from a calibrated response to the offender's unique propensity to reoffend.[1] It is thus against the backdrop of such consequentialist aims that the uptake of data-driven risk assessment has taken place.

Next to consequentialism, however, lies a more immediate source of inspiration for the use of data-driven methods in sentencing, namely, evidence that actuarial procedures for assessing risk are generally more reliable than unaided clinical (or "professional") judgment (Meehl 1954; Dawes et al. 1989). The higher accuracy—or rather *perceived* accuracy—of actuarial procedures, in turn, raises an important issue concerning their adoption, particularly in their machine-learning/big-data guise. The subfield of cognitive psychology known as "human factors" is relevant here.

"Human factors" is concerned with the psychological and ergonomic aspects of human-machine interaction. Its exploration of principles of optimal interface design and task allocation is both experimental and applied—theories of how human cognitive and physiological constraints bear upon human interaction with machines are tested empirically, and the findings of these empirical investigations are then regularly fed back into the design of human-machine systems. The aim of human factors researchers is to discover principles that enable humans to interact with technology in the

John Zerilli, *Algorithmic Sentencing* In: *Sentencing and Artificial Intelligence*. Edited by: Jesper Ryberg and Julian V. Roberts, Oxford University Press. © Oxford University Press 2022. DOI: 10.1093/oso/9780197539538.003.0009 safest, most productive, error-minimizing, and comfortable way. In the usual domains in which such investigations have occurred (marine transportation, aviation, and a number of industrial and manufacturing arenas), the most persistent findings are striking. It appears that once a system reaches a particular threshold of accuracy and reliability, its human invigilators are likely to fall into a state of complacency or deferred criticism: the system, in effect, is assumed to be all-knowing, so that outputs which might otherwise be viewed with suspicion by a diligent and conscientious observer tend to be overlooked or excused on the assumption that "the machine knows best" (see Parasuraman and Manzey 2010 for reviews). So understood, the phenomenon is not unlike the so-called CSI effect, in which police, jurors, and even judges are liable to overestimate the importance of forensic evidence (Marks et al. 2017; see also Damaška 1997).

The consequences of human factors research are potentially far-reaching for sentencing policy, though the field of human factors itself has had very little to say about the use of technology in the legal profession. For as automated decision aids become ever more widespread in the sentencing of offenders, it is natural to worry that judges will fall prey to the same tendencies to which other professionals, technicians, and experts have succumbed when using state-of-the-art software tools (Cummings 2004). It was just this worry to which a recent French report on artificial intelligence gave expression when it noted that "it is far easier for a judge to follow the recommendations of an algorithm which presents a prisoner as a danger to society than to look at the details of the prisoner's record himself and ultimately decide to free him" (Villani 2018, 124). The New York-based AI Now Institute expressed fears along similar lines: "[w]hen [a] risk assessment [system] produces a high-risk score, that score changes the sentencing outcome and can remove probation from the menu of sentencing options the judge is willing to consider" (AI Now 2018, 13).

The question remains, however, whether we really should be worried by all this. In this chapter, I describe and analyze some pertinent human factors results and assess the extent to which they pose a serious problem for the use of algorithms in the sentencing of offenders. While the findings from human factors research are themselves robust, they do not seem to translate neatly to the judicial sphere. The incentives, objectives, and ideologies of sentencing judges appear to upset the usual pattern of results seen in many other domains of human factors research.

9.1 The Field of Human Factors

Human-computer interaction has been studied since at least the late 1960s (Pazouki et al. 2018; see Kelley 1968, Edwards and Lees 1974, and Sheridan and Ferrell 1974, for early reviews). While initially the topics receiving greatest attention concerned optimal task allocation, interface design, and software ergonomics (Rouse 1981; Hatvany and Guedj 1982; Williges and Williges 1982), these fairly niche research projects can be seen to form part of a broader preoccupation with the psychology of computer-aided decision-making. Still, it was not until the publication of Lisanne Bainbridge's (1983) paper on the "Ironies of Automation" that the most pressing psychological challenges of computer-aided decision-making were diagnosed.[2] In her work, the contradictions inherent in computer-aided decision-making were made explicit, the principal one being "that the more advanced a control system is, so the more crucial may be the contribution of the human operator" (1983, 775). By this she meant that because no system can ever quite be fail-safe, a human must always play at least some invigilatory or oversight role (rendered all the more crucial precisely because the system is so advanced); but because automation gives rise to the kinds of cognitive phenomena already mentioned, it may be that no human *can* adequately perform an invigilatory role (Bainbridge 1983, 776).

In other work (Zerilli et al. 2019; Zerilli et al. 2021), I have subdivided the overarching human factors problem into four distinct subproblems, which can also be seen as four distinct (but closely allied) areas of human factors research (see Box 9.1). Roughly, the introduction of automation can lead to the following: a *capacity problem* when automated systems compute over many more variables than human cognitive limits allow the human to process or keep pace with; an *attentional problem* when the task at hand involves little more than monitoring a system's generally seamless transactions, making it very difficult for the human to sustain visual attention and maintain proper "situation awareness"; a *deskilling problem* when human skills are not adequately maintained through regular exercise, and consequently degrade; and finally, an *attitudinal problem* when a system reaches such a level of proficiency as to induce overtrust in its human overseer. These problems may occur on their own or together in any combination. They may also reinforce one another in particular cases (e.g., the first three problems could easily exacerbate the last one).

BOX 9.1 Four Problems Investigated in the Field of Human Factors

---

1. The capacity problem
   Humans are not able to keep track of the systems they are tasked with supervising because the systems are too advanced and operate at incredible speeds.
2. The attentional problem
   Humans get very bored very quickly if all they have to do is monitor a display of largely static information.
3. The deskilling problem
   Skills that are not regularly maintained will degrade over time (also known as "deskilling").
4. The attitudinal problem

Humans have a tendency to overtrust systems that perform reliably *most* of the time (even if they are not reliable *all* of the time).

Adapted from Zerilli et al. (2021, 85)

The capacity problem is a potentially serious one for the law. In many of the most socially consequential and normatively loaded applications of machine learning (such as risk assessment), knowing that an automated system works properly *just is* knowing its reasons for deciding, and to be satisfied with those reasons. A judge relying on a risk assessment tool, for example, would want to know that the system reasoned legitimately to its conclusion, and did not (let us say) take an offender's race, religious beliefs or sexual orientation into account when assigning a risk score. In fact, without some such understanding of the system's operations, it is hard to see how a risk score could inform a judge's discretion in a rational way. How, for instance, would a score enter into a judge's calculations without the judge knowing what importance to place upon the score, as determined (among other things) by the quality of the reasoning that led to it? A judge's being unable to understand why a system assigns the scores it does (as the capacity problem implies could be the case) seems to pose a genuine ethical and legal conundrum.

Be that as it may, I shall not pursue the capacity problem any further in this chapter. For one thing, the explanation of machine learning decisions is a topic that interests researchers well beyond human factors, and which in fairness merits separate treatment.[3] For another, much of the interest of the capacity problem from a human factors point of view lies in its exacerbation of the attitudinal problem.[4] Indeed, to the extent that both problems arise in a particular case, the capacity problem could make some efforts at alleviating the attitudinal problem somewhat futile. If I am tempted to overtrust a system that is very complex—indeed, overtrust it partly because it is so complex—exhorting me *not* to overtrust it, and use my better judgment, is unlikely to jolt me out of my dependence if my dependence results partly from my inability to understand how the system works.

The deskilling problem, too, is likely to have important ramifications for sentencing practice, inasmuch as being less exercised in traditional (algorithmically unassisted) sentencing tasks could over time lead to sentencing judges becoming gradually less adept in the kind of practical reasoning required for sentencing deliberation. Nevertheless, sentencing is not wholly unlike other forms of judicial and forensic deliberation which today are still conducted manually (so to speak) and at which judges can therefore be expected to maintain their skills—for example, when making findings of credibility, or setting levels of aggravated and punitive damages in civil trials. Moreover, the exact nature of and potential for this sort of "moral deskilling" remain to be clarified, both as a philosophical and empirical matter (see Vallor 2015). Thus I shall not pursue the deskilling problem any further here. And given that risk scores are not "monitored" in any relevant sense of the word, the attentional problem does not really arise. So for the remainder of this chapter, I shall restrict my analysis to the attitudinal problem alone.

9.2 Bad Attitudes: Automation Complacency and Automation Bias

Two manifestations of the attitudinal problem have received significant attention over the past few decades (see, e.g., Skitka et al. 2000; Parasuraman and Manzey 2010; Pazouki et al. 2018). *Automation-induced complacency* describes conditions in which, owing to the highly automated nature of a task, the human operator's role has ceased to *actively* involve them, so that they are no longer impelled to assess a system's outputs critically, and lapse into an unduly diffident, deferential, or unsuspecting state of mind with respect to the system (Pazouki et al. 2018). *Automation bias* occurs when human operators preference a system's signals over other sources of information, including the evidence of their own senses (Pazouki et al. 2018). These two closely related phenomena "describe a conscious or unconscious response of the human operator induced by overtrust in the proper function of an automated system" (Parasuraman and Manzey 2010, 406). Disturbingly, they seem obstinately resistant to intervention. There is evidence that explicit briefings about the risks associated with the use of a particular tool are not enough to counteract the strength of automation bias, and that extended practice likewise is ineffective against automation complacency (Parasuraman and Manzey 2010).

Intriguingly—and fortunately—these problems only appear to arise within a fairly narrow band or "sweet spot" of system performance. When a system is not regarded as especially reliable, the effects are not seen (Bagheri and Jamieson 2004; Parasuraman and Manzey 2010; Banks et al. 2018a; Banks et al. 2018b). The effects are seen only when reliable *but imperfect* systems are used, so that automation is considered "most dangerous when it behaves in a consistent and reliable manner *for most of the time*" (Banks et al. 2018b, 283, emphasis added). On the other hand, when a system functions reliably *all* of the time, or at any rate more reliably than its human counterpart (by some margin), the effects *are* seen, but arguably do not matter, or matter less in proportion as the system exceeds human performance (Zerilli et al. 2019; Zerilli et al. 2021). Hence the sweet spot: the problem arises at a certain threshold of system performance, but wanes (at least in terms of the danger it poses, if not its existence) once the system measurably outperforms an expert human counterpart.

How worried should we be about all this when it comes to the use of risk assessment tools in sentencing? If these results were to generalize to the judiciary, I submit that we should be very worried. First, on a typical construal of the judicial function in sentencing, risk assessment is not meant to be delegated to an algorithm, any more than a judge can delegate the task of fact-finding to an expert witness. Despite the expert being more knowledgeable about a particular province of learning, the judicial fact-finding role is still one which the judge is personally expected to discharge. In a similar vein, automated risk assessment tools are intended to serve in the literal sense of automated decision *support* tools, so that the decision-maker exercises their own independent judgment, ideally before consulting the tool. On this picture, the tool functions as little more than a check on the decision-maker's intuitions, and should in no way be seen as a substitute for the decision-maker's actual discretion. This is a crucial point. There are in fact many ways that an algorithm could be said to "support" a human decision-maker

(Administrative Review Council 2004, 14–15, 20). Extended along a scale of types of support, these would range from least instructive to most instructive—from merely scaffolding, prompting, or perhaps supplementing human judgment at one end, to more actively coaxing or even replacing the human decision-maker at the other end. I have previously suggested that risk assessment tools can be situated on the "less instructive" end of this scale, as systems that *supplement* human judgment by carrying out functions in such a way as to augment human capacities (Zerilli et al. 2019). So if it turns out that the risk of a judge succumbing to automation complacency is real, we should all be worried, since it amounts to no less than the risk of a vital judicial responsibility being abdicated.

Second, the credentials of risk assessment instruments locate them firmly in the problematic "sweet spot" zone I mentioned earlier—the zone where their perceived reliability and accuracy vis-à-vis human decision-makers is liable to induce overtrust in them. As I mentioned earlier, statistically guided methods of decision-making have been shown to have a certain edge over unstructured clinical/professional judgment. But this superiority is not unqualified. Statistical methods and data-driven algorithms may be reliable, but they are not unequivocally reliable—that is, significantly better-than-human in a preponderance of hard cases. The main reason for this is that not all relevant factors to a determination will be codified into an algorithm, and even when they are, the determination itself (such as whether someone poses a risk of recidivism) may be only one component of a larger decision (such as regarding what sentence to impose). Marion Oswald (2018, 16), when addressing the use of algorithms in the public service, rightly warns that assuming "that the forecast or classification represents the only or main factor on which the 'rightness' or 'wrongness' of the overall decision is to be judged . . . may risk changing the question that the public sector decision-maker has to answer." While her remarks were made with public sector decision-makers in mind, they are no less relevant to sentencing judges. Sentencing never reduces to brute prediction. No jurisdiction is so fixed on a single objective. Thus even if the human "gets it wrong" (i.e., mispredicts) while the machine "gets it right" (e.g., the offender *did* end up reoffending, though the judge let them out), the fact remains that there will always be more to sentencing than a sole consideration, and the judge always obliged to take stock of factors not feasible (or even possible) to encode in an algorithm (such as retributive considerations, general deterrent considerations, remorse/contrition, and the like). Proper decision-making will have regard to all of these factors, even if the outcome *looks* wrong. (This is to underscore a point I made earlier when discussing the capacity problem: reasons for a decision matter, and *how* a judge (or machine) decides is arguably even more important than *what* the judge (or machine) decides.) The use of algorithms in sentencing may obscure this fact, because algorithms do have a certain edge over human caseworkers where predictions are concerned, and it is this very superiority that can make a foil of human judges. The conditions, we could say, are ripe for automation complacency and bias.

The upshot of the foregoing discussion, then, is that yes, *if* the human factors results were to hold in the judicial sphere, we should indeed be concerned. But now the question is, *do* those results, in fact, hold? The limited research record suggests that the results do not hold; and it is worthwhile inquiring into why this might be the case.

9.3 Preliminary Investigations

Angèle Christin's (2017) ethnographic study compared the use of algorithms by web journalists and legal professionals, including court staff and judges. She notes that "the discussion [regarding the uptake of algorithmic instruments] has largely focused on the instruments themselves," and that "[w]e know less about the practices . . . of the people who rely on algorithmic technologies in their work and lives" (Christin 2017, 2). Her work takes place against a backdrop of previous investigations into sociotechnical systems (e.g., Orlikowski 1992, 2007) that prize open the organizational contexts in which technological artifacts operate. An important aim of this work is to expose how an artifact's meaning (and therefore reception) within an organizational setting may be actively shaped by the organization's practices, policies, chains of command, and the like. Such work arguably provides grounds for skepticism about the impact that risk assessment instruments are likely to have in the criminal justice system, for it is by no means a given that the techno-utopian rhetoric that often surrounds the arrival of a new technology will prove justified in this organizational setting in particular.

While Christin did not directly set out to address the salience of human factors in the criminal justice system, the questions she asked are certainly pertinent here: "How do people make sense of the recommendations provided by algorithmic tools? Do they blindly follow the algorithms' suggestions, manipulate the instruments, or ignore them? How do algorithmic practices and representations vary depending on their context?" (Christin 2017, 2). Her methodology involved in situ observation of criminal proceedings in three courts in the United States, as well as interviewing 22 court personnel, including court administrators, probation officers, judges, and defense lawyers. She found discrepancies between managerial claims and the actual day-to-day use of algorithms by those on the ground ("During misdemeanor and felony hearings, most judges and prosecutors did not use the analytics, dashboards, and risk assessment tools at their disposal"). She quotes one judge as saying:

> I don't look at the numbers. There are things you can't quantify . . . You can take the same case, with the same defendant, the same criminal record, the same judge, the same attorney, the same prosecutor, and get two different decisions in different courts. Or you can take the same case, with the same defendant, the same judge, etc., at a two-week interval and have completely different decision [sic.]. Is that justice? I think it is. (Christin 2017, 9)

She discusses a variety of strategies used by court staff to minimize the impact of algorithms. One of them (so-called foot-dragging), involves simply "ignoring or bypassing risk scores" altogether (Christin 2017, 9). Another strategy involves conscious gaming of the system to achieve a desired output. Overall, despite a great deal of hype and ongoing controversy regarding their various biases, Christin found that little attention is paid to algorithms in practice.

Much the same conclusions were reached by Megan Stevenson's (2018) study of the US state of Kentucky's experiment with several pretrial risk assessment tools since 2011. She notes that while Kentucky's statutes, via a clear set of "action directives," strongly favored pretrial release as the default setting, these directives were not followed. Had they been followed, 90% of defendants would have been granted "immediate non-financial release" (Stevenson 2018, 311). In fact, only 29% were granted such terms at the first bail setting. As she observes: "If judges are not convinced or coerced to follow statutory guidelines, a risk assessment tool will not be an effective method of liberalizing release" (2018, 311).

Garrett and Monahan's (2020) study reports inter alia on a set of investigations into the US state of Virginia's experience with the use of non-violent risk assessment (NVRA) instruments in sentencing. Very much in line with Christin and Stevenson's findings, their surveys of Virginian judges reveal "highly divergent attitudes towards risk assessment" and that "[a] sizable minority of judges [have] great discomfort with the goals and the use of risk assessment at sentencing" (Garrett and Monahan 2020, 445). Eight out of ten judges endorsed the view that sentencing should be based on more than just the gravity of the offense committed and so should factor in the offender's risk of reoffending. But by implication, two out of ten judges did not agree with the use of risk assessment in sentencing, and perhaps endorse purely retributivist sentencing aims: either way "a significant minority of judges excluded considerations of risk when sentencing eligible drug and property offenders and were largely unfamiliar with the NVRA" (Garrett and Monahan 2020, 468). This is consistent with around half the judges stating that they "always" or "almost always" considered NVRA results in drug and property matters, and around a third stating that they "usually" did so in such cases (Garrett and Monahan 2020, 467). A further interesting result is that seven out of ten judges believed the availability of noncustodial and rehabilitative options to be "less than adequate," and 75% considered that the availability of more options would "change their sentencing practices" (Garrett and Monahan 2020, 467).

A final study (Grgić-Hlača et al. 2019) examined the effects of algorithms on bail determinations, using civilian volunteers instead of judges to test a range of hypotheses. While the use of risk assessment instruments for bail determinations might not be immediately relevant to sentencing, the study's primary results are still worth citing. In general, the authors report that receiving machine advice has only a small effect on decisions ("For most cases, the fraction of participants who predict recidivism is very similar with and without advice") (Grgić-Hlača et al. 2019, 8). Where participants make their predictions before receiving machine advice, and their predictions diverge from the machine's, in only a minority of cases (19.9%) will they change their pre-advice predictions so as to concur with the machine's advice after learning of it. This minority (290 out of 5,150 cases) is a subset of a somewhat larger minority of cases (390 out of 5,150) in which participants change their predictions in response to machine advice (thus in 100 of 5,150 cases participants changed their predictions but not their advice). Furthermore, participants are not more likely to follow machine advice when they are given (positive) information about its accuracy. On the other hand, *incentivizing* participants to follow machine advice does seem to make them more sensitive to the advice (although interestingly "the effect is not more pronounced if the incentive is stronger") (Grgić-Hlača et al. 2019, 16).

9.4 The Role of Incentives, Objectives, and Ideology in Sentencing Practice

Why might the judicial use of algorithms fail to conform to patterns of algorithmic use in other domains of activity which human factors researchers have investigated?

Perhaps the fact that sentencing judges must by law exercise their own judgment in sentencing, with many judges taking this to mean that they should do so *before* consulting the algorithm, could be upsetting the usual pattern of results. The bail study provides modest evidence that this could be the case, for in only a minority of cases where participants made their predictions *before* receiving machine advice did they then go on to change their predictions *after* receiving that advice (and fewer still actually changed their advice). What makes this interpretation a little less compelling, however, is the fact that participants were told in advance that the machine had an accuracy rate of 68%, and might therefore have "read this as a hint not to take the advice seriously" (Grgić-Hlača et al. 2019, 9). In fact, the bail study could be interpreted as offering solid evidence for another hypothesis entirely: that warnings to judges about the relatively low accuracy of a risk assessment tool are effective in counteracting some of the effects of automation complacency and bias. If so, while there would still be a discrepancy between what is observed in the courts and what has been observed in other forums, the discrepancy would also be easy enough to explain in human factors terms: automation complacency and bias do not occur when an autonomous system is perceived to be only moderately reliable. Telling judges that a tool is accurate in fewer than 7 cases out 10 may be enough to knock them out of their complacency. Perhaps the most effective warning would give a quantitative indication of accuracy *as well as* an instruction to use the tool merely as a check on one's working *after* one has already made up one's mind. This is a worthwhile proposal that should be the subject of future criminological/ human factors inquiry. (Of course, to the extent that one remains in the dark about how an algorithm arrives at its conclusions—even in general terms that cite the various factors in a decision and their weights—using the algorithm as "check" on one's work still seems rather like a stab in the dark.)

Yet another possibility is that there simply *is* no discrepancy to speak of here: judges *are* being influenced by risk assessment instruments, perhaps in salutary ways too—for example, in their desire to reduce incarceration rates—it is just that they are constrained from giving effect to algorithmic recommendations by a lack of adequate resources. Garrett and Monahan (2020) did find, after all, that a large majority of judges were potentially willing to follow NVRA advice if only the interventions it recommended were actionable. A plausible twist on this scenario might posit that when judges already have reason to expect that it will not be possible to follow through with an algorithm's recommendations (say, because of resource constraints), they will systematically discount or ignore them.

But a few other hypotheses have better empirical support. The first emphasizes the likely crucial role that the *incentives* of judges play in structuring their patterns of algorithmic reliance and aversion. Human factors scholars have long known that accountability mechanisms can be effective in offsetting tendencies to automation bias. As the authors of one experiment put it, "making participants accountable for either their overall performance or their decision accuracy led to lower rates of automation bias" (Skitka et al. 2000, 701). What is implicit in this result is that when participants are given prudential reasons to use instruments carefully, they are more likely to do so. To some extent this is also borne out by the bail study, which found that incentives to find ground truth, or to avoid false positives or false negatives, do not induce reliance on machine advice. Fair enough, then: users of algorithms can be induced to handle algorithmic information more rationally and discriminatingly when given prudential reasons to do so. And perhaps sentencing judges have enough of these prudential motivations operating in the background to explain why they do not easily succumb to automation bias. But while incentives are almost certainly operating in the background of sentencing deliberations, they do not seem to be the kinds of incentives that necessarily lead to more careful sifting of algorithmic information.

Firstly, incentives can be perverse. The bail study is a case in point. In addition to finding that participants could be incentivized to find ground truth in spite of machine advice, it also revealed that participants could be incentivized to rely on machine advice. I interpret these results to mean that incentives can be effective in any direction: where the incentives are targeted to finding ground truth, *that* behavior is what the incentives are likely to elicit, not reliance on machine advice (especially when machine advice is distrusted); when the incentives are instead geared toward reliance on machine advice, *that* behavior is what the incentives are likely to elicit (to some extent even if machine advice is distrusted); and so on.

Secondly, there is evidence that sentencing judges can indeed be incentivized in less than ideal ways—they may be prudentially motivated to follow or to ignore algorithmic recommendations in ways that do not track their perceptions of an algorithm's reliability. (In other words, there is evidence that sentencing judges are not wholly motivated to find ground truth.) More concretely, incentive schemes may encourage judges to discount algorithmic outputs *even when they consider the outputs to be reliable*, and, conversely, to follow algorithmic outputs *even when they consider the outputs to be unreliable*. The following is by no means a far-fetched scenario (see, e.g., Stevenson and Doleac 2019, 20). A judge might (consciously or otherwise) rely on an algorithm to take some of the pressure off them for releasing a "low risk" offender that they believe has a very slight chance of reoffending (say, a likelihood just better than chance). In such a case, the judge technically disagrees with the algorithm (which assigns "low risk"), but acquiesces to the recommendation regardless, because the judge is willing to give the offender the benefit of the doubt and can cite the algorithm in defense in the event that the offender recidivates. It is true that the judge here does not *strongly* disagree with the algorithm, and could in some sense be said to be following its recommendation. The point, however, is that the algorithm has tipped the scales of justice in favor of lenience partly because it offers the judge an excuse for a poor outcome in a case that could have gone either way (Stevenson and Doleac 2019, 5, 20; see also Van Dam 2019). At all events, the situation is not one where we can say that the judge "uncritically" followed the algorithm: the judge would personally prefer to ignore its recommendation, but chooses to heed it for partly self-interested reasons. In the converse situation, a judge may bypass an algorithm's designation of an offender as "low risk" out of fear of a public backlash and a need to be (seen to be) tough on crime—even though the judge personally agrees with the algorithm and would otherwise release the offender. In these and similar ways, incentives may structure patterns of algorithmic dependence and deviation in ways that do not track judicial perceptions of an algorithm's reliability.

Another set of incentives may make judges less disposed to place their trust in algorithms overall. Christin (2017, 11) observes that "the long training process and high barriers to entry in the field of law shape the professional identity of judges and prosecutors in powerful ways, making them more likely to doubt the benefits of using external tools to complement or replace their own expertise." That professional incentives could operate in these ways should not be surprising. Incentives are woven into the fabric of the legal profession. It is known that career advancement and professional esteem are strong motivators on the bench (Shepherd 2011; Cooter 1983). In jurisdictions where elevation to judicial office depends on being elected, such motivations are even more plain (Brace et al. 1999). And once appointed (or elected), judges obviously strive to avoid being overturned on appeal (Randazzo 2008). It is therefore not surprising that these incentives would mesh in complex ways with external pressures to use algorithms in sentencing, and potentially render the latter less effective as a result.

Apart from operating under unique incentive structures, judges are plausibly less prone to automation complacency and bias because they also have unique *objectives*. A judge may think that a risk score is reliable enough, but also happen to think that risk scores should not inform sentencing—for example, in accordance with a retributive theory of punishment (see Garrett and Monahan 2020, 445, 468). Such a judge will not set crime prevention as a sentencing objective. They may, for example, view a young offender as being less culpable, and consequently impose a lighter sentence, despite youth being a high predictor of recidivism and an algorithm assigning a high-risk score. But even when a judge is not a retributivist, and simply takes account of more than just an offender's recidivism risk in sentencing (as indeed they must), the effect of such competing objectives will likely mitigate the influence of an algorithmic assessment, even if it will not eliminate that influence entirely (Stevenson and Doleac 2019).

Finally, judges bring unique *ideologies* to sentencing. Ideologies overlap with incentives and objectives, but can be singled out too as uniquely influencing judicial behavior. As Christin (2017, 10) notes once again: "In criminal justice, innovation does not come with the glitter and appeal that it has in other sectors: it is often a source of uncertainty, because by definition an innovation arrives without the vetting of precedent." One might say that the ideology of the legal profession as a whole is against innovation, quantitative analysis, and forecasting—its vehicles of reasoning (precedent) and redress (compensation, restitution, retribution, etc.) are predominantly backward-looking. Legal culture is nothing if not steeped in tradition. This ideology plausibly frames an a priori suspicion of algorithmic techniques in criminal justice that manifests as algorithmic aversion and the belief (rightly or wrongly) that risk assessment instruments are less than reliable. This is another way of saying that algorithmic aversion may itself be an ideology, to which the tradition-steeped ideology of the legal profession naturally leads.

One factor I have not mentioned is judicial bias, which could well be lumped in with ideology. Judges are obviously not above holding biases against certain demographics, and there is emerging evidence that algorithms, far from mitigating their effects, can give them license (Albright 2019). Importantly, this phenomenon is not always due to the algorithms themselves being biased (which is a separate issue) (Stevenson 2018, 309). Entrenched stereotypes may affect the way a judge will interpret the same risk score assigned to two offenders differing only in their socioeconomic status, so that the disparity cannot really be attributed to the risk score. Skeem et al. (2019) found that judges who, without a risk assessment to hand, might have been more lenient on relatively poor offenders than more affluent ones, may impose harsher penalties on poor offenders—and lighter penalties on more affluent offenders—the moment a risk assessment tool forms part of the sentencing calculus. This is not because risk assessment tools are necessarily biased against poor offenders. Indeed, all the offenders who were assigned risk scores in the study were assigned exactly the same risk scores, regardless of their socioeconomic status.

It is an arresting result, which apparently held even after controlling for the gender, race, political orientation, and jurisdiction of the judges. The study's authors speculate that it arises from the difference between assessments of blameworthiness and assessments of risk. They reason that low socioeconomic status often plays an exculpatory role in sentencing, in contrast to affluence. But when attention is diverted from the assessment of blameworthiness to the assessment of *risk*—as it inevitably is under risk assessment—low socioeconomic status becomes a disadvantage to the extent that it is prejudicially perceived as indicative of higher recidivism risk. The perception can probably aptly be described as "prejudicial" here because affluent offenders assigned the *same* risk score did not receive penalties that were as harsh as those visited on the poorer ones. In the authors' own words (references omitted, emphasis added):

Adding formal risk assessment information may have cued judges to process poverty as a factor that increased the likelihood that the defendant would continue committing offenses . . . This context may have activated stereotypes of poverty and affluence that led judges to interpret *identical risk scores* as signaling a much higher risk of rearrest for the relatively poor defendant than his more affluent counterpart. (Skeem et al. 2019, 57)

9.5 Conclusion

In this chapter, I have described and analyzed some pertinent human factors results, and assessed the extent to which they pose a problem for the use of algorithms at sentencing. I conclude that while the findings from human factors research are robust, they cannot be applied straightforwardly to sentencing judges. The incentives, objectives, and ideologies of judges may exert a significant gravitational pull away from algorithmic sentence recommendations or risk predictions, so that judges are unlikely to blindly accept what a machine tells them about an offender's risk of recidivism. Judicial incentives and ideologies in particular may be such as to make judges less prone to the allure of data-driven and high-tech innovation.

To be sure, algorithmic sentencing may pose genuine challenges— challenges of transparency, bias, data protection, and so on. It can also be expected to pose many of the same challenges as those posed by the human processing of statistical information more generally, such as the various heuristics and biases discussed by psychologists and behavioral economists (e.g., the availability heuristic, anchoring bias, overconfidence, etc.). However, the fear that judges will fall victim to *automation* bias, unthinkingly parroting whatever an algorithm happens to say in a spirit of "Computer says NO," is not one that preliminary evidence suggests is well-founded.

I have, in passing, suggested that appropriately crafted warnings may have something going for them in any event. It is true that a warning to judges not to place too much stock in an algorithm would not tell them *how* to discount it, and, for reasons I explained, discounting becomes virtually impossible to do rationally when a judge does not understand how a given algorithmic assessment is calculated. Nevertheless, there are some early signs that warnings may be enough to dispel any illusions judges might have about a technology, sufficient to encourage them to consult risk assessments only *after* they have come to their own conclusions. While this would not resolve the discounting issue, it could be enough to mitigate automation-induced complacency and bias. Further research should investigate this matter directly.

Notes

1. For penological arguments against the use of predictive instruments, and more generally against preventative aims in sentencing, see von Hirsch (1976, ch. 3; 1986, 176–178).
2. For precursors to Bainbridge, see Wickens and Kessel (1979) and Wiener and Curry (1980).

3. See Ryberg, this volume, ch. 2, and Chiao, this volume, ch. 3; Zerilli (Forthcoming) (for a philosophical account of the problem and a framework within which to approach its resolution); and Zerilli et al. (2018) (for an earlier attempt at the same).
4. Cf. Ryberg, this volume, ch. 2.

References

Administrative Review Council. 2004. Automated Assistance in Administrative Decision Making. Barton, ACT: Commonwealth of Australia.

AI Now. 2018. Litigating Algorithms: Challenging Government Use of Algorithmic Decision Systems. New York: AI Now Institute.

Albright, A. 2019. "If You Give a Judge a Risk Score: Evidence from Kentucky Bail Decisions." John M. Olin Center for Law, Economics, and Business Fellows' Discussion Paper Series No. 85. Available at: http://www.law.harvard.edu/programs/olin_center/fellows_papers/pdf/Albright_85.pdf.

Bagheri, N., and G. A. Jamieson. 2004. "Considering Subjective Trust and Monitoring Behavior in Assessing Automation-Induced 'Complacency.'" In Human Performance, Situation Awareness, and Automation: Current Research and Trends, edited by Dennis A. Vicenzi, Mustapha Mouloua, and Peter A. Hancock, pp. 54–59. Mahwah, NJ: Erlbaum.

Bainbridge, L. 1983. "Ironies of Automation." Automatica 19 (6): pp. 775–779.

Banks, V. A., A. Erikssona, J. O'Donoghue, and N. A. Stanton. 2018a. "Is Partially Automated Driving a Bad Idea? Observations from an On-Road Study." Applied Ergonomics 68: pp. 138–145.

Banks, V. A., K. L. Plant, and N. A. Stanton. 2018b. "Driver Error or Designer Error: Using the Perceptual Cycle Model to Explore the Circumstances Surrounding the Fatal Tesla Crash on 7th May 2016." Safety Science 108: pp. 278–285.

Brace, P., M. G. Hall, and L. Langer. 1999. "Judicial Choices and the Politics of Abortion: Institutions, Context, and the Autonomy of Courts." Albany Law Review 62 (4): pp. 1265–1302.

Christin, A. 2017. "Algorithms in Practice: Comparing Web Journalism and Criminal Justice." Big Data and Society 4 (2): pp. 1–14.

Cooter, R. D. 1983. "The Objectives of Private and Public Judges." Public Choice 41 (1): pp. 107–132.

Cummings, M. L. 2004. "Automation Bias in Intelligent Time Critical Decision Support Systems." AIAA 1st Intelligent Systems Technical Conf. (https://doi.org/10.2514/6.2004-6313).

Damaška, M. R. 1997. Evidence Law Adrift. New Haven, CT: Yale University Press.

Dawes, R. M., D. Faust, and P. E. Meehl. 1989. "Clinical versus Actuarial Judgment." Science 243 (4899): pp. 1668–1674.

Edwards, E., and F. P. Lees. (eds.). 1974. The Human Operator in Process Control. London: Taylor and Francis.

Garrett, B. L., and J. Monahan. 2020. "Judging Risk." California Law Review 108: pp. 439–493.

Grgić-Hlača, N., C. Engel, and K. P. Gummadi. 2019. "Human Decision Making with Machine Assistance: An Experiment on Bailing and Jailing." Proceedings of the ACM Human-Computer Interaction 3 (CSCW 178): pp. 1–25.

Hatvany, J., and R. A. Guedj. 1982. "Man-Machine Interaction in Computer-Aided Design Systems." Proc. IFAC/IFIP/IFORS/IEA Conf. Analysis, Design and Evaluation of Man-Machine Systems, Baden-Baden, Sept. Oxford: Pergamon Press.

Kelley, C. R. 1968. Manual and Automatic Control. New York: Wiley.

Marks, A., B. Bowling, and C. Keenan. 2017. "Automated Justice? Technology, Crime, and Social Control." In The Oxford Handbook of Law, Regulation, and Technology, edited by Roger Brownsword, Eloise Scotford, and Karen Yeung, pp. 705–730. New York: Oxford University Press.

Meehl, P. E. 1954. Clinical versus Statistical Prediction: A Theoretical Analysis and a Review of the Evidence. Minneapolis: University of Minnesota Press.

Orlikowski, W. J. 1992 "The Duality of Technology: Rethinking the Concept of Technology in Organizations." Organization Science 3 (3): pp. 398–427.

Orlikowski, W. J. 2007. "Sociomaterial Practices: Exploring Technology at Work." Organization Studies 28 (9): pp. 1435–1448.

Oswald, M.. 2018. "Algorithm-Assisted Decision-Making in the Public Sector: Framing the Issues Using Administrative Law Rules Governing Discretionary Power." Philosophical Transactions of the Royal Society A 376: pp. 1–20.

Parasuraman, R., and D. H. Manzey. 2010. "Complacency and Bias in Human Use of Automation: An Attentional Integration." Human Factors 52 (3): pp. 381–410.

Pazouki, K., N. Forbes, R. A. Norman, and M. D. Woodward. 2018. "Investigation on the Impact of Human-Automation Interaction in Maritime Operations." Ocean Engineering 153: pp. 297–304.

Randazzo, K. A. 2008. "Strategic Anticipation and the Hierarchy of Justice in US District Courts." American Politics Research 36 (5): pp. 669–693.

Rouse, W. B. 1981. "Human-Computer Interaction in the Control of Dynamic Systems." ACM Computing Surveys 13: pp. 71–99.

Shepherd, J. 2011. "Measuring Maximizing Judges: Empirical Legal Studies, Public Choice Theory and Judicial Behavior." University of Illinois Law Review 2011 (5): pp. 1753–1756.

Sheridan, T. B., and W. R. Ferrell. 1974. Man-Machine Systems: Information, Control, and Decision Models of Human Performance. Cambridge, MA: MIT Press.

Skeem, J. L., N. Scurich, and J. Monahan. 2019. "Impact of Risk Assessment on Judges' Fairness in Sentencing Relatively Poor Defendants." Law and Human Behavior 44 (1): pp. 51–59.

Skitka, L. J., K. L. Mosier, and M. Burdick. 2000. "Accountability and Automation Bias." International Journal of Human-Computer Studies 52: pp. 701–717.

Stevenson, M. 2018. "Assessing Risk Assessment in Action." Minnesota Law Review 103: pp. 303–384.

Stevenson, M. T., and J. L. Doleac. 2019. "Algorithmic Risk Assessment in the Hands of Humans." Available at: https://ssrn.com/abstract=3489440 or http://dx.doi.org/10.2139/ssrn.348944.0

Vallor, S. 2015. "Moral Deskilling and Upskilling in a New Machine Age: Reflections on the Ambiguous Future of Character." Philosophy and Technology 28: pp. 107–124.

Van Dam, A. 2019. "Algorithms Were Supposed to Make Virginia Judges Fairer. What Happened Was Far More Complicated." Washington Post, November 19.

Villani, C. 2018. For a Meaningful Artificial Intelligence: Towards a French and European Strategy. Available at: https://www.aiforhumanity.fr/pdfs/MissionVillani_Report_ENG-VF.pdf.

von Hirsch, A. 1976. Doing Justice. New York: Hill and Wang.

von Hirsch, A. 1986. Past or Future Crimes. New Brunswick, NJ: Rutgers University Press.

Wickens, C. D., and C. Kessel. 1979. "The Effect of Participatory Mode and Task Workload on the Detection of Dynamic System Failures." IEEE Transactions on Systems, Man, & Cybernetics 9 (1): pp. 24–31.

Wiener, E. L., and R. E. Curry. 1980. "Flight-Deck Automation: Promises and Problems." Ergonomics 23 (10): pp. 995–1011.

Williges, R. C., and B. H. Williges. 1982. "Human-Computer Dialogue Design Considerations." Proc. IFAC/IFIP/IFORS/IEA Conf. Analysis, Design and Evaluation of Man-Machine Systems, Baden-Baden, Sept. Oxford: Pergamon Press.

Zerilli, J. Forthcoming. "Explaining Machine Learning Decisions." Philosophy of Science.

Zerilli, J., A. Knott, J. Maclaurin, and C. Gavaghan. 2019. "Algorithmic Decision-Making and the Control Problem." Minds and Machines 29 (4): pp. 555–578.

Zerilli, J., A. Knott, J. Maclaurin, and C. Gavaghan. 2018. "Transparency in Algorithmic and Human Decision-Making: Is There a Double Standard?" Philosophy and Technology 32 (4): pp. 661–683.

Zerilli, J., J. Danaher, J. Maclaurin, C. Gavaghan, A. Knott, J. Liddicoat, and M. Noorman. 2021. A Citizen's Guide to Artificial Intelligence. Cambridge, MA: MIT Press.

10

Plea Bargaining, Principled Sentencing, and Artificial Intelligence

Richard L. Lippke

Recently, we have seen the introduction of forms of artificial intelligence into criminal justice system decision-making. One form this can take involves the use of sophisticated algorithms, either developed by or run through computers, which are then employed in making decisions about how to sentence individuals convicted of crimes. Assuming that such algorithms incorporate relevant and defensible sentencing inputs and weight them appropriately, they hold out the promise of helping us to achieve more consistency in sentencing. If we are apprised of the nature of the relevant inputs and their weights in the algorithm, greater transparency in sentencing will be possible as well. It will not come as a surprise to those who study criminal justice systems throughout the world that forms of racial, ethnic, or gender bias infect them, including at the sentencing stage of their operations (Davis 2007; Tonry 2011; Alexander 2010). Even in the absence of such distorting influences, the judges who are tasked with sentencing might exercise their considerable discretion in ways that are worrisomely variable or ad hoc. Appropriate AI technology might therefore be brought in to usefully "instruct" them in determining sentences, thus constraining their discretion in ways that are socially desirable.

There is considerable debate about the feasibility and advisability of using AI technology in shaping, or perhaps determining, the many decisions that officials in criminal justice systems have to make (Simmons 2018; Slobogin 2012, 2018; Starr 2014; Hutton 1995; Bagaric and Wolf 2018). That debate extends to the use of sentencing algorithms by judges. I intend to sidestep much of that debate in what follows. I will assume both the plausibility and advisability of introducing more transparency and consistency into sentencing and grant, for the sake of argument, that AI technology, in the form of properly developed and deployed sentencing algorithms, would help us

Richard L. Lippke, *Plea Bargaining, Principled Sentencing, and Artificial Intelligence* In: *Sentencing and Artificial Intelligence*. Edited by: Jesper Ryberg and Julian V. Roberts, Oxford University Press. © Oxford University Press 2022. DOI: 10.1093/oso/9780197539538.003.0010 to achieve them. My focus, instead, will be on the value such sentencing algorithms have in what I term "robust" plea bargaining regimes, ones exemplified by charge adjudication practices and procedures in the United States. Such regimes bestow not only substantial and unchecked charging discretion on prosecutors, they permit prosecutors to engage in charge and sentencing bargaining with accused persons, or more typically, their attorneys. Also, and crucially, in robust plea regimes, the outcomes of such bargaining, in the form of charging and sentencing recommendations to the courts, are often acceded to by judges.

Granted, judges in robust plea regimes will typically have the authority to reject the sentence bargains agreed to by prosecutors and the accused. In cases in which prosecutors and accused persons reach what are termed "binding agreements," judicial non-acquiescence in plea deals entails that the accused can withdraw their guilty pleas (Ross 2006, 719). However, it does not entail that the accused (or prosecutors) can compel sentencing judges to accept the terms of such agreements. Also, in the absence of such binding agreements, the accused can only hope that the sentencing judge will accept the sentence proposed by the prosecutor. Again, depending on the jurisdiction, the judge might not be bound by any agreement between the prosecutor and the accused with regard to sentencing. Despite this official independence of sentencing judges, observers of US-style plea bargaining routinely note that many judges are reluctant to confound the plea deals reached between prosecutors and accused persons (Heumann 1977). In part, this is because judges, like prosecutors, face caseload pressures which discourage them from second-guessing the plea deals presented to them for fear of slowing down the work of the courts. Also, judges in robust plea bargaining regimes might not have much access to the information contained in the relevant case dossiers (Turner 2016, 223). This will obviously limit their abilities to evaluate the plea deals which they are asked to ratify.

Most observers of charge adjudication in the United States characterize it as a robust plea bargaining regime (Alschuler 1968; Schulhofer 1992; Bibas 2004; Lippke 2011; Brown 2016). Perhaps it is an outlier in this regard and should simply be regarded and treated as such. However, there is reason to believe that forms of charge and sentencing bargaining exist elsewhere in the world, and that they are on the increase (Langer 2020; Turner 2009, 2016). Hence, I believe that examining how such regimes undercut the case that can be made for welcoming AI assistance into the criminal justice realm is instructive.

The challenge that US-style plea bargaining poses to the promise of employing AI in sentencing is apparent. Even if such technology would aid judges in determining sentences in ways that are more "principled," because based on relevant sentencing factors that are defensible, transparent, appropriately weighted, and applied consistently, these virtues of AI assistance will exist only to the extent that judges actually determine sentencing outcomes. If judges routinely defer to prosecutors' sentencing recommendations, transparency and consistency will be reduced unless prosecutors can be convinced to employ the algorithms to guide them in making sentencing recommendations. This is a possibility I explore in section 10.2. More troubling still is the possibility, or likelihood, that since it is the charges that the accused plead to that significantly shape their sentences, any gains in principled sentencing produced by the use of AI will be confounded by charge bargaining that is less than transparent in its structure and whose outcomes might by influenced by myriad factors, some of which will seem dubious or obviously inapt. Few who have examined US-style charge bargaining describe it as a highly principled or structured process.[1] It might be suggested that charging itself could be rendered more principled by the use of AI algorithms. That possibility is explored in section 10.3.

The conclusions I reach in sections 10.2 and 10.3 are that the promise of AI technology as a source of more transparent and consistent criminal justice outcomes is apt to be thwarted in robust plea bargaining regimes. In the main, this is because prosecutors in such regimes will sometimes view both charge and sentence bargaining strategically. By this I mean that prosecutors will view them as means to inducing accused persons to accede to guilty pleas. As such, prosecutors may be rather indifferent to considerations of transparency and consistency in producing criminal justice outcomes in lots of cases. To some scholars, such an analysis will simply reveal the indefensible character of such charge adjudication regimes. In response to this, in the section 10.4, I note briefly some of the challenges to principled criminal justice outcomes that will likely remain even if we eschew robust forms of plea bargaining.

In the first section, to which I now turn, I offer some clarifying remarks about what I regard as the most defensible character and uses of AI technology in sentencing.

10.1 Some Preliminary Points

First, I believe that the most plausible way to conceive of the use of AI technology by the officials of the criminal justice system tasked with assigning sentences to the convicted is in terms of aiding them to make more consistent and transparent decisions (Hutton 1995; Slobogin 2018). It is hard to imagine the circumstances in which criminal justice officials, or the public which they are supposed to serve, would accept the complete displacement of officials' judgments on sentencing, and perhaps other matters, by computer generated or applied algorithms. Are we supposed to imagine, for instance, that upon conviction, a technician would enter the relevant sentencing inputs with regard to an individual—the charges of conviction, any aggravating or mitigating factors, and criminal history scores—and then sit back and let a computer calculate the applicable sentence which would then be assigned to the individual, without any further scrutiny by an actual criminal justice official, and especially a judge? That would seem not only an unattractive practice but one that would engender legitimacy concerns among officials and members of the public (Simmons 2018). By contrast, if we imagine officials using AI technology to guide them in making decisions, perhaps by providing a check against their tendencies toward bias or other forms of inconsistency, such an approach seems worth entertaining as an improvement over current practices (Schwarze and Roberts 2021).

Second, it would seem that the most defensible way to think about sentencing algorithms is in normative rather than descriptive or summative terms. In other words, in coming up with such algorithms, we should debate what inputs they ought to include, along with the weights of those inputs (Ryberg 2021). Again, with regard to such an algorithm, relevant inputs would presumably include the charge or charges of conviction, any aggravating or mitigating factors in the offender's conduct, and the criminal history of the offender. Whether other characteristics ought also to be included, such as the offender's gender, neighborhood of habitation, or employment history, would have to be debated. Also, if they were included, then like the other relevant sentencing inputs, they would have to be assigned some weight in the sentencing algorithm. What seems much less defensible is the generation of a sentencing algorithm by having a series of past case dispositions fed into a computer and then having it come up with

188 SENTENCING AND ARTIFICIAL INTELLIGENCE

a sentencing algorithm based on those dispositions. Such an approach is bound to simply reproduce, in the algorithm, whatever biases or inconsistencies the case dispositions reflect (Hannah-Moffat and Struthers Montford 2019; Thomsen 2021). If most judges in their sentencing practices are arbitrary at times, or biased, or permit their own personalities or political ideologies to influence their decisions, the computer analysis will simply mush all of these together to yield an "average" way in which sentences have been determined in the past, which will then be applied to future cases. I am not sure why anyone would regard such an algorithm as having an instructive or defensible role in determining how sentences ought to be assigned to the individuals convicted of crimes. To appreciate how problematic such a summative algorithm would be, suppose that one of more of the judges whose case dispositions were used to generate it decided the cases that came before them by spinning a needle which, when it stopped, determined the sentence to be assigned to a recently convicted offender. Such "spinning" judges' case dispositions would thus form part of the basis for the resulting algorithm. That seems an unacceptable outcome. Instead, we should rely on careful debate and analysis of the appropriate factors to be used in sentencing, along with their respective weights, and develop an algorithm that reflects the conclusions reached.

Third, it is apparent that many of the uses to which AI-generated algorithms are being used by criminal justice officials are mostly predictive in character. This is true, for instance, of their use in making decisions about who to keep in pretrial detention and who to release back into their communities while they await adjudication of the charges against them. It is also true of the use of such algorithms to help police decide when and where to allocate their limited resources, or to identify potentially "dangerous" individuals based on their social media posts (Simmons 2018). However, I would argue that when it comes to sentencing, the use of AI technologies by judges to assist them in making decisions should not be conceived as primarily about prediction. Instead, if they use such technologies, it should be to help them make decisions about "appropriate" sentences given the charge or charges of which individuals have been convicted. In this way, sentencing is primarily "backward-looking," in the sense that it looks back in time to nature of the criminal conduct which individuals committed and assigns sentences accordingly. This is not to say that sentencing cannot accommodate predictive elements. Judges will often be guided or constrained by legislatively or common law-determined sentence ranges for the various offense types. They will then have to determine where, in the relevant range, the individuals being sentenced ought to be located. Arguably, judges might defensibly assign an offender a somewhat higher sentence in the relevant range based on evidence that he or she is dangerous and so should be incapacitated for a longer period of time (Frase 2013; Bagaric and Hunter 2021). But the relevant sentence range might be set by other factors, such as the severity of the harms inflicted or threatened by crimes of the type in question and the culpability of the offender in inflicting or threatening them. Even if we conceive of sentence ranges for types of crimes being determined entirely by forward-looking crime reduction considerations, the task of sentencing judges will be to determine where, in the relevant range, to locate the offender being sentenced. Doing so will require the judge to focus on the charge or charges of conviction and the degree of blameworthiness of the offender, not solely or primarily the offender's future risk of offending. Defensible sentencing algorithms should, it seems, incorporate such "backward-looking" elements, which is not to say that they should not include any "forward-looking" ones.

Fourth, it would seem advisable to provide the relevant criminal justice officials some input into the generation of the normative algorithm, if only to increase its legitimacy in their minds and thus make more likely their acceptance of its "dictates" (Hutton 1995). One of the problems with the development of proprietary sentencing algorithms is that we do not know what went into their generation in some cases, thus undermining any claim to the effect that their use improves transparency in sentencing (Ryberg 2021). Also, we are not able to tell whether such algorithms are counting relevant or defensible inputs or to what extent they are doing so. This is apt to make judges or other officials wary, if not outright skeptical, of them. There is evidence that criminal justice officials will refuse to adhere to rules, procedures, or sentencing mandates that they regard as too harsh or unfair or in other ways counterproductive (Tonry 2013). Providing them some input into the algorithms thus seems advisable. Short of this, since it may be difficult to provide officials such input on a continuing basis, the inputs, their weights, and the rationales for including them in the algorithm should be made public so that officials can, perhaps, be convinced of the appropriateness of the relevant algorithm. Feedback mechanisms in which officials offer suggestions and criticism should also exist in order to update or refine the algorithms. This would hopefully sustain or enhance their perceived legitimacy.

190 SENTENCING AND ARTIFICIAL INTELLIGENCE

10.2 Prosecutors and Sentencing Algorithms

If one of the concerns about robust forms of plea bargaining is that they might relegate sentencing judges to passive or secondary roles in determining sentences in many cases, in that they will often accept plea deals worked out by prosecutors and the accused (or the attorneys for the accused), it might be suggested that a partial solution is to ask prosecutors themselves to accept guidance from AI sentencing algorithms. Once prosecutors reached agreements with the attorneys of accused individuals on the charges to which the accused were willing to plead, prosecutors could seek the input of the algorithm in determining the appropriate sentences to recommend to judges. Also, attorneys for the accused could be given access to the algorithm and its recommendations in a given case, so that they could be assured (on behalf of their clients) that prosecutors were agreeing to reasonable sentences given the charges to which their clients were willing to plead guilty. Assuming that all of the parties, including judges, deferred to the algorithm's suggested sentences, we would gain some assurance that like cases were being treated alike, at least when it came to sentencing. Also, assuming that it was clear what sentencing inputs that, along with their respective weights, the algorithm incorporated, transparency in sentencing would be enhanced.

Set to one side, for the time being, the problem that such a procedure would do little to introduce transparency and consistency into the process by which prosecutors (and defense attorneys) settled on the charges to which the accused were willing to plead. The more telling difficulty with this proposal is that it presupposes something about the way in which prosecutors in robust plea bargaining systems view sentencing that is probably false or at least misleading in many cases. Prosecutors in such regimes may not be concerned primarily to ensure that persons suspected and thus accused of crimes receive sentences that reflect all and only their criminal misconduct, or perhaps their provable criminal misconduct. They are not even concerned primarily, or exclusively, with ensuring that accused persons receive sentences that accurately reflect the gravity of the charges to which accused persons are willing to enter guilty pleas. Instead, prosecutors are frequently most concerned to elicit guilty pleas. Admittedly, this might more often be the case when the criminal conduct in question is not terribly serious. How often is it not terribly serious? Well, quite often, as a matter of fact. Estimates are that close to 80% of the cases processed by the criminal justice system in the United States involve misdemeanors and thus crimes that are typically punished by sentences of less than a year in custody and quite often punished by noncustodial sentences (Natapoff 2010). Legal scholars suggest that prosecutors in such cases seek to maximize convictions rather than sentences (Bowers 2007). In fact, almost any sentence will suffice, in the minds of prosecutors, in lots of these cases. Observers of the system routinely note that prosecutors are willing to cut very generous deals in order to attract pleas (Bowers 2007). Granted, there might be, in some jurisdictions, something like "going rates," in the form of typical sentences, for the various mostly minor criminal offenses that clog the system. However, such "going rates" are typically presumptive only. Problems with evidence in a case or obstacles posed by defense attorneys who are motivated and competent might convince prosecutors to "sweeten" their offers by proposing substantial sentence discounts in order to convince reluctant defendants to enter guilty pleas. Prosecutors might also offer generous sentence discounts to accused persons who provide useful information that enables them to resolve other cases.

In short, prosecutors in robust plea bargaining systems tend to view sentencing somewhat strategically. By this I mean they view sentencing recommendations as tools for extracting guilty pleas. They offer to "go easy" on accused persons to smooth the process of gaining the cooperation of the accused in keeping the caseload moving (Heumann 1977). Once prosecutors have offered the accused (through their attorneys) substantial sentencing discounts in exchange for such pleas, they will not be all that interested in, or likely to accede to, whatever sentence an AI algorithm suggests is appropriate given the charge or charges to which the accused are willing to plead guilty. Importantly, defense attorneys also might not be all that interested in what a sentencing algorithm recommends given the charges to which their clients have agreed to plead guilty—at least not if the prosecutor is willing to offer a lenient sentencing recommendation in order to ensure that the accused's guilty plea will be forthcoming when they appear before a judge. Again, in many of the mostly minor kinds of cases that predominate in many criminal justice systems, sweet deals of these kind will often be on offer simply in order to expeditiously move the caseload (Bowers 2007, 1142–1143).

Of course, prosecutors in robust plea bargaining schemes do not always offer to go easy on accused persons when it comes to sentencing in order to attract their pleas. In cases of more serious crimes, and especially ones the resolution of which the public might be anticipated to pay more attention, prosecutors might be more unyielding, offering the accused, at most, modest sentencing discounts in exchange for guilty pleas. More importantly, prosecutors will employ charging strategies to put pressure on accused persons to plead guilty. They might stack charges in order to menace accused persons with cumulatively frightening custodial sentences. As legal scholars who write about US criminal law have shown, it often contains numerous overlapping provisions upon which prosecutors can draw in crafting criminal charges (Stuntz 2001). Also, US double jeopardy law does little to discourage charge stacking, since multiple charges regarding an incident can be lodged so long as they each contain some distinctive element (Stuntz 2001, 566). Stacked charges pose grave threats to the accused, since conviction on all or most of them can produce cumulative sentences that are long and hard. Alternatively, prosecutors might charge individuals with crimes that carry harsh mandatory minimums, even if prosecutors do not believe that the accused are really deserving of such penal outcomes, given their criminal misconduct. Prosecutors might then offer to withdraw such charges in exchange for guilty pleas to charges that do not carry mandatory minimums. These forms, and others, of charge bargaining reveal the severe limitations of any proposal to "fix" robust plea bargaining by convincing prosecutors to accept guidance from sentencing algorithms. To the extent that charge bargaining determines charges, there will be little gain in "principled" sentencing through the employment of sentencing algorithms, even assuming that prosecutors could be convinced to abide by the outcomes of their deployment in specific cases. If prosecutors are inconsistent, and perhaps substantially so, about the ways in which they offer, modify, or withdraw charge bargains, and the grounds for their decisions on these matters remain opaque, as they often will, there will be little by way of "principle" injected into the penal outcomes that result.

Before turning to the possibility of development of AI-assisted charging algorithms, one last point about sentencing algorithms should be made. The debate about AI-assisted sentencing seems, at times, to assume a somewhat simplified set of sentencing circumstances, ones in which individuals are being sentenced by judges for a single offense of conviction. However, it is well-known that individuals are often convicted of or plead guilty to more than a single charge for which they must then be sentenced (Reitz 2010). Such "multiple offense" sentencing poses difficulties concerning which, at present, there seems little theoretical consensus (Ryberg et al. 2018). Should multiple offenders receive the appropriate sentence for their worst offense with the sentences for the other offenses folded under that sentence? Or should they be assigned separate sentences for each offense, with them all then added together to achieve a cumulative sentence? Or should they receive an overall sentence somewhere in-between, which means that they get what are known as "bulk discounts" in sentencing? The lattermost option appears to be the one taken in most criminal justice systems. Yet if we lack a normative solution to multiple offense sentencing, we will also struggle to construct a sentencing algorithm to aid judges in deciding how to sentence multiple offenders (or prosecutors in deciding what sentences to recommend for them). This, in turn, suggests that judicial discretion will be hard to limit or control in such cases, contrary to the goal of having criminal justice systems that produce more "principled" outcomes.

10.3 AI and Charging Decisions

Given the strategic way in which prosecutors are apt to view plea bargaining in robust plea bargaining regimes, it might appear useless to suggest that their charging decisions could be rendered more principled by development of an algorithm to aid them in making those decisions. As we have seen, prosecutors in such regimes are not solely interested in "capturing" accurately and fully the criminal conduct of suspects in the charges they file. They also deploy their charging discretion in order to elicit guilty pleas from the suspects that come under their purview. They might undercharge some of them, especially when the criminal conduct in question is not too serious, in order to efficiently clear cases. Alternatively, if they encounter stubborn or well-represented suspects, they might overcharge them in order to convince them of the virtues of pleading guilty to some charges or other. But before we too quickly dismiss the usefulness of charging algorithms in such regimes, I believe that it is instructive to examine the notion, to see just how difficult it would be to devise such algorithms. I will not claim that concocting charging algorithms is impossible. My knowledge of the possibilities afforded by AI technology is too limited for me to plausibly make such a claim. However, I do believe that coming up with charging algorithms involves complexities that cast considerable doubt on the feasibility of the project.

Start with a list of the kinds of considerations that it seems reasonable to believe go into charging decisions, especially in jurisdictions that grant prosecutors considerable discretion in setting charges and bargaining about them. We can then turn to questions about which of these considerations ought to be included in a normative algorithm, their relative weights, and some of the difficulties the defensible inputs pose to developing algorithms. Here is a list of considerations that the literature on plea bargaining suggests prosecutors will pay at least some attention to in arriving at charges against individuals suspected of crimes:

a. Reliability of the evidence: obviously, some pieces of evidence will be more reliable than others in sustaining charges against suspects. A confident eye-witness identification of a suspect will be more reliable than an eye-witness who says she is "pretty sure" it was the person under investigation who she saw in the vicinity of a crime. DNA evidence will be more reliable than partial fingerprint evidence, which, in turn, is likely to be more reliable than fiber evidence as interpreted by an expert.

b. Probative force of the evidence: even if an eyewitness is sure about her identification of the suspect as being in the vicinity of the crime, such evidence will often constitute, at most, part of what a prosecutor needs to convict a suspect at trial, assuming a burden of proof on the state of "beyond a reasonable doubt." A DNA match at the scene is also reliable and might have strong probative force in some circumstances, but not others. If lots of possible perpetrators of a crime are identified through DNA evidence at the scene, obviously, the probative force of such evidence is weaker. In some cases, prosecutors may need only a relative few pieces of reliable evidence to put together a strong case. In others, they might need numerous such pieces, each of which might have to be assessed for probative force.

c. Anticipated legal challenges to the evidence: prosecutors may be aware that a piece of reliable and probative evidence was obtained under circumstances in which the police or investigators either ignored or bent the procedural rules. If so, prosecutors will have to consider the likely outcomes of legal challenges and where successful challenges will leave them in terms of the strength of the overall case they have against the accused.

d. Anticipated legal defenses: prosecutors might be aware that a suspect intends to assert a justification or excuse to the anticipated charges against him. The viability of such defenses will have to be examined and weighed by the prosecutor.

e. Quality of the suspect's defense counsel: prosecutors will know that some suspects are more likely to have competent and motivated defense attorneys than others, depending on the nature of the charges being contemplated by the prosecutor, the resources suspects have at their disposal, and the funding provided in the jurisdiction for indigent defense. Competent and motivated defense attorneys will tend to offer more legal challenges to the evidence or more defenses to charges, other things being equal. They will also be better at raising problems with the reliability or probative force of evidence.

f. The resource constraints on prosecutors: all criminal cases exact some toll on the limited resources at the disposal of prosecutors, with more serious cases usually exacting more of a toll. It seems likely that prosecutors will weigh, at least to some extent, resource costs in deciding what kinds of sentence and charge bargains to offer the accused.

g. Prosecution priorities in a jurisdiction: jurisdictions differ somewhat in their charging and adjudication priorities. If a prosecutor has been elected on a pledge to pursue vigorously certain kinds of crimes, then doing so might require her or his subordinate prosecutors to resolve other kinds of cases more expeditiously. That might lead them to engage in more charge bargaining in the latter kinds of cases. Also, other kinds of political pressures or government policies might elevate in importance the prosecution of some offenses over others. These too will force difficult choices on prosecutors who have limited resources.

h. Victim desires or vulnerabilities: prosecutors might have to pay some attention to what crime victims want in their efforts to secure convictions. Victims might publicly protest a too generous charge or sentence bargains. Also, in some cases, victims will be vulnerable in ways that might convince prosecutors to accept plea deals to lesser offenses, because putting victims through the ordeal of a trial to secure conviction on more veridical charges would be damaging or cruel.

i. Perceptions about certain suspects: in some cases, prosecutors might believe that some suspects are dangerous and so should not be offered charge bargains that would reduce their sentences. When a suspect has a long history of well-documented violence, for instance, the concern to incapacitate him might be an urgent and understandable one.

j. Strategic considerations: there will be cases in which prosecutors want or need the cooperation of one or more accused persons in producing evidence against others who are suspected of or formally accused of crimes. To gain that cooperation, prosecutors might believe it is desirable to tender charge or sentence bargains to the accused persons who can provide them with vital evidence. Or, to take another kind of case, sometimes there will be evidence that a crime was committed but it will not be clear who should be charged with it. A significant quantity of illicit drugs might be found in a vehicle with four occupants, all of whom deny knowing anything about them. A prosecutor might charge them all with possession with intent to distribute, hoping that one or more of them will subsequently admit ownership, at which point charges could be dropped against the other occupants.

k. Need to maintain comity with police and criminal investigators: the literature suggests that prosecutors are under some pressure to pursue cases that are brought to them by police or investigators, if only to maintain the quality of their working relationships with those on whom they rely to bring them cases and, at times, gather additional evidence (Findley and Scott 2006). If prosecutors are too quick to dismiss charges in some cases, or lower them too dramatically in order to gain guilty pleas, police and investigators might come to distrust them.

It is probably safe to say that the preceding list is not exhaustive, but it covers enough of the possible considerations to show just how complex are the decisions that prosecutors have to make as they contemplate plea bargains. Some of these considerations will be regarded as inappropriate by legal scholars, especially ones from jurisdictions in which charge bargaining is not permitted or is strongly discouraged. In particular, it might be argued that prosecutors should mostly be moved by the evidence against suspects, not by concerns about politics or how many of their limited resources pursuing a case will exact. However, even if we focus more narrowly on the considerations related to the evidence against suspects, there are a number of them and, more importantly, they seem significantly different from those that sentencing algorithms tend to incorporate. Sentencing algorithm inputs seem more "objective" than "evaluative" (Bagaric and Wolf 2018). The charges of which individuals have been convicted or pled guilty are "facts," of sorts, as is the existence (or lack thereof) of aggravating or mitigating factors, and the criminal histories of those being sentenced, especially if their inclusion in the algorithm involves a criminal history "score" of the kind calculated in some jurisdictions (Frase 2013). Likewise, if factors like an offender's gender, neighborhood of residence, or employment history are deemed defensible sentencing factors, they seem to be more or less matters of fact. Granted, it might be that some of these considerations involve some element of evaluation.

One suspects that if neighborhood of residence is to be included as a mean-ingful element, some metric of "good" and "bad" neighborhoods will have to be employed. More significantly, there might have to be some evaluation of the aggravating and mitigating factors introduced if the algorithm is to get beyond a simple listing of such factors. But compared with the consid-erations that will go into making charging decisions, and the construction of any algorithm to adequately "capture" the complexity of such decisions, devising an algorithm to aid in sentencing seems fairly straightforward.

By contrast, most of the considerations that go into making charging decisions are ineluctably "evaluative." Clearly, this is so with regard to such factors as the reliability of a piece of evidence or its probative force. How reliable a witness or other bit of evidence or how helpful, if reliable, it is in building a conclusive case for the guilt of an accused person will not only be matters of degree but open to differing interpretations. The same will be true for the significance of possible legal challenges to one or more pieces of evidence and to the problems that might be posed by anticipated legal defenses that individuals charged with crimes might have at their disposal. If considerations such as the resource toll pursuing a case might exact on the prosecutor's office, or the caliber and cooperativeness (or lack thereof) of the accused's attorney are to be taken into account, then these too will involve complex and somewhat contested evaluations. Assuming that these various evaluative elements can be creatively accommodated by the designers of a charging algorithm, the designers will then have to determine how much weight each of them is to be given in the algorithm, a task which also will be complicated and contested.

We will also have to determine what it is we want such an algorithm to yield and how it will do so. One plausible answer to these questions is this: we will want the algorithm to offer some assessment of the strength of the overall case for prosecutors going forward with some charge or charges against those whom they suspect of crimes. Perhaps the algorithm would be tasked with assigning some probability of success at securing conviction, beyond a rea-sonable doubt, on the charge or charges. Or, instead of assigning a proba-bility, perhaps the algorithm would yield some more crude assessment of success, such as "highly likely," "likely," "unlikely," or "very unlikely." If trial success seems too high a standard, which it might to prosecutors inclined toward and permitted to plea bargain, perhaps the algorithm could be tasked with determining whether the evidence in a case meets some minimum threshold of "feasibility" or "confidence" that would encourage prosecutors to go forward with the charges. There is also the question whether it would be the prosecutors themselves who entered the possible charges for assessment, or whether descriptions of all of the various criminal charges could be somehow "built into" the algorithm. In the latter case, its use might not only provide some assessment of the charges being contemplated by prosecutors, its use could offer assessments of other possible charges.

All of these complexities lead me to wonder whether a charging algorithm is feasible. If it is not, then the motivating premise of AI assistance— that it can be used to render more principled decisions by criminal justice officials—seems inapplicable to the charging context. But perhaps I am not giving the designers of criminal justice algorithms enough credit. It might be argued that the problems posed by the evaluative character of many of the considerations prosecutors must weigh in making charging decisions can be addressed to some extent in the design of a charging algorithm. We could incorporate the evaluative features of things like the reliability or probative force of evidence into the algorithm by assigning each of them numerical scores on, say, a 1 to 10 scale, with "1" signifying the lowest level of reliability or probative force, and "10" signifying the highest levels of these. In similar ways, we might be able to devise numerical scores for the likely success of legal challenges or for the plausibility of possible legal defenses that might be proffered by the defense. We would still have to determine the weight in the algorithm to be given to each of these evaluative elements, but it might be claimed that doing so is, in principle at least, no different than the task of assigning weights to the various inputs that comprise a defensible sentencing algorithm.

Suppose that some way of assigning evaluative "scores" to each of the relevant inputs could be devised and, once weights to each of the inputs was determined, the algorithm would be complete and could be used to assist prosecutors in making charging decisions. One question that arises at this point is this: Who would be tasked with determining the relevant evaluative "scores" that serve as the inputs of the algorithm? With sentencing algorithms, it might be possible to have trained technicians simply enter the relevant charges and other "objective" factors and then let the algorithm do its work. It seems unlikely that this would suffice for the charging algorithm. Rather, someone trained in the law and with relevant kinds of experience in making charging decisions would have to determine the scores for the evaluative elements and enter them. More importantly, it seems doubtful that prosecutors would accept the entry of evaluative scores determined by individuals other than themselves, for how would they know that the scores were appropriate to the case at hand (Hutton 1995)? At the very least, the prosecutor who is supposed to be aided by this bit of AI technology would want to check, and possibly correct, the scores entered by someone else, to ensure their accuracy. Yet if that is correct, one is left wondering how much real use the algorithm would be to prosecutors. Once they have done the work of figuring and entering the inputs, it would seem that they will have a pretty good sense of where the case against a suspect stands. Prosecutors, and especially veteran ones, will have their own "charging algorithms" in their heads that they will become pretty adept at applying. In the crush of minor cases of criminal offending with which many prosecutors will have to deal, relying on their own sense of where a case stands might be all they have the time or inclination for.

Still, AI technology might be of some use in promoting principled charging, if prosecutors can be convinced to use it. At the very least, the computer-applied algorithm would employ agreed-upon weightings of the relevant charging factors, once those factors were entered. Prosecutors operating without the algorithm might routinely make mistakes in calculating the weights of the various inputs, which mistakes would then be reflected in their decisions about what charges to file. Or they might be inconsistent about calculating the weights correctly in ways the algorithm would not be. If we imagine that some of these mistakes or inconsistencies are born of forms of gender, class, racial, or ethnic bias, then employing AI technology would serve as a corrective. But only as a partial corrective. After all, if prosecutors are prone to such biases, they will be apt to influence their determinations of the evaluative scores of the various algorithm inputs. Maybe a prosecutor routinely but subconsciously sees evidence as more reliable or probative when it concerns the suspected crimes of African Americans or Latinx. Or, prosecutors might be more disinclined to see legal challenges to evidence as significant when male recidivists are involved than when female first-time offenders are involved. Granted, once their problematic evaluative scores with respect to these various elements were entered, the algorithm would produce results that reflect the appropriate weights of the various elements in charging decisions. However, the algorithm would not correct the biases of prosecutors in determining the evaluative scores.

A different kind of problem is posed by the ways in which many US prosecutors will view and treat charging as a strategic process. As we have seen, they will not be solely interested in the matching of charges to apparent criminal misconduct, or in the overall strength of the evidence for one or more charges. They might well realize, independently of assistance by a charging algorithm, that the evidence against a suspect is weak. They could, of course, simply drop the charges in such cases. But they also might offer the suspect (through her attorney) such an attractive plea offer on a reduced charge that the suspect will agree to enter a guilty plea. The prosecutor thus gains a conviction, which is all he or she might desire in certain cases. Alternatively, a prosecutor might know, without having to consult an algorithm, that the evidence relative to a charge against an individual is decisive. Yet the individual in question has retained an attorney who is known to be recalcitrant in ways that will cost the prosecutor considerable time and effort if the prosecutor is to secure a conviction. Hence, the prosecutor suggests a plea to a lesser charge, perhaps with a generous sentence reduction thrown into the mix. These kinds of decisions by prosecutors appear to be everyday phenomena in legal jurisdictions that permit robust forms of plea bargaining (Alschuler 1968; Schulhofer 1992; Brown 2016). And there may be very little that is transparent or consistent about such decisions.

I suspect that prosecutors used to making them will be somewhat uninterested in what a charging algorithm, assuming we can devise a defensible one, tells them about the cases with which they must deal. They will prefer to trust their own instincts, or to follow office policies, which policies might yield some consistency across cases. However, I suspect that such policies will be presumptive only and might be based on factors that have varying and sometimes tentative relations to the strength of evidence in cases. It will hardly be surprising if such policies give some, or perhaps considerable, weight to things like the resource toll to the office that the pursuit of charges in a case might exact, or the need to maintain good relations between the office and the police, or the political priorities of the chief prosecutor. Incidentally, I have mostly ignored some of these considerations in analyzing the feasibility of coming up with an AI charging algorithm. They have less to do with the strength of cases against suspects and more to do with the organizational or political realities which prosecutors must accommodate. I am not sure how one could incorporate them into the charging algorithm; I am pretty sure that they will often be taken into account by prosecutors not only in the United States but elsewhere. The latter is a point I will come back to.

One further point about charging algorithms should be made. As I have characterized the prospect of them to this point, they would be employed prior to any challenges to the state's case against a suspect being raised by the suspect's attorney before a judge. Granted, prosecutors will often anticipate such challenges on their own and the problems they might pose to the state's case could be added to the evaluative inputs in a case. Yet defense attorneys might have various kinds of surprises up their sleeves that prosecutors will simply not foresee.[2] These might include witnesses who contradict the state's witnesses or who raise other kinds of problems with the state's evidence. Or they might include novel legal challenges to the state's evidence or the procedures used to acquire it. Ideally, it would seem, prosecutors should "run the charging algorithm" after being apprised of all of the obstacles they are likely to face, and a court's willingness to allow or credit them. But this would require some sort of hearing, presumably before a judge, in which the state's case and defense challenges to it were at least preliminarily vetted (Lippke 2011). Again, when it comes to sentencing, things are different, and official deployment of algorithms seems more straightforward. The charges are settled; all that is left for disputation might be the plausibility or weight of aggravating or mitigating factors, but these are things that both prosecutors and defense attorneys presumably will have been permitted some say in before a judge or other official enters the relevant inputs required by the algorithm.

10.4 Conclusion

It will be easy for critics of US-style plea bargaining to make the point that since the system is rife with opaqueness and inconsistencies—indeed, it almost seems set up to produce these—that, of course, there is little to be gained by way of "principled sentencing" through the use of AI technology. Unless we are prepared to rein in charge bargaining, or prohibit it outright, and regularize and limit the kinds of sentence reductions that accused persons who are willing to admit their guilt receive, the tendency of prosecutors to view and treat possible charge and sentence reductions as strategies to induce pleas will render them hostile to efforts to constrain their decision-making through the employment of charging or sentencing algorithms. Even judges who do not routinely defer to prosecutors' sentencing recommendations in such a system, and who seek help from sentencing algorithms that are normatively defensible, will only be able to produce limited consistency in sentencing outcomes. Prior decisions by prosecutors about charges will have significantly shaped the criminal justice outcomes in ways that undercut the gains in transparency and consistency promised by the use of AI technologies.

Although the United States is a bit of outlier in the discretion it gives prosecutors to determine criminal justice outcomes, we might want to be cautious with claims about the extent to which AI technology can produce more "principled" criminal justice outcomes in other kinds of adjudication regimes. There is, after all, evidence of charge bargaining, albeit perhaps of more limited kinds, elsewhere in the world (Turner 2009; Campbell, Ashworth, and Redmayne 2010: 324; Brook et al. 2016) In particular, one suspects that things like resource constraints, reluctant witnesses or vulnerable victims, and organizational priorities often play some role in prosecutors either declining to file charges, or reducing them in order to more easily gain the "cooperation" of accused persons in admitting their guilt. Again, all of this might more often be true when we are dealing with less serious criminal offenses, ones which, after all, are rather more commonplace. For instance, it seems likely that prosecutors in many jurisdictions will elect to drop charges in such cases when the evidence appears weak, rather than push police or investigators to come up with more or better evidence. The resource toll of persevering will be harder for prosecutors to justify when the crimes in question are mostly minor.

Likewise, once charges are initially filed, discussions with defense attorneys might produce "alterations" in the charges once prosecutors are made more fully aware of the obstacles and challenges they will face if cases proceed to trials. How much pause these discussions give prosecutors might well depend on the quality of defense counsel available to accused persons, which, in turn, will depend on the resources the accused have at their command. Yet charge "adjustments," whatever their apparent causes, might also be influenced by the kinds of factors (race, ethnicity, gender, class) that AI sentencing technologies should be designed to counter or reduce. Granted, nothing I am describing here comes close to the kind of strategic bullying by prosecutors that marks some US-style plea bargaining, where charges are added or dropped to encourage, or in some cases, compel, guilty pleas.

Further, it is important to keep in mind that lots of decisions about who falls under the scrutiny and control of the criminal justice system are made by the police. Scholars of policing point to the enormous discretion the police have in deciding who to be suspicious about, where to look for offending, who to stop and question, who to search, and who to let go with warnings or who to arrest and refer to prosecutors (Kleinig 1996; Davis 1969). All of these kinds of decisions are apt to be influenced by things like racial, ethnic, gender, and class biases. Whether and to what extent policing decisions might be "regularized" by AI technologies—something I would be skeptical about given the enormous variety and complexity of such decisions, as well as the speed with which they must be made—is no doubt open to debate. But if they cannot be harnessed by such technologies, and some charging decisions resist taming as well, then the reality is that sentencing algorithms offer "principled" criminal justice outcomes at a point that is rather late in the processes that produce those outcomes. Maybe a bit more transparency and consistency near the end of the process is better than nothing. But to my way of thinking, the prospects of AI assistance in rendering criminal justice systems more transparent and consistent appear modest.

Notes

1. For three recent and rather bluntly negative assessments of US-style plea bargaining, focusing on the power that prosecutors wield to secure guilty pleas from accused persons, see Klein (2006) Brown (2016) and Capers (2016).
2. Wright and Miller (2002) describe the practices of a New Orleans district attorney who insisted that lawyers in his office carefully screen cases before levying charges. The lawyers were also told not to engage in charge bargaining once the charges were screened and filed. However, Wright and Miller note that some charge adjustments did appear to occur, perhaps because the screening occurred without the input of defense attorneys in cases and thus prosecutors subsequently found themselves having to compromise on charges once they met with defense attorneys.

References

Alexander, M. 2010. The New Jim Crow: Incarceration in the Age of Colorblindness. New York: The New Press.
Alschuler, A. 1968. "The Prosecutor's Role in Plea Bargaining." University of Chicago Law Review 36: pp. 50–112.
Bagaric, M., and D. Hunter. 2021. "Enhancing the Integrity of the Sentencing Process Through the Use of Artificial Intelligence Systems." This volume.
Bagaric, M., and G. Wolf. 2018. "Sentencing by Computer: Enhancing Sentencing Transparency and Predictability and (Possibly) Bridging the Gap between Sentencing Knowledge and Practice." George Mason Law Review 25: pp. 653–709.
Bibas, S. 2004. "Plea Bargaining Outside the Shadow of Trial." Harvard Law Review 117: pp. 2463–2547.

Bowers, J. 2007. "Punishing the Innocent." University of Pennsylvania Law Review 156: pp. 1117–1179.

Brook, C. A., B. Fiannaca, D. Harvey, and P. Marcus. 2016. "A Comparative Look at Plea Bargaining in Australia, Canada, England, New Zealand, and the United States." William and Mary Law Review 57: pp. 1147–1224.

Brown, D. K. 2016. "Judicial Power to Regulate Plea Bargaining." William and Mary Law Review 57: pp. 1225–1276.

Campbell, L., A. Ashworth, and M. Redmayne 2019. The Criminal Process. 5th ed. Oxford: Oxford University Press.

Capers, I. B. 2016. "The Prosecutor's Turn." William and Mary Law Review 57: pp. 1277–1308.

Davis, A. L. 2007. Arbitrary Justice: The Power of the American Prosecutor. New York: Oxford University Press.

Davis, K. Culp. 1969. Discretionary Justice: A Preliminary Inquiry. Baton Rouge: Louisiana State University Press.

Findley, K. A., and M. S. Scott 2006. "The Multiple Dimensions of Tunnel Vision in Criminal Cases." Wisconsin Law Review 2006: pp. 291–397.

Frase, R. S. 2013. Just Sentencing: Principles and Procedures for a Workable System. New York: Oxford University Press.

Hannah-Moffat, K., and K. Struthers Montford. 2019 "Unpacking Sentencing Algorithms: Risk, Racial Accountability, and Data Harms." In Predictive Sentencing: Normative and Empirical Perspectives, edited by Jan De Keijser, Julian V. Roberts, and Jesper Ryberg, pp. 175–195. Oxford: Hart Publishing.

Heumann, M 1977. Plea Bargaining: The Experiences of Prosecutors, Judges, and Defense Attorneys. Chicago: University of Chicago Press.

Hutton, N 1995. "Sentencing, Rationality, and Computer Technology." Journal of Law and Society 22: pp. 549–570.

Klein, S. R. 2006. "Enhancing the Judicial Role in Criminal Plea and Sentence Bargaining." Texas Law Review 84: pp. 2023–5203.

Kleinig, J. 1996. The Ethics of Policing. Cambridge: Cambridge University Press.

Langer, M. 2020. "Plea Bargaining, Conviction without Trial, and the Global Administratization of Criminal Convictions." Annual Review of Criminology, available at: https://www.annualreviews.org/doi/10.1146/annurev-criminol-032317-092255 (accessed September 16, 2020).

Lippke, R. L. 2011. The Ethics of Plea Bargaining. Oxford: Oxford University Press.

Natapoff, A. 2010. "Misdemeanors." Southern California Law Review 85: pp. 1313–1375.

Reitz, K. R. 2010. "The Illusion of Proportionality: Desert and Repeat Offenders." In Previous Convictions at Sentencing: Theoretical and Applied Perspectives, edited by Julian V. Roberts and Andrew von Hirsch, pp. 137–159. Oxford: Hart Publishing.

Ross, J. E. 2006. "The Entrenched Position of Plea Bargaining in United States Legal Practice." American Journal of Comparative Law 54: pp. 717–732.

Ryberg, J., J. V. Roberts, and J. W. De Keijser. 2018. Sentencing Multiple Offenders. Oxford: Oxford University Press.

Ryberg, J. 2021. "Sentencing and Algorithmic Transparency." This volume.

Schulhofer, S. 1992. "Plea Bargaining as Disaster." Yale Law Journal 101: pp. 1979–2009.

Schwarze, M., and J. Roberts. 2021. "Reconciling Artificial and Human Intelligence: Supplementing Not Supplanting the Sentencing Judge." This volume.

Simmons, R. 2018. "Big Data, Machine Judges, and the Legitimacy of the Criminal Justice System." University of California-Davis Law Review 52: pp. 1067–1118.

Slobogin, C. 2012. "Risk Assessment." In The Oxford Handbook of Sentencing and Corrections, edited by Joan Petersilia and Kevin R. Reitz, pp. 196–214. New York: Oxford University Press).

Slobogin, C. 2018. "Principles of Risk Assessment: Sentencing and Policing." Ohio State Journal of Criminal Law 15: pp. 583–596.

Starr, S. B. 2014. "Evidence-Based Sentencing and the Scientific Rationalization of Discrimination." Stanford Law Review 66: pp. 803–872.

Thomsen, F. C. 2021. "Judicium ex Machinae: The Ethical Challenges of Automated Decision-Making in Criminal Sentencing." This volume.

Stuntz, W. J. 2001. "The Pathological Politics of Criminal Law." Michigan Law Review 100: pp. 505–600.

Tonry, M. 2011. Punishing Race: A Continuing American Dilemma. New York: Oxford University Press.

Tonry, M. 2013. "Sentencing in America, 1975–2025." Crime and Justice: A Review of Research 42: pp. 141–198.

Turner, J. I. 2009. Plea Bargaining Across Borders. New York: Aspen Publishers.

Turner, J. I. 2016. "Plea Bargaining and International Criminal Justice." McGeorge Law Review 48: 219–246.

Wright, R., and M. Miller. 2002. "The Screening/Bargaining Tradeoff." Stanford Law Review 55: pp. 29–118.

11
Reconciling Artificial and Human Intelligence

Supplementing Not Supplanting the Sentencing Judge

Mathis Schwarze and Julian V. Roberts

How might machine learning improve judicial decision-making, or the sentencing process in general? Proposals to incorporate AI into the sentencing process range from the modest to the ambitious, from merely supporting judges, to replacing them entirely. Three principal[1] approaches exist:

1. Replace judges completely with an algorithm which determines sentence having taken into account all relevant case characteristics and all relevant principles, purposes, and guidelines. The sentence is determined as soon as the necessary information has been entered, so there is no need, or purpose to mounting a sentencing hearing. Few scholars advocate this approach.

2. Replace judges (as in Option 1), unless the parties specifically elect sentencing by judge instead of the AI sentence.[2] This implies a twin-track system, with defendants electing "mode of sentencing" in the same way that in some jurisdictions they elect mode of trial.[3] The algorithmic sentence would not be decisive unless accepted by both parties. Sentencers would therefore share the determination of sentencing outcomes with the program.

3. Employ AI to support judicial decision-making. This approach guided the various sentencing information systems developed in recent decades. The judge consults a computer-derived recommendation much as courts in jurisdictions with guidelines consult the guideline's sentence recommendations. Under this approach AI would also make other contributions to more consistent and principled sentencing; it

could inform the sources of guidance at sentencing: appellate courts or Sentencing Commissions (in countries with both institutions).

We regard Option 1 as dystopian and unlikely to prove acceptable to most people, particularly litigants and victims. Option 2 renders AI the default option—a troubling prospect as well. As with other simplified criminal proceedings bypassing courts (see Enescu 2019 for the German penal order), it would risk unfair outcomes. Some defendants will fail to elect sentencing by a judge simply due to a lack of understanding or insufficient legal advice. The result would be disparities of outcome and unresolvable conflicts between a judicial sentence and one derived from AI.

That leaves Option 3, which is the subject of this chapter. The third way employs an AI-derived sentence to guide judges. Machine learning is also employed to identify flaws in sentencing decisions—unjustified disparities; discrimination; and violations of key principles such as equity. Since the algorithm learns from human judgments, we refer to this as Human-Algorithmic Learning (HAL). HAL may also enhance sentencing by improving the guidance provided by the Courts of Appeal, and in a growing number of jurisdictions, sentencing guidelines. Since their objectives overlap, HAL can be of particular assistance in shaping and enhancing these guidelines in ways overlooked in the literature to date.

11.1 Overview

The chapter begins by briefly noting some reasons why a machine-learned sentence represents an unconvincing alternative to judicial decision-making (section 11.2). This section touches on the central feature of sentencing in common law countries: the sentencing hearing, which constitutes a distinct phase of the criminal process. Under many proposals, the sentencing hearing would be unnecessary in most cases. Section 11.3 explores some of the ways that AI may supplement judicial decision-making. Computer-assisted information systems are the most-discussed approach and several have been implemented going back as far as the 1980s. This section discusses the problems in constructing an adequate database and the benefits of an AI-derived *Advisory Sentence*. Section 11.3.2 briefly considers other ways in which AI may improve the sentencing process, for example, by detecting sources of bias and departures from principled sentencing more effectively than conventional means. Lastly, section 11.4 examines the unexplored ways in which AI may improve the guidance provided to courts.

11.2 Why AI Should Supplement Not Supplant Judges

Bagaric and Wolf (2018) offer an upbeat evaluation of computerized sentencing, arguing that sentencing is "extremely amenable to computerised decision-making" (681; see also Stobbs, Hunter, and Bagaric 2017, 272). They conclude that "computerised sentencing is preferable to judicial sentencing" (2018, 708). In our view sentencing is less amenable to being determined by computer than they suggest, and AI is unlikely to replace judicial decision-making at sentencing, for reasons both technological and deontological. The technological difficulties of programming a "computer judge" stem from the nature of judicial reasoning, and challenges to entering the appropriate data relevant to the sentencing decision.

Human legal reasoning is not a purely logical process. Some legal questions might be solvable using relatively logical "textbook rules." However, judges will sometimes be confronted with "hard cases" for which the existing rules are insufficient. These cases require the interpretation of a rule or the creation of new rules by reference to "policy goals or the requirements of justice" (Dworkin 1963, 628). This task requires fundamentally *human* qualities such as common sense, moral, social, and cultural awareness (Susskind 1986, 133). By its nature, the sentencing of an offender is an example of a "hard case." It operates on the basis of judicial discretion and individualization and has a moral element. Therefore, replacing sentencing judges by computers would require "human level" AI or "artificial general intelligence"—the field's "holy grail"—which remains elusive (Boden 2016, 21).

It is also unclear how AI could assist in clarifying the normative significance of elements of the sentencing process. Assume a jurisdiction where the legislature has prescribed that sentences should conform to the principle of retributive proportionality. The challenge for courts is implementing this principle—for example, by taking factors related to proportionality into account and disregarding or down-weighting other factors. Under such a regime, the level of harm inflicted would carry much weight, while the offender's risk of reoffending would have little effect on the sentence. Judges must then decide which of a myriad of sentencing factors are relevant to the principle. Is remorse relevant? Should premeditation carry a great deal or little weight? Judges make these individual decisions at present. It is hard to conceive how AI could be programmed to distinguish factors on the basis of their relevance to a proportionate sentence. Machine learning could be useful, however, in establishing whether courts were conforming to the proportionality principle (see discussion in Chiao 2018).

The ethical concerns are rooted in the inaptitude of computers for any "human function that involves interpersonal respect, understanding, and love" (Weizenbaum 1976, 269). A comparison between the application of AI to law and medicine illustrates this point. The medical field is amenable to the spread of machine intelligence as patients' primary concern is the accuracy of diagnosis and the effectiveness of subsequent treatment. In the future most diagnoses will be made remotely by AI diagnostic tools and the movement toward "telemedicine" has likely been accelerated by the 2020 pandemic. Unlike medicine, however, sentencing has a normative dimension. Most importantly, a computer would surely be less effective in communicating censure as it lacks a moral commitment to its output. Receiving a letter or some other form of communication is likely to have less censuring effect than a statement of reprobation, expressed by a legitimate authority operating in a public forum.[4]

A related issue is legitimacy, or perceived legitimacy. In the medical domain, legitimacy is established through professional accreditation and the regulation of licensed practitioners. Legitimacy in the sphere of justice is more complicated. Questions of perceived legitimacy will linger, even if the judiciary are highly qualified appointees whose work is supervised by higher authorities. Put simply, some defendants may, for example, perceive a panel of white, middle-class, middle-aged magistrates to lack legitimacy,[5] even though they are sworn members of the judiciary who have passed through a rigorous appointment process. Representativeness may also be critical to ensuring an adequate degree of perceived legitimacy. The class or ethnicity of the practitioner is less likely to affect patients' perceptions of the legitimacy of doctors. Evaluations of competence will determine perceptions of legitimacy; the same may not be true for judges.

11.2.1 Loss of Hearing?

As the term implies, sentencing hearings (or in jurisdictions without a separate sentencing hearing, the closing speeches) give the parties an opportunity to air their views, perspectives, and recommendations to the judge. In this phase of the process, defendants and victims alike seek a fair *hearing*. True, at present sentencing hearings may be perfunctory affairs in which the court imposes a sentence upon a silent defendant whose lawyer communicates on his or her behalf. This reality should not blind us to the potential benefits arising from a thorough discussion of the issues involved. The domain of sentencing procedure, often overlooked in the substantive literature, requires some consideration as the use of HAL (and other technological advances such as remote hearings) proliferates. Advocates of AI say little about the procedure to be followed when the program has generated a sentence. Does it simply appear as an attachment to an email addressed to the offender? Is it read aloud in open court without any opportunity for response from the parties?

If HAL is more effective than human judges at determining the most appropriate sentence—whether this refers to retributive or preventive principles—it is hard to see a role for an in-person hearing. Assuming all relevant information has been entered into the program, what remains to be discussed? There appears no role or opportunity for offenders to express their perspective. Allocution is an important due process right, acknowledged across all legal systems. Offenders are always entitled to speak to sentence, and advocates make a speech in mitigation at sentencing. These submissions may contain substantive information unavailable until that point, or the interpretation of agreed facts may influence the sentence of a human judge. This element of sentencing is abandoned when a computer program decides sentence. De Mulder and Gubby (1983) noted this almost 40 years ago: "If there is no human agent available to whom he may express his point of view, his purpose will be frustrated. Such frustration of purpose could easily affect the legitimation of the authority" (302).

Of course, some kind of "speak to sentence" option could be devised. The offender could have an opportunity to submit a statement to be entered prior to HAL's final sentence. This might take the form of an excuse, regret, apology, or explanation for the offense. Consistent with the adversarial model it could be the subject of commentary by the prosecution. Or a judge could review the statement and if convinced of the need to intervene, might enter a "correction for personal mitigation," which would modify HAL's final sentence. But from the perspective of the actors, this is a poor substitute for an offender's opportunity to address the judge in open court.

Without a hearing, other participants in the hearing may also lose their voice. Although few hearings involve victims reading their statements aloud in open court, there is evidence that when this occurs, victims benefit from the experience (Roberts 2009). They may feel a sense of vindication or participation. This would not be the case if they submitted their Victim Impact Statement (VIS) through an online portal, or worse if they simply responded to a series of prompts (e.g., "Were you physically harmed? If not, proceed directly to Q8"). Finally, there is some evidence that hearing about the impact of the crime from the victim him- or herself has a more powerful effect upon offenders. When the VIS simply forms part of the prosecution submission on sentence, the offender may be less attentive. This (and other) communicative functions of the sentencing hearing—or closing speeches—are lost when HAL occupies the bench.[6] Defendants sometimes complain that their perspectives are not heeded by judges in a busy court. But if judges are hard of hearing, HAL is stone deaf.

11.2.2 The Input Problem

The principal barrier to creating a functioning sentencing algorithm lies at the input stage. The complexities of inputting appropriate information have been overlooked by AI advocates. In order to construct a database of sentencing decisions on which AI will operate, judgments need to be routinely input. Constructing a database for a medical diagnostic tool is relatively straightforward. Patients respond to a series of questions: Is the pain sharp or dull? How severe is the pain on a 10-point scale? Once many patients have input responses, the program determines the correlates and predictors of symptoms and pathologies. Then, drawing upon the outcomes of previous therapeutic outcomes, the program recommends a specific treatment.

Sentencing is qualitatively different. A sentencing court considers many subtle and interacting factors, which vary in weight depending upon the offense and the offender. Stobbs et al. claim that "the only data which would need to be inputted [into the program] in a particular case is the aggravating and mitigating factors which were relevant" (2017, 272). This suggests the process is as straightforward as entering the number, nature, and duration of symptoms into a diagnostic program. Hardly. Sentencing is more complicated; sentencing factors carry different weights in different contexts, and their significance cannot be determined in advance or necessarily reduced to a specific value (e.g., remorse: "high"; criminal history: "modest").

Some case characteristics may readily lend themselves to entry into the database. For example, the offender's gender or age (assuming these are deemed relevant to sentencing). Other variables are as clear as the medical ones: Did the offender plead guilty? Was the plea entered early or late in the proceedings? Does he or she have any relevant prior convictions? If so, how many? Previous convictions illustrate the benefits and limitations of AI-assisted sentencing. An offender's criminal record could be reduced to a mechanical computation, but again AI would only be capable of crude weightings of prior crimes. How relevant for current sentencing for manslaughter is a previous conviction for robbery? If two offenders have the same prior conviction of assault, but one occurred two years ago and the other ten years previously, to what extent, if at all, should the court discount the older conviction? AI could apply simple rules such as assigning a severity increment for each prior crime, but one which diminishes over time. But human judgment will still be required. AI may recommend a one-year sentence enhancement when the offender has a prior, serious conviction of the same crime for which he is now being sentenced. Legally significant details will likely escape the AI analysis. If the prior crime had occurred as a result of some situational pressure which re-emerged in the offender's life at the time of the current crime, a human decision maker may be inclined to discount the prior record enhancement or ignore the prior conviction altogether (see Frase and Roberts 2019).[7]

Turning to the victim—who would input the contents of the Victim Impact Statement, to note one near-universal component of sentencing in common law jurisdictions? The extent to which the information in the VIS should affect sentencing is challenging for judges; programming HAL to evaluate and assign weight to the contents of the VIS may be impossible.

Many other qualitative judgments that would have a significant effect would be missed: the deeply remorseful individual vs the offender who perfunctorily expresses remorse through his lawyer; the offender with previous convictions yet who has a compelling explanation for the prior offending. A great deal of information about sentencing factors may be entered into the database, but it is hard to see how interpretation, context, and explanation—provided by the defense lawyer in the speech in mitigation may be taken into account.

Sentencers could enter the data when they sentence an offender, indicating in more qualitative ways how much weight was assigned to different factors. This would lead to a more accurate prediction, but would be very labor-intensive for judges. That's a problem in itself. One of the challenges in existing databases is judicial fatigue in terms of inputting data.[8]

To summarize, AI's sentence recommendation would only approximate the "true" sentence which reflects all relevant case characteristics, because the data on which it is based only imperfectly captures all the components which determined previous sentences. Overall, therefore, *replacing* the sentencing judge by AI is neither a realistic nor a salutary option. This is not to say a "computer judge" would not be conceivable in relatively simple and inconsequential legal matters (for example, Estonia is exploring the use of AI to decide small civil claims (cf. Dymitruk 2019)). Criminal sentencing, however, is not one of them.

11.3 The Advisory Sentence

How then, could AI support sentencing judges? HAL could follow in the footsteps of the pioneering computer-assisted "Sentencing Information Systems" trialed in the 1980s and 1990s (e.g., Doob and Park 1987; Simon and Gaes 1989), the principal difference being the vast increase in computing power available today. These systems were developed because a method was lacking "for anyone . . . to know in a systematic, up-to-date, and accessible manner, on a continuing basis, what kinds of sentences are being handed down" (The Canadian Sentencing Commission 1987, 60). The emergence of sentencing guidelines improved judicial information on the sentencing practice these instruments mirrored, but the depth of information is inevitably limited. HAL would fill this gap by drawing upon prior practice to provide a sentence for an individual case, which we term an *Advisory Sentence* (AS). As HAL would operate based on past practice, the AS would be able to incorporate preventive as well as proportionality-oriented considerations, depending on the relevant sentencing framework (Hutton 1995; Chiao 2018).

HAL's AS is derived using machine learning classifiers. This technological approach seems favorable over encoding fixed rules into the program by hand (Bagaric and Wolf 2018). While such a logic-based approach would provide a high degree of transparency (rules such as "*if* the offender has x prior convictions, *then* . . ." are easily comprehensible for humans), an example-based method promises much more fine-tuned and accurate results (on the "transparency—accuracy trade-off," see Ryberg and Petersen, this volume). Further, for the purposes envisaged here, a machine learning capability is essential because it would allow HAL to keep in synch with a changing sentencing practice.

Judges could operate HAL parallel to consulting relevant sentencing guidelines. To avoid giving the impression of a precise and unique sentence, the program would provide confidence intervals around its recommendations in the form of sentence ranges. For example, the program might recommend a sentence of 18 months, with a 95% confidence interval running from 15 to 25 months and a midpoint of 20 months, which captures 95% of the custodial sentences imposed for this offense.

The AS would serve as a point of departure to consider the circumstances of the case appearing for sentencing, along with lawyers' submissions, Pre Sentence Reports, victim impact statements, and sources of guidance such as appellate decisions. The system would be publicly available and transparent, conforming to the requirements set out by several contributors to this volume. The parties would use the AS to prepare their sentencing submissions. Members of the public could input information and receive an AS on the details they provide in the same way that people enter driver and vehicle details into a website in order to obtain an estimate of automobile insurance premiums.

11.3.1 Deficits of Past Judicial Practice as a Data-Source

If courts used the AS, sentencing would become more consistent and transparent. However, using past judicial practice as a frame of reference also carries with it some inherent difficulties. One challenge in feeding the program's database with prior judgments is ensuring that the predictions have a principled foundation. This is particularly the case in sentencing systems affirming both retributive and preventive rationales. For example, in the aftermath of the 2011 English riots, courts deviated from a proportionate punishment in order to promote general deterrence (cf. Pina-Sánchez et al. 2017). This approach was endorsed by the Court of Appeal, which stated that "the imposition of severe sentences, intended to provide both punishment and deterrence, must follow" (*R v. Blackshaw and others* [2011] EWCA Crim 2312 [4]). If these judgments were entered into the program's database, its prediction for a "standard" proportionate sentence would become distorted. This would compromise the principled elements of the algorithm's predictions, thus undermining the communicative function of punishment (e.g., Duff 2001). One solution would be for the sentencing framework to be embedded within the algorithm. It could affirm retributive proportionality as a primary rationale, or prevention. If retributive proportionality was deemed primordial, deviations from the proportionate punishment for reasons of deterrence, incapacitation, and rehabilitation would become apparent. In this way, the program could predict "pure" proportionality but indicate where deviations might be warranted.

Another disadvantage of reflecting current sentencing practice in the program's predictions is that any existing biases would become institutionalized. For example, a guilty plea is supposed to reduce sentence regardless of the nature or seriousness of the offense. Yet some judges tend to "downweight" plea in the most serious cases, contrary to published guidance. This misuse of the factor would be captured by the database and then reinforced through the AI recommendations or other kinds of output. Moreover, it is possible that the algorithm's architecture (and outputs) changes over time in ways the guidelines authority does not approve. For example, a specific aggravating or mitigating factor listed in the guidelines might largely be ignored by the courts, thus having no impact on the AS issued by the program. If judges are guided *only* by the AS, this would mean the trial courts were determining sentencing practice, rather than the relevant guidelines authority or appeal court. Other stakeholders in the criminal process such as victim representatives, barristers, or academics that currently take part in shaping the guidelines would lose any influence on sentencing.

For these reasons, there is a need for an institution that assumes a corrective function. This function would fall within the remit of the existing sentencing guidelines authorities. By issuing sentencing guidelines and thus shaping judicial practice, the sentencing commission or council would *indirectly* influence the algorithm's database. This would allow it to counteract any biases or unwarranted developments becoming apparent in the program. Over time, the sentencing program and sentencing guidelines would merge into a single system. The sentencing commission or council would be given the authority to adjust the algorithm directly. This would render the AS a combination of both an AI prediction based on prior practice and normative interventions carried out by the sentencing commission or council. In any event, sentencing commissions should not cede jurisdiction to the algorithm.

11.3.2 Benefits of the Advisory Sentence System: Promoting Greater Uniformity

Even if HAL cannot (or should not) replace judges at sentencing, it is capable of making a much greater contribution to the sentencing process than is currently the case. Beyond the limited (and controversial) role of risk prediction, at present AI makes no contribution to the sentencing process. In the remaining sections of this chapter, we identify other ways in which AI may improve sentencing decisions (see Bagaric and Wolf 2018; Hutton 1995, for additional discussion of the benefits of computer-assisted sentencing). We begin with the most obvious target: unjustified variation in sentencing outcomes.

Research for over a century has documented disparity at sentencing due to the personality and attitudes of the judge. The early attempts to employ computers at sentencing aimed to reduce disparity by providing judges with a sentence recommendation based upon key case characteristics and other information. The principal goal of sentencing reform has long been to reduce disparities and discrimination at sentencing. This is particularly true for sentencing guidelines (Crackanthorpe 1900; Frankel 1972). In the United States and England and Wales (and many other jurisdictions), sentencing guidelines were introduced to structure judicial decision (Frase 2019; Roberts and Ashworth 2016). Research suggests that these reforms have achieved greater consistency at sentencing (Pina-Sánchez and Linacre 2014), although concerns about disparity and discrimination persist (e.g., Pina-Sánchez and Linacre 2013). Will HAL perform this task more effectively? Its potential to reflect complex combinations of criteria is a distinct advantage over sentencing guidelines, which can only operate based on a simple grid or flow-chart logic.

Using the AS, judges would benefit from an unbiased source of information about the impact that sentencing factors have had upon sentence outcomes. This information may influence their subsequent sentencing decisions. At present, guidance is either episodic (from appellate decisions) or potentially distorted by adversarial bias. Regarding the former, some guideline judgments will indicate the strength that a factor should carry; as for the latter, counsel may point to prior decisions which suggested the impact that a given factor should have on the sentence. AI's calibration would provide a far more accurate and unbiased guide to the weight that courts have assigned sentencing factors.

Consistency would likely increase as courts reflected the totality of current practice in their judgments. The algorithm would predict the same sentence regardless of where, when, and by whom it was used, provided that the same set of facts were entered into it. There would be a trend for sentences to become less disparate around the average sentence, as judges seeing that a sentence is outside the normal distribution would likely move closer to the average sentence. However, the transfer process between judges' impressions during the trial and what is in fact being entered into the sentencing algorithm remains a gateway for inconsistencies. Similar to the effect of sentencing guidelines, judges will be able to "generate" a desired prediction outcome if they enter the right criteria. In the following, some specific areas in which AI could increase consistency are highlighted.

11.3.2.1 Reducing and Identifying Direct and Indirect Discrimination

One of the most troubling cognitive biases relates to legally protected characteristics such as race and gender. Racial disparities in criminal justice are a phenomenon present in most Western jurisdictions (Phillips and Bowling 2017). However, there is insufficient knowledge on the extent and causes of these disparities, partly due to a lack of adequate sentencing data (Pina-Sánchez et al. 2019). Research on racial bias suggests that judges "think about race as a relevant and useful heuristic for determining the blameworthiness of the defendant and the perniciousness of the crime" (Eberhardt et al. 2006, 385).

AI could help reduce discrimination at sentencing—a function, however, that is far from straightforward. As Bagaric and Wolf (2018) note: "computers have no instinctive, unconscious bias, are incapable of inadvertent discrimination, and are uninfluenced by extraneous considerations and by assumptions and generalizations that are not embedded in their programs" (696). Thus, excluding race and other protected offender characteristics as variables from the algorithm's predictions ostensibly promises unbiased sentence recommendations. However, employing a machine learning tool entails the specific risk of generating "algorithmic bias." If discrimination were present in the HAL's database, simply excluding the protected factors would be insufficient for ensuring unbiased predictions. The algorithm would learn to substitute the excluded factors with "proxy variables" (see in detail Davies and Douglas, this volume). Therefore, the introduction of HAL would have to be accompanied by a research function scrutinizing even ostensibly neutral factors for disproportionate impact. The most thorough way to tackle biased predictions, however, would be to address the sources of discrimination influencing the algorithm's training data directly.

AI might support this task by more effectively identifying the sources of direct and indirect discrimination at sentencing. The current approach to detecting *direct* discrimination entails conducting multivariate analyses comparing sentencing outcomes for, say visible minority and white defendants. After controlling for as many legal characteristics as possible, to what extent do sentencing patterns for the racial groups differ? Such analyses have been published in most Western nations (e.g., Sentencing Council 2019; Hood 1992; Roberts and Doob 1997). A sentencing algorithm could greatly facilitate this research. Assuming it operated on the basis of an extensive range of legal variables, it could show racial disparities simply by manipulating the variable "race" and track changes in racial disparity over time. *Indirect* discrimination arising from some element of the sentencing regime is harder for human researchers to detect. For AI, it would be relatively straightforward. A defendant's plea and criminal record are two examples of such indirect sources of disproportionate impact.

Plea-based sentencing reductions may indirectly discriminate against minorities (see discussion in Johnson and Richardson 2019). Black defendants are less likely to plead guilty, for a range of reasons, including "overcharging" by prosecutors, lack of trust in the CJS, or inadequate legal advice (Lammy 2017; Hood 1992). The consequence is that such defendants are less likely to benefit from the plea-based sentence reductions—more likely to be imprisoned, and for a longer term. A number of authors have called for the abolition of plea-based discounts for this reason (e.g., Tonry 2009). A similar argument has been made against prior record enhancements which result in higher custody rates and longer sentences for racial minorities. The result is racial disproportionality in prison populations (see Frase and Roberts 2019). There are likely other ostensibly neutral aspects of sentencing, which trigger indirect discrimination, and AI would be far more effective at uncovering these effects.

11.3.2.2 Detecting Local Sentencing Anomalies and Departures from Principle

Thus far, our focus has been upon the sentence, not the sentencer. Assuming a relatively comprehensive database including case characteristics and reasons for sentence, AI could focus on the judge. AI would be useful in identifying aberrant courts or rogue judges—in terms of current practice. If AI revealed evidence of regional sentencing disparity, this would permit the Sentencing Council to pinpoint these courts or judges, in order to permit remedial action.

Some local courts may evolve their own disproportionate practices. For example, regional sentence disparity is widespread in Germany: a recent study found regional differences in the average sentence length amounting up to 25% across all offenses when comparing the regions of Upper Bavaria and Baden (Grundies 2018). While the regional variability may be less striking in England and Wales, local variation exists for certain offenses and sentencing factors (Pina-Sánchez 2015). In a similar fashion, whether true or not, some judges acquire a reputation for being particularly severe toward certain categories of offending, for example, domestic violence or drink driving. This can lead to "judge shopping"—as lawyers seek to secure a particular judge for a bail application, trial, or sentencing hearing. Defendants who fall foul of one of these kinds of anomalous sentencing cultures may not be aware of the fact, and may fail to appeal their sentence as a result. AI would easily (and accurately) identify such aberrant sentencing practices (or judges who are outliers), leading to remedial action from the sentencing guidelines authority, court of appeal, or the senior judiciary. HAL would monitor the performance of its employer, the court.

11.3.2.3 Facilitating Appellate Review of Sentencing

AI could also facilitate appellate review of trial court sentences. The conventional test for appellate intervention in the common law world takes the form of determining whether there has been an error in law, or the sentence was "manifestly unfit." Most appeals will turn upon the second ground (Trotter 2020). Yet the phrase "manifestly unfit" is slippery and subjective; the concept of fitness can be interpreted in different ways.

A statistical definition may be useful in determining whether a given sentence—say three-years imprisonment—is "manifestly unfit." AI would be capable of generating a much more accurate calibration of whether the characteristics of the current case justify the sentence imposed. And whether, in light of these and a comprehensive matching with previous decisions for the same offense, this sentence was unfit. For example, if 95% of prior sentences for the crime were under 30 months, would this render the 3-year sentence unfit? Or if 95% were under 24 months? This kind of "statistical fitness" alone may be insufficient grounds for appellate intervention. However, an appeal court could incorporate this information along with submissions from counsel as it determines whether there is a basis for interfering with the trial court sentence. The AI *Advisory Sentence* may also make the appellate review process more efficient. The program's determination as to whether, taking into account all case characteristics, this sentence should be overturned could be provided to counsel. Armed with this information, lawyers would be better placed to know whether their client's appeal is likely to succeed, and be more able to advise clients contemplating an appeal. This kind of application has been routine for years in the area of civil litigation.

11.3.2.4 Constraining Adversarialism in Sentencing Submissions: Offender Risk

Sentencing in the common law countries is adversarial in nature, particularly in the United States, Canada, and Australia. While plea negotiations often result in joint submissions on sentencing, the parties' initial (and sometimes final) positions will normally be far apart. American prosecutors in particular have a reputation for robust and adversarial positions on sentence. Prosecutorial submissions often stress the offender's high risk of reoffending and the consequent threat to society. The search for relevant precedent will be party-driven, and only minimally constrained by codes of professional conduct. Defense counsel are obliged to mount a speech in mitigation that will reflect the defendant's interests, and will have no need to consider wider concerns such as consistency. The consequence is that at sentencing in adversarial systems, a judge is often confronted by two very divergent recommendations for sentence. Counsel for the defendant may argue his or her client represents a low risk to reoffend, pointing to various steps taken to address various addictions. In light of these actions by the defendant since the offense and while awaiting sentencing, a community-based punishment may be appropriate. In response, the prosecutor may point to the offender's history of noncompliance with previous court orders, including terms of probation, and advocate imprisonment.

Who's right? The conclusions of a sentencing submission will inevitably reflect the perspectives and interests of the party. The current solution to this problem in many countries involves the use of probation services who prepare a report on the offender, his or her social milieu, criminal history and suitability for particular sanctions. Probation officers often provide a sentence recommendation—(e.g., "this individual is (or is not) a suitable candidate for a community-based sentence"). Yet probation caseloads and limits on ongoing training mean that probation recommendations are often subjective and occasionally cursory. AI could provide both a risk score and a "suitability for sentence" recommendation. Predicting offender risk is a close approximation to medical algorithms, which predict the likelihood of various pathologies. AI could incorporate a much wider range of information relevant to risk, including variables related to the offense and the offender. The score would be uncontaminated by human bias, or adversarialism. Concerns will remain that factors which disadvantage certain groups will be incorporated into the program.

The applications described thus far all attempt to improve judicial decision-making, directly by offering an AS, and indirectly through improving the quality of submissions. AI also has great potential to improve the nature of existing guidelines.

11.4 Enhancing Sentencing Guidelines

Sentencing guidelines originated in the United States during the 1970s, and have now spread to many other jurisdictions (see Frase and Mitchell 2020; Roberts and Harris 2019). Although they assume different forms, the guidelines share a common objective: promoting more principled and consistent sentencing. Guidelines are generally based on existing practice, and contain sentence recommendations for courts to follow. Usually, sentencing commissions or councils devise and issue the guidelines. This is the case across the United States, in England and Wales, South Korea, Scotland, and other jurisdictions. Elsewhere the senior judiciary creates the guidelines for lower courts to apply at sentencing. To date, AI has played no role in constructing or amending these systems. In jurisdictions operating guidelines, most of the applications of AI discussed so far—enhancing consistency and sentencing research—are currently performed by the relevant guidelines' authority, the sentencing commission or council. AI would contribute to the work of the Commission, assisting in monitoring guidelines compliance and improving the guidelines.

11.4.1 Identifying Problematic Areas of Guidance

AI can assist in shaping the guidelines themselves. This may mean identifying problematic aspects of guidelines and ways in which the courts are misapplying current guidance, whether in statutes, judgments, or sentencing guidelines. This task is currently undertaken by sentencing commissions and councils; AI would perform the same task more effectively. The judicial use of alternate forms of custody found in Canada and England and Wales illustrates.

Many countries operate suspended prison sentences or home confinement sanctions. Canada has a Conditional Sentence of Imprisonment (CSI), which is a sentence of custody served at home. In England and Wales, courts may impose a Suspended Sentence Order (SSO), which is also a form of imprisonment. In both jurisdictions, before it may impose an SSO or a CSI, a court must first be satisfied that a custodial sentence is inevitable.[9] These sanctions may be imposed only after the court has taken a decision to imprison the offender. This is made clear by one of the guidelines (see Sentencing Council 2016).

Despite this requirement, research has suggested that courts in England and Wales and Canada do not always follow this logic. In some cases, defendants receive a CSI or an SSO as a replacement for a community penalty rather than a term of custody (see Webster and Doob 2019; Irwin-Rogers and Roberts 2019). When this occurs, "net-widening" has taken place: the alternate forms of imprisonment have drawn upon the community rather than custodial caseload. Determining whether and to what extent cases receiving a CSI or SSO were originally bound for a community punishment rather than prison is a complex research challenge (see Webster and Doob 2019). Yet AI would easily be able to identify CSIs or SSOs with characteristics that are significantly closer to the profile, which in the past attracted a community penalty. In this way it would be possible to far more accurately estimate the extent to which "net-widening" occurs, with a view to correcting this misapplication of the guidance and misuse of the sanction.

11.4.2 Refining Elements of the Guidelines

Guidelines outside the United States are generally offense specific in nature (Roberts and Harris 2019). Each guideline contains sentencing factors relevant to the specific crime, and these factors are distinguished in terms of their importance. The guidelines in England require courts to proceed through a series of steps at sentencing, applying different factors at separate stages of the process. For example, the English guidelines assign the most important sentencing factors to the first step of the guideline.

At Step 1 these factors determine which of three sentence ranges is used. The first step in the sequence has the most important impact on the sentence ultimately imposed. In order to promote proportionality, only factors relevant to harm and culpability are considered at Step 1. Less important factors appear at Step 2, where they only affect movement *within* the range of sentence established at Step 1 (see Roberts 2019). "Factor placement" is therefore important: it is necessary to ensure that the primary factors (reflecting harm and culpability) are appropriately assigned to Step 1 while less important factors appear at Step 2. A glance at any guideline will reveal the challenge in ensuing appropriate placement of sentencing factors. Two factors from the burglary guideline are "occupier at home (or returns home) while offender present," and "gratuitous degradation of the victim." Which factor should carry more weight and be assigned to Step 1? It is far from clear.

At present, factors are selected and assigned to Steps of the guidelines by the Council members, in discussion at Council meetings. AI can better perform this task: it could empirically verify the weight carried by different factors in previous sentencing decisions, and placement could reflect these weights. Step 1 factors could then be defined as any factor carrying a certain weight in terms of predicting sentence severity. Based upon the AI analysis the Council might wish to re-allocate certain factors, for example if a Step 2 factor turns out to account for a very high degree of variance in sentencing outcomes. Of course, this empirical analysis assumes that courts to date have used the factors appropriately, and with many of the AI applications we propose, a careful judicial review of outcomes would be necessary.

AI could also identify any overarching misapplications of the guidelines. One of the central puzzles in proportionate sentencing is the relationship between the two components of a proportional sanction: Which is more important, harm or culpability? Guidelines in England and other countries are structured to reflect these twin dimensions. The English guidelines duck the issue by treating both dimensions equally. Most of the Council's guidelines require a court to assign the case to one of three levels of offense seriousness and one of three levels of culpability. (These may be broadly conceived as low, medium, and high levels, although different terms are used in the guidelines.)[10]

Increments in severity track both in equal measure. For example, the increase in recommended sentence length from the intermediate to the highest level of harm is 7 years (9 to 16 years). A shift from medium level of culpability to the highest level has the same effect: an additional 9 years. But does this structure mean that in practice courts impose sentences where harm and culpability are equally weighted, as intended by the Sentencing Council? Courts have much discretion to depart from the recommended sentence starting point and ranges, with the result that empirically one of the two factors may explain significantly more variance. Or, more likely, for certain offenses the offender's culpability score will be far more predictive of sentence length than harm; for other crimes, the reverse may be true. In this context, AI would be able to accurately determine how courts are weighing the twin components of proportional sentencing, and identify any offenses where in practice courts depart from the equal weighting of harm and culpability mandated by the guidelines. At present, the degree to which sentences actually correspond to the balance prescribed by the guidelines is unknown.

11.4.3 Enhancing Sentence Recommendations: Identifying the Most Effective Sentence

Sentencing guidelines usually provide specific sentence recommendations. In the United States, these track the seriousness of the offense and the offender's criminal history. AI would be able to suggest a recommendation which would incorporate much more information—for example, regarding offender risk, and the effectiveness of alternative sanctions. HAL would be equally superior at the task of deciding which of a range of sanctions is most likely to achieve desistance for different profiles of offenders. Assuming a database containing a rich array of data about the offender, his or her offending history, the current crime, and history of prior contacts with the CJS—to name a few variables—AI could recommend the most "effective" sanction in the same way that medical AI predicts which patients will be most likely to benefit from which therapies. AI could go even further. When imposing a community order, judges in England and Wales may choose to impose any or all of a range of up to 15 conditions or requirements such as a curfew, a residence requirement, or an unpaid work requirement (Wasik 2014, 138–150).

When crafting sentence judges attempt to individualize the restrictions imposed, with a view to determining the most effective combination. This determination is assisted, haphazardly by counsel ("my client informs me he would find a program to treat alcohol abuse useful, and he is happy to comply with a 7pm curfew"), and by advice from probation services ("this offender would benefit from a mobility restriction preventing him from entering the city centre or having any contact with known criminal associates"). Ultimately, however, the conditions imposed are likely to reflect judges' experience and intuitions about which conditions are most useful or effective. AI would be particularly useful in establishing the most appropriate release conditions for prisoners released on parole, where the decision is purely preventive. Again, at present, decisions on mobility restrictions, reporting requirements and the like are made by parole boards, without the benefit of machine intelligence.

11.5 Conclusion

In this chapter, we have attempted to put HAL in its place by mapping the proper role of AI at sentencing along with its potential applications. We share the view expressed by others (e.g., Donohue 2019) that sentencing is a judicial function which should remain in human hands. Defendants, victims, and the wider community are unlikely to regard HAL's sentencing as a satisfactory substitute for human decision-making. Nevertheless, machine learning will likely play an increasingly important role in supporting judicial decision-making. A sentencing algorithm would provide sentencers with a far more comprehensive picture of current sentencing practice, thus improving consistency. Specifically, it could mitigate human cognitive biases and discrimination at sentencing. It would help detect local sentencing disparities and facilitate appellate review. In addition, AI can improve the guidance provided to assist courts, by identifying problematic aspects of guidance. Lastly, it could foster a deeper understanding of the sentencing practice, which might influence the guidelines' elements.

How realistic is the establishment of an AI program as devised here within existing sentencing systems? Earlier we outlined that HAL would be well suited to perform many of the tasks currently covered by sentencing guidelines. Therefore, the transition to AI supported sentencing should be easier in those jurisdictions where sentencing guidelines are already in place. An incremental development toward AI informed sentencing might begin, for example, with AI supported research carried out within the sentencing authority and corresponding adjustments to the guidelines. One of the main hurdles to HAL's establishment, however, will be judicial acceptance (Tata 1998, 204). In jurisdictions such as Australia and Germany, which strongly affirm an individualistic (or "instinctive") approach to sentencing, judges will likely be less inclined to accept the relevance of information on penalties passed for prior ("unalike") cases. It is also possible, however, that judges in these jurisdictions will be enticed by the prospect of HAL achieving a much higher degree of individualization than traditional discretion-structuring instruments. In fact, HAL has the potential to address some of the perennial problems of the "instinctive" approach to sentencing such as identifying an appropriate starting point sentence (Schöch 1972, 128).

Expanding the role of AI in support of the sentencing process requires careful consideration in order to preserve sentencing as what it is: an essentially human enterprise. Yet, if employed responsibly, HAL has considerable potential for making sentencing more consistent and principled—just don't let it take over the bench.

Notes

1. Other approaches are possible. For example, under a hybrid scheme, minor offenses might be sentenced by a computer program while more serious cases would be handled as now, by judges. Or, a judge could review and consider all the relevant information and then feed into the computer for final determination of the sentence.
2. Bagaric and Wolf (2018) advocate use of a computer determined sentence, but suggest that if the parties disagree on the appropriate sentence, a hearing is held at which the judge makes "relevant factual determinations" (681). This accomplished, the judge then cedes jurisdiction to HAL to "set the penalty" (681).
3. For example, defendants in England and Wales can choose between trial in the magistrates' courts or the Crown Court.
4. Even if a computer could give reasons for a particular sentence, these would not reflect empathy for the victim or censure of the offender. Further, insofar as notions of restorative justice play a role and sentences are supposed to have a "healing" function, this would not be reconcilable with a computer simply providing a sentence.
5. One perennial critique of the lay magistracy in England and Wales is that magistrates (who are unpaid volunteers) are unrepresentative of the communities from which they are drawn. As a result, there has been a push for greater diversity in recent years.
6. There is a counterargument. Some may argue that an in-person hearing exposes the adjudicator to extralegal factors, thereby undermining principled sentencing. There is no shortage of potential threats: very emotional victim impact statements; powerful, but class-linked character references; adverse inferences about defendants who fail to express remorse for serious crimes. Without a hearing, the effect of these influences is likely to be limited.

7. Research in England and Wales has demonstrated that for a variety for reasons, courts disregard a large proportion of prior convictions at sentencing (see Roberts and Pina Sanchez 2015).

8. The Sentencing Council of England and Wales operated a survey of Crown courts for a four-year period (2011–2015). Sentencers were required to input data about each sentencing decision. The survey was ultimately discontinued largely because judges considered the task too onerous.

9. In England and Wales, this is phrased by reference to a general restriction on the use of imprisonment known as the "custody threshold." Courts must not pass a custodial sentence unless the offense is so serious that this threshold has been passed (s. 152, Criminal Justice Act 2003). A suspended sentence order is considered a sentence of custody, and hence subject to the so-called custody threshold.

10. See, for example, Sentencing Council of England and Wales. 2016. Robbery Offences. Definitive Guideline. Available at: https://www.sentencingcouncil.org.uk/publications/item/robbery-definitive-guideline-2/.

References

Bagaric, M., and G. Wolf. 2018. "Sentencing by Computer: Enhancing Sentencing Transparency and Predictability, and (Possibly) Bridging the Gap between Sentencing Knowledge and Practice." George Mason Law Review 25 (4): pp. 653–709.

Boden, M. A. 2016. AI: Its Nature and Future. Oxford: Oxford University Press.

The Canadian Sentencing Commission. 1987. Sentencing Reform: A Canadian Approach: Report of the Canadian Sentencing Commission. Ottawa: Minister of Supply and Services Canada.

Chiao, V. 2018. "Predicting Proportionality: The Case for Algorithmic Sentencing." Criminal Justice Ethics 37 (3): pp. 238–261.

Crackanthorpe, M. 1900. "Can Sentences Be Standardised?" The Nineteenth Century 47: pp. 103–115.

De Mulder, R. V., and H. M. Gubby. 1983. "Legal Decision Making by Computer: An Experiment with Sentencing." Computer Law Journal 4: pp. 243–303.

Donohue, M. 2019. "A Replacement for Justitia's Scales?: Machine Learning's Role in Sentencing." Harvard Journal of Law and Technology 32: pp. 657–678.

Doob, A. N., and N. W. Park. 1987. "Computerized Sentencing Information for Judges: An Aid to the Sentencing Process." Criminal Law Quarterly 30 (1): pp. 54–72.

Duff, A. 2001. Punishment, Communication, and Community. Oxford: Oxford University Press.

Dworkin, R. 1963. "Judicial Discretion." The Journal of Philosophy 60: pp. 624–638.

Dymitruk, M. 2019. "Artificial Intelligence as a Tool to Improve the Administration of Justice?" Acta Universitatis Sapientiae: Legal Studies 8: pp. 179–190.

Eberhardt, J. L., P. G. Davies, V. J. Purdie-Vaughns, and S. L. Johnson. 2006. "Looking Deathworthy: Perceived Stereotypicality of Black Defendants Predicts Capital-Sentencing Outcomes." Psychological Science 17: pp. 383–386.

Enescu, R. 2019. "Simplified Procedures in Criminal Matters and the Risk of Judicial Errors: The Case of Penal Orders in Germany." Journal on European History of Law 10: pp. 182–187.

Frankel, M. E. 1972. "Lawlessness in Sentencing." University of Cincinnati Law Review 41: pp. 1–54.

Frase, Richard S. 2019. "Forty Years of American Sentencing Guidelines: What Have We Learned?" Crime and Justice 48: pp. 79–135.

Frase, R., and K. L. Mitchell. 2020. "Sentencing Guidelines in the United States." In Handbook on Sentencing Policies and Practices in the 21st Century. Corrections and Sentencing, edited by Cassia Spohn and Pauline Brennan, pp. 43–67. New York: Routledge.

Frase, R. S., and J. V. Roberts. 2019. Paying for the Past: Prior Record Enhancements in the US Sentencing Guidelines. New York: Oxford University Press.

Grundies, V. 2018. "Regionale Unterschiede in der gerichtlichen Sanktionspraxis in der Bundesrepublik Deutschland. Eine empirische Analyse." In Kriminalsoziologie: Handbuch für Wissenschaft und Praxis, edited by Dieter Hermann and Andreas Pöge, pp. 295–313. Baden-Baden: Nomos.

Hood, R. 1992. Race and Sentencing: A Study in the Crown Court: A Report for the Commission for Racial Equality. Oxford: Oxford University Press.

Hutton, N. 1995. "Sentencing, Rationality, and Computer Technology." Journal of Law and Society 22 (4): pp. 549–570.

Irwin-Rogers, K., and J. V. Roberts. 2019. "Swimming Against the Tide: The Suspended Sentence Order in England and Wales, 2000–2017." Law and Contemporary Problems 82: pp. 137–162.

Johnson, B. D., and R. Richardson. 2019. "Race and Plea Bargaining." In A System of Pleas, edited by Vanessa Edkins and Allison Redlich, pp. 83–106. New York: Oxford University Press.

Lammy, D. 2017. An Independent Review into the Treatment of, and Outcomes for, Black, Asian and Minority Ethnic Individuals in the Criminal Justice System. HMSO. Available at: https://assets.publishing.service.gov.uk/government/uploads/system/uploads/attachment_data/file/643001/lammy-review-final-report.pdf.

Phillips, C., and B. Bowling. 2017. "Ethnicities, Racism, Crime, and Criminal Justice." In The Oxford Handbook of Criminology, edited by Alison Liebling, Shadd Maruna, and Lesley McAra, pp. 190–212. Oxford: Oxford University Press.

Pina-Sánchez, J. 2015. "Defining and Measuring Consistency in Sentencing." In Exploring Sentencing Practice in England and Wales, edited by Julian V. Roberts, pp. 76–92. Basingstoke: Palgrave Macmillan.

Pina-Sánchez, J., and R. Linacre. 2014. "Enhancing Consistency in Sentencing: Exploring the Effects of Guidelines in England and Wales." Journal of Quantitative Criminology 30 (4): pp. 731–748.

Pina-Sánchez, J., and R. Linacre. 2013. "Sentence Consistency in England and Wales: Evidence from the Crown Court Sentencing Survey." British Journal of Criminology 53 (6): pp. 1118–1138.

Pina-Sánchez, J., C. Lightowlers, and J. Roberts. 2017. "Exploring the Punitive Surge: Crown Court Sentencing Practices Before and After the 2011 English Riots." Criminology & Criminal Justice 17: pp. 319–339.

Pina-Sánchez, J., J. V. Roberts, and D. Sferopoulos. 2019. "Does the Crown Court Discriminate Against Muslim-named Offenders? A Novel Investigation Based on Text Mining Techniques." British Journal of Criminology 59 (3): pp. 718–736.

Roberts, J. V. 2009. "Listening to the Crime Victim: Evaluating Victim Input at Sentencing and Parole." Crime and Justice 38: pp. 347–412.

Roberts, J. V. 2019. "The Evolution of Sentencing Guidelines: Comparing Minnesota and England and Wales." Crime and Justice 48: pp. 187–254.

Roberts, J. V., and A. Ashworth. 2016. "The Evolution of Sentencing Policy and Practice in England and Wales, 2003-2015." Crime and Justice 45: pp. 307–358.

Roberts, J. V., and A. N. Doob. 1997. "Race, Ethnicity and Criminal Justice in Canada." Crime and Justice 21: pp. 469–522.

Roberts, J. V., and L. Harris. 2019. "Sentencing Guidelines Outside the United States." In Handbook on Sentencing Policies and Practices in the 21st Century. Corrections and Sentencing, edited by Cassia Spohn and Pauline Brennan, pp. 68–86. New York: Routledge.

Roberts, J. V., and J. Pina-Sanchez, J. 2015. "Previous Convictions at Sentencing: Exploring Empirical Trends in the Crown Court." Criminal Law Review (8): pp. 575–588.

Schöch, H. 1972. "Möglichkeiten und Grenzen einer Typisierung der Strafzumessung bei Verkehrsdelikten mit Hilfe empririscher Methoden." In Kriminologische Gegenwartsfragen, edited by Hans Göppinger and R. Hartmann, pp. 128–137. Stuttgart: Enke.

Sentencing Council of England and Wales. 2016. Imposition of Community and Custody Penalties. Definitive Guideline. Available at: https://www.sentencingcouncil.org.uk/wp-content/uploads/Imposition-definitive-guideline-Web.pdf.

Sentencing Council of England and Wales. 2019. Investigating the Association between an Offender's Sex and Ethnicity and the Sentence Imposed at the Crown Court for drug Offences. Available at: https://www.sentencingcouncil.org.uk/wp-content/uploads/Sex-and-ethnicity-analysis-final-1.pdf.

Simon, E., and G. Gaes. 1989. "ASSYST - Computer Support for Guideline Sentencing." In Proceedings of the Second International Conference on Artificial Intelligence and Law–ICAIL '89: pp. 195–200. Vancouver: ACM Press.

Stobbs, N., D. Hunter, and M. Bagaric. 2017. "Can Sentencing Be Enhanced by the Use of Artificial Intelligence?" Criminal Law Journal 41: pp. 261–277.

Susskind, R. E. 1986. "Detmold's Refutation of Positivism and the Computer Judge." The Modern Law Review 49: pp. 125–138.

Tata, C.1998. "The Application of Judicial Intelligence and 'Rules' to Systems Supporting Discretionary Judicial Decision-Making." Artificial Intelligence and Law 6: pp. 203–230.

Tonry, M. 2009. "Abandoning Sentence Discounts for Guilty Pleas." In Principled Sentencing. Readings on Theory and Policy, edited by Andrew von Hirsch, Andrew Ashworth, and Julian V. Roberts, pp. 351–353. 3rd ed. Oxford: Hart Publishing.

Trotter, G. T. 2020. "The Role of Appellate Courts in Sentencing." In Sentencing in Canada, edited by David P. Cole and Julian V. Roberts, pp. 169–182. Toronto: Irwin Law.

Wasik, M. 2014. A Practical Approach to Sentencing. Oxford: Oxford University Press.

Webster, C., and A. N. Doob. 2019. "Missed Opportunities: A Postmortem on Canada's Experience with the Conditional Sentence." Law and Contemporary Problems 82: pp. 163–197.

Weizenbaum, J. 1976. Computer Power and Human Reason: From Judgment to Calculation. San Francisco: Freeman.

12

Artificial Intelligence and Sentencing

Humans against Machines

Sigrid van Wingerden and Mojca M. Plesničar

12.1 Introduction

According to Chiao in his contribution to this book, the desirability of the use of AI in sentencing should be evaluated by comparing computers to the status quo ante, rather than to an unrealistic, and in any case unrealized, ideal. Although we agree that changes to the legal process such as adopting algorithmic sentencing methods can be beneficial when the change is an incremental improvement over the status quo, in order to assess whether the change is an improvement, we need to know what this "ideal" is toward which improvements are aimed. Therefore, the question whether AI is better at making sentencing decisions than human judges is approached differently in this chapter. We compare human with AI judges by evaluating the extent to which they are able to make a legitimate sentencing decision: Is legitimacy better achieved by machine than by human judges?

To answer this question, we developed a theoretical model for a legitimate sentencing regime. As explained later in the chapter, this model comprises both normative and empirical legitimacy, wherein normative legitimacy contains different levels and empirical legitimacy separate components. We use this model to compare the capabilities of AI and human judges. In reviewing human judges' performance, we draw upon research into the nature of human decision-making at sentencing. In doing so, we do not distinguish between different systems of sentencing, but rather look at universal decision-making dynamics. Regarding "AI judges," we first need to explain what we mean by the term AI judges.

Sigrid van Wingerden and Mojca M. Plesničar, *Artificial Intelligence and Sentencing* In: *Sentencing and Artificial Intelligence*. Edited by: Jesper Ryberg and Julian V. Roberts, Oxford University Press. © Oxford University Press 2022.
DOI: 10.1093/oso/9780197539538.003.0012

12.1.1. AI Judges

Defining AI is challenging. There is a myriad of definitions, and they are not static, but rather ever evolving. Generally, AI involves technology or methods that tackle problems which require intelligence to be solved (Plant 1994). Simple rule-based algorithms are usually insufficient to place in this category; the problem-solving needs to require some sort of autonomy on the side of the agent (e.g., EU-Commission 2018). The general AI sought by AI pioneers (and still being developed today, albeit at a slower pace) would be capable of competing with human intelligence: it would learn and adapt to new situations and different problems. It should, however, still be distinguished from artificial "superintelligence," AI past the point of singularity: the point after which it would greatly surpass human intelligence (Boden 2016).

Contrarily, narrow AI is generally designed to perform limited tasks (e.g., facial recognition or web search) and is increasingly successful in doing so. The task is performed within relatively narrow constraints and parameters. Narrow AI cannot be used for more complex tasks or easily move from one task to a different one: its success is dependent on it remaining in its own specialized area (Boden 2016; Franklin 2014).

All modern tools, including the ones being used and developed for sentencing purposes, fall within this last category. Sentencing machine learning-based models are not generally intelligent: they operate within the preconceived or pre-learned parameters and are unable to adapt to new situations and different problems. In the comparison of human and AI judges, however, we will consider both the existing narrow AI and the developing futuristic general AI, pointing out the differences this distinction involves for our debate.

12. 2 Legitimacy of Sentencing

Legal punishment "is (a) unpleasant, (b) imposed for conduct that has breached legal rules, (c) targeted against the individual responsible for that conduct, (d) imposed intentionally by State agents other than the subject, who are (e) acting under the authority of the breached law" (Hayes 2018, p. 236). Deciding whether to deprive people of their liberty is one of the most difficult decisions we make as a society and for most modern societies, the

232 SENTENCING AND ARTIFICIAL INTELLIGENCE

most severe restriction of human rights we can imagine. Considering the harm that is inflicted upon the defendant (but not only the defendant!) punishment requires justification; without it, such behavior would be regarded as wrong or evil (De Keijser, Van der Leeden, & Jackson 2002). People have sought justifications for punishment in many different places and ideas. Society (and academics') views on why and how we punish have evolved and are still evolving—with more and more facets being uncovered and alternatives to traditional views being developed. What is often lacking, however, are concepts by which we legitimize the act of sentencing itself. If we accept that punishment is an (essential) part of society, we need to discuss how coming to that punishment needs to be accomplished in order for the punishment and the process to be viewed as legitimate. Therefore, in order to assess whether AI judges are better at achieving legitimacy in sentencing than human judges, we first develop a model in which legitimate sentencing is partitioned into different elements. This model is abstract and a significant simplification of reality, but enables us to analyze the different aspects of legitimacy of sentencing. The first step in the development of the model is distinguishing normative from empirical legitimacy, building upon Roberts and Plesničar (2015).

12.2.1 Normative Legitimacy

Normative legitimacy means that sentencing must have a coherent moral justification. Moral legal theories serve as a critical standard against which sentencing practices are to be judged (De Keijser et al. 2002). The two main moral justifications for criminal punishment are the retributive and the utilitarian. Retribution requires that the severity of the punishment is proportionate to the severity of the crime and the blameworthiness of the offender (von Hirsch 1992). A punishment imposed with utilitarian aims is justified if it maximizes the happiness in society (Michael 1992) taking into account the various costs (e.g., financial, social, emotional to the offender or their family) and benefits (e.g., crimes prevented) of imposing a punishment (Ewald & Uggen 2012). Deterrence, incapacitation, and rehabilitation are utilitarian sentencing strategies. In reality, systems usually have a mixed or hybrid justification model, in which the retributive and utilitarian approaches are combined. Moreover, in recent decades alternative justifications have emerged, including restorative and therapeutic justice—which can hardly be reconciled with classical justifications for punishment (Snedker 2018; Strang & Braithwaite 2017).

When assessing in more detail whether sentencing practices are normatively legitimate, there are several questions in need of answering. The model we developed to evaluate the normative legitimacy of sentencing distinguishes three different levels: (1) the fundamentals of the system, (2) the actual sentencing decisions as regards the principles, and (3) the effects of the principles in practice.

12.2.1.1 The Fundamentals of the System

The first set of questions addresses the foundation of the system: Is it grounded in moral principles? Are, for example, the aims of sentencing stipulated in the law? Or are there sentencing guidelines that promote moral legal theories for sentencing, for instance, by reflecting ideas about proportionality? Are these ideas and aims coherently implemented throughout the system, and thus providing a coherent framework of sentencing?

The extent to which a sentencing system is grounded in moral theories differs among countries. Systems also differ: some are based on retribution, others have rehabilitation as the core objective, yet others have a mixed set of rationales for punishment. And some systems do not explicitly state the moral theories they are grounded in (Tonry 2011).

The differences between the systems in different countries show that there is no one universal way to ground a sentencing system in moral theories: the moral fundamentals of the system depend on context and culture. However, some sort of moral grounding is vital for both a sense of justice and for a functioning sentencing system. Ashworth (2010), for example, believes that not having a clear sentencing ideology undermines the rule of law, as too much discretion is left to sentencers: not just in terms of adjusting the sentence to the circumstances of the case, but by allowing (too much) space for potential personal beliefs to replace a common rationale. Moreover, not having a clear idea about what sentencing aims to achieve is a cause of disparity (Henham 2013; Hogarth 1971; Palys & Divorski 1986; Wandall 2008).

12.2.1.2 Sentencing Decisions and Principles

Our *second* level of normative legitimacy surrounds the question of the sentencers' attitudes to moral principles: When judges make their sentencing decision, what principles do they apply? And are these the same principles underlying the system?

If judges apply the moral principles that lie at the foundation of the system, normative legitimacy is enhanced. But judges may also intentionally or un-intentionally deviate from the system's moral foundations by promoting other sentencing goals (De Keijser et al, 2002; Greenblatt 2008; Morris 1974). Normative legitimacy can still be achieved: what matters is that sentencing decisions reflect moral principles. A lack of explicit moral justification at the foundational level might even be compensated by a strong application of moral theory at the level of the sentencing decision. However, this can also work the other way. A system can have a strong moral foundation that is not discernible in the individual sentencing decisions of the judges. Then there is no normative legitimacy at this second level.

12.2.1.3   Effects of Principles

The *third* question refers to the extent to which the sentencing goals are actu-ally met—or whether they can be met at all: What are good intentions if they do not bring the intended consequences? For a system to be normatively le-gitimate, the purposes that the system sets out in theory thus need to be met in practice as well; this is the requirement that makes the punishment neither wrongful nor evil (De Keijser et al. 2002). If punishments are meted out with the goal of rehabilitation or deterrence, for instance, have future crimes actu-ally been prevented by the imposition of the punishments?

12.2.2   Empirical Legitimacy

However, as hard as it seems to fulfill our model's elements of normative legit-imacy, fulfilling them does not ensure that a sentencing regime is perceived as legitimate. In order to be perceived as such, the sentencing system must also be aligned with the views of the public, a trait we call *empirical legiti-macy*. Such alignment with public views will enhance compliance with the law and cooperation with the criminal justice system (Roberts and Plesničar 2015). If people perceive the courts to impose inappropriate sentences or to take into account the wrong factors, the legitimacy of the entire system may be called into question (Henham 2013). In order to have a sentencing re-gime that is aligned with public views, it needs to be clear and transparent, consistent in application, and sensitive to the input of all relevant parties (Roberts and Plesničar 2015). Effective communication is key. Consequently, we expand our model to assess the legitimacy of sentencing by distinguishing three requirements for sentencing to be empirically legitimate: (a) transparency, (b) consistency, and (c) communicative effectiveness.

12.2.2.1 Transparency

Legitimate sentencing requires that the public understands why a certain punishment is imposed. In his chapter in this book, Ryberg (2020) explains that clarity and transparency of the sentencing decision are needed to improve the quality of the decisions, to provide accountability of the decisions, and to guide the general public's moral compass as well as manage the public's expectations. They may promote confidence and perceived legitimacy by contributing to a better public understanding of sentencing (Ryberg, 2020).

12.2.2.2 Consistency

The second requirement for legitimate sentencing is that sentencing decisions must be consistent and thus predictable. Similar cases should be punished similarly, and dissimilar cases should be punished dissimilarly to the degree of their dissimilarity. Judges use their discretionary powers to fit the punishment to the case at hand (Saleilles & Ottenhof 2001; Sutherland, Cressey, and Luckenbill 1992). However, this individualization of punishments can undermine legitimacy, if disparity in outcomes cannot be explained by legally relevant factors. For example, when the mood of the judge has affected sentencing, the punishment should not depend on whether the judge suffers from a headache, stress, tiredness, or relationship problems. Disparity in outcomes between judges is also unwarranted: it should not matter if one is sentenced by judge A or judge B. Judges have to be impartial professionals who only take legally relevant factors into account. Decision-making without bias is not only important for the acceptance of the sentencing practices by the public at large (cf. empirical legitimacy) but also for the acceptance of the punishment by the defendant (cf. Tyler's (2003) procedural justice).

12.2.2.3 Effective Communication

The last element of legitimate sentencing is the ability of the system to foster good communication. The public needs to know how and why punishments are meted out and how the sentencing system is performing. In addition, the public also needs to feel able to, within limits, influence how the system is shaped. Good two-way communication is key then. Moreover, effective communication does not only apply to the public, but more importantly, to the participants in the process: the defendant, the prosecution, the victim, and the witnesses. For a procedure to be considered fair, one of the crucial elements is that people have an opportunity to participate in the situation by explaining their perspective and expressing their views about how problems should be resolved (Tyler, 2003). This is a key element to achieve procedural justice: defendants who perceive that they have been treated with respect and fairness by courts are likely to be more cooperative and compliant with the law and its various agents than those who perceive they have not been treated respectfully and fairly (Walters and Bolger 2019).

12.2.3 The Legitimacy of Sentencing Model

To evaluate whether AI is better at achieving legitimacy in sentencing than human judges, we have thus developed a multilayered model that distinguishes empirical from normative legitimacy (see Figure 12.1). However, albeit separate, these two pillars of our model are interrelated. Public views on sentencing can affect the moral principles that are strived for in the foundation of the sentencing system. For example, public concern over released sex offenders can result in changes in the legal framework that increase the possibilities for incapacitation (McDonald 2012). Public views can also affect the implementation of the moral principles at the level of the actual sentencing decision, for example, when the public demands harsher punishment (Cochran et al 2020). There are three elements of normative legitimacy: (i) the moral principles in the foundations of the system, (ii) the extent to which they are applied through actual decision-making, and (iii) the extent to which sentencing decisions achieve the sentencing goals. These

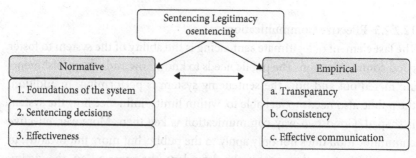

Figure 12.1 Elements of legitimacy at sentencing

all affect public views of sentencing. They are the basis on which public views rest. Normative and empirical legitimacy are thus interrelated.

Generally, the more the individual elements are present in the system, the more legitimate it is and vice versa. We see legitimacy as a continuum, although there are obviously endpoints, where a system might be fully legitimate at one end, and completely illegitimate at the other. Having set this abstract model as the background to our further discussion, we now evaluate whether human or machine judges are better at achieving legitimacy in sentencing.

12.3 Humans vs. Machines

12.3.1 Normative Legitimacy: Foundations of the System

The first level is that of the foundation of the system: Is it coherently grounded in moral principles? We feel that at this level, there is currently no role for AI. Humans have created sentencing systems and chosen the moral theories underpinning these systems. There is currently no realistic prospect of AI assuming those tasks.

But should we allow AI to adjust the foundations of our systems? This requires moral judgment in a novel situation, and at present, AI does not have these capacities (Donohue 2019). However, perhaps a future version of Hal-like super-AI past the point of singularity could develop the ability to make moral judgments and create new conceptions of justice. While this is unlikely for the foreseeable future, we feel very reluctant to accept that this super-AI morality would surpass human morality. Such important decisions about the essence of humanity and the fundamental elements of sentencing should not be left to algorithms that we would not even be able to understand—no matter how well they may perform.

12.3.2 Normative Legitimacy: Sentencing Decisions

The second level of normative legitimacy considers the sentencing decisions of judges: Are humans better at making morally justified decisions than machine judges?

Donohue (2019) asserts that sentencing comes down to a singular moment of moral judgment involving the jurist and the defendant. To make a normative assessment about the punishment to impose, the judge must understand the significance of conceptions of blame, desert, responsibility, excuse, and so forth (Chiao 2019). Virtues such as empathy and compassion are also important for moral judgment, as are intuition and understanding of the human condition (Donohue 2019). Human judges have these capacities although the conceptions differ among judges. Making a moral judgment is inherently subjective. Further, human judgment is responsive to an indefinitely broad range of relevant factors and hence is suited to addressing decision-making contexts in which each case is unique (Chiao 2019). Human judges are also capable of making normative judgments in novel situations (Donohue 2019). Making moral judgments is thus a particularly human ability.

But does the capacity to make moral judgments result in principled sentencing? As de Keijser et al. (2002) have shown, judges may adhere to certain moral principles, but this is not always discernible in their individual sentencing decisions. The punishments judges impose do not always reflect their sentencing goals. Instead of reflecting a consistent moral justification, sentencing seems to be driven by pragmatism and eclecticism (de Keijser et al. 2002). Human judges thus have the capacity to make moral judgments and this allows them to apply moral theories of sentencing when they determine sentence. In practice, however, the sentences they impose are not always in line with these principles.

How about AI? Can AI make moral judgments? Currently, the answer is no. When we consider if/then algorithms, where the rules for sentencing as well as all the normative assessments would have to be programmed into codes, the problems confronting human judges amplify. Legal rules are general and abstract in nature, while algorithms need specific yes/no rules. Moreover, manually programmed algorithms can never fully encompass all the factors and combinations of factors that should affect the sentencing outcome (but see Bagaric and Wolf (2018) for a different view). Not because of the magnitude of these factors and combinations which computers may grasp more efficiently than humans, but because it would require programmers and drafters to have the wisdom to make concise "if/then" rules to convert the moral principles of the system into computer code. Moreover, it is currently impossible to capture human values like empathy and compassion in algorithms. Ethics are too complex to transfer to a computer code (Moor 2006). Moor (2006) notes another difficulty—the computer's absence of common sense and general knowledge. One could program a machine with Asimov's first law of robotics: "do no harm," but this would only be of use if machines understand the meaning of harm in the real world (Moor 2006).

However, complex AI today works differently and is typically not coded with precise rules. Today's most functional AI is based on the concept of machine learning. At sentencing, this means large datasets of prior judgments are used by the machine to find correlations between characteristics of cases and the imposed punishments on its own—without specific prior "if/then" rules. This learning produces a model able to make decisions and to improve on them by learning from prior experience. This type of algorithmic justice thus tries to replicate prior sentences in similar new cases.

One of the main problems with this approach is that it is based on existing cases. If we wanted the algorithm to propose ideal solutions, these existing cases should have been ideally decided on—but we know this is far from the truth. In fact, as stated before, human sentencing often lacks a moral justification, and many human judgments will probably not be a good basis for principled sentencing. Prior research has shown that these decisions are biased in several ways, for example, with regard to the offender's gender and race (Završnik 2020). These biases will thus be replicated in the decision-making of AI judges. The dangers of "garbage in, garbage out" are apparent here. Moreover, this type of machine learning is less impressive when the past is unlike the future: future cases may be very different from past ones. While humans in these cases make novel decisions, machine learning-based AI will not be able to extrapolate past rules to new circumstances—it is made for replication and not innovation (Fagan and Levmore 2019). This type of AI is not equipped to deal with developments in society or changing views of crime seriousness. As such, it cannot be used for some form of dynamic justice that tracks the developments in the norms of society.

Finally, in the future, general AI should be able to function as an ethical agent. A full ethical agent has human-like qualities: it can make independent moral judgments but also exhibits qualities like intentionality, consciousness, free will, and empathy (Segun 2020). It can also be held accountable for its decisions. The question is then whether virtues such as empathy may also be self-learnable for general AI. And if so, should humans then accept the punishments handed out by full ethical agent machine judges as superior to human decision-making? Again, our strongest objection against the idea of AI making sentencing decisions is that this function is too important to be entrusted to an entity whose reasoning we do not understand.

12.3.3 Normative Legitimacy: Effects of Principles

After the foundation of the system and the actual sentencing decisions of judges, the final level in our model of normative legitimacy is the effect level: Are the moral principles of the sentencing system met in practice? Are the sentencing goals that judges aimed for achieved?

In theory, a system founded in retribution, or judges aiming for retribution, is effective when sentencing is proportionate to the seriousness of the crime and the blameworthiness of the offender. But in practice, this is difficult to assess: What is a proportional punishment? What is considered to be a just punishment is ambiguous and not universal: it is culturally dependent and subjective (Plesničar & Šugman Stubbs 2018). An evaluation of the severity of the harm that the offender caused by his crime requires an evaluation for which subjective sentiments like empathy and compassion are key. There is no objective answer to the question of what a proportionate punishment exactly is, beyond the sentencing ranges set out for individual offenses. While the concepts of cardinal and ordinal proportionality help to promote proportional sentencing, we cannot say the same about individual sentencing decisions. We thus find it hard to evaluate the extent to which human judges are capable of meting out proportionate punishments. But since imposing a proportionate punishment requires moral considerations, we think it safe to assume that machine judges (who lack the ability for moral judgment) will perform worse than humans.

If we look at the utilitarian perspective, effects might be easier to assess— in theory. In theory, a punishment is justified from a utilitarian perspective when it maximizes happiness in society. In practice, this justification is hard to assess, since the costs and benefits are unknown, or even unknowable to the judge: How many crimes are prevented if the offender is locked up for a certain amount of time? And how much weight should be given to, for example, a prevented rape? Or, moreover, how much weight should be assigned to the suffering of the defendant's children left without a parent for a prolonged time? If the costs and the benefits are unclear, how can we tell whether the punishment was effective? Moreover, recidivism rates are high, so the effectiveness of punishment in terms of deterrence and rehabilitation is questionable. And if punishments imposed with the aim of preventing future crimes are not effective, their imposition cannot be morally justified at this level of the model. With the current knowledge about the consequences of punishment, achieving legitimacy at this effect level of the model seems almost impossible, both for human and AI judges.

Perhaps this is where future AI may prove most effective. By connecting many different datasets that contain information on the consequences of punishment, AI could develop more insights into the effects of punishment. AI could, for example, follow offenders over time to determine whether they commit new crimes, whether they have a job, where they live and—by connecting to social media—even see what their social networks look like and what their hobbies are. This information on the offender's progress could be crucial to learning about the effects of punishment. Machine judges could use this information to learn about which offenders are deterred and when. Or to learn about the effectiveness of different rehabilitation programs for different types of offenders. Connecting all these datasets and letting AI use it for sentencing might increase the effectiveness of sentencing, but comes with high social costs, like privacy issues. Again, the issue is this: Do we want to entrust AI with this power?

12.3.4 Empirical Legitimacy: Transparency

As noted earlier, clarity and transparency of sentencing decisions are both important for legitimacy in sentencing. Clarity is needed to check how moral justification theories are applied in the actual sentencing decisions, while transparency allows the public to see how decisions are made.

Human judges provide insight into their sentencing decisions by giving reasons. However, these reasons do not explain everything. The same rationale, even the exact same wording, can be used to justify a prison sentence of six, seven, or eight years. Moreover, the judge can only refer to characteristics of the crime or of the offender that she *consciously* took into account. However, we know that sentencing decisions are also shaped by factors that the judge unconsciously considers, for example, because of stereotyping (Albonetti 1991). When the judge is unaware of the factors influencing her decision, she cannot account for them (see the contribution of Chiao (2020) to this book for examples of unconscious influences on sentencing decisions). Thinking thus remains hard to explain and giving reasons is not the same as reasoning. There is "no generally accepted theory of how cognitive phenomena arise from computations in cortex" (Valiant 2014, 15). What happens in the mind of the judge when she makes her sentencing decision is a black box in itself.

Moreover, at the systemic level, modern sentencing systems are complex and difficult to comprehend. The problem goes beyond just judges having difficulty explaining their decision-making. For a layperson, understanding how sentencing operates is often hard: accounting for different levels of culpability, combinations of factors, etc., makes for a very complex system, one which is far from clear or transparent.

The two issues combine when stepping into the zone of AI judges. Individual decisions should be the direct result of what the system had predicted. The transparency of the algorithms of machine judges depends on the type of AI that is used. "If/then" algorithms (that are not yet AI) producing decision trees are very transparent, although extensive codes can make it difficult to see the forest for the trees. Models based on machine learning are much less transparent, especially because it is not always or immediately clear *why* certain factors have a certain value for the sentencing decision. Machine learning looks for relations between characteristics that best predict the outcome. It does not look for characteristics that should affect the punishment according to legal principles. The transparency is limited to showing which factors predict the sentencing outcome, and this makes the sentencing decision unclear. Moreover, today's most effective machine learning uses the black box method: data come into the model and results come out—the process and method by which that happens are not the focus of the task. Further developments might improve this current lack of transparency, but for now, it seems an illusion (Goebel et al. 2018).

Clarity and transparency would be even more of an issue with futuristic AI. Such AI might then be the only one who understands how the system works: not even experts in the field of computer science could audit the process. In that case, no one could assess whether the sentencing determinants are reliable at all (Chiao 2019). This is the type of opacity that Ryberg calls "technically caused opacity" in his chapter.

Transparency is thus not well achieved by human judges. For AI judges, while simplistic algorithms can be very transparent, more sophisticated or self-learning AI will necessarily lead to further opacity.

12.3.5 Empirical Legitimacy: Consistency

Sentencing should not only be transparent, but it should also be consistent and thus predictable. Similar cases should be punished similarly, and only legally relevant factors should be taken into account by the judge. For human judges, consistency in sentencing is a challenge because human reasoning is flawed. Setting aside intentional wrongdoing, human judges are as prone to making judgment mistakes as humans in general (Schauer 2010). For example, cognitive biases may very likely affect judges' decision-making when assessing the blameworthiness and dangerousness of the offender. Such decisions are made in a context where time and information are limited (Albonetti 1991; Steffensmeier, Ulmer, and Kramer 1998). In order to deal with these uncertainties, judges develop a decision-making schema that draws upon past experiences and societal stereotypes to determine the defendant's risk and blameworthiness. Relying on stereotypes could be one of the causes of unwarranted sentencing disparity. Research has shown for example that—in some contexts—Black defendants are punished more severely than White defendants, and male defendants more severely than female (Baumer 2013; Bontrager, Barrick, and Stupi 2013). Research has also demonstrated differences in sentencing outcomes between judges in similar cases (Spohn 2008; Wooldredge 2010). Subjective assessments of the facts of the case, the relevant circumstances of the offender, the preferred sentencing goals, and the punishment that is deemed just may cause sentencing disparity.

Disparity was the main reason for the introduction of sentencing guidelines across common law jurisdictions (Ashworth 2009; Frankel 1972; Stith & O'Neill 2003). Sentencing guidelines limit the discretionary powers of judges to leave less room for a subjective assessment to affect sentencing outcomes. This is particularly true for the restrictive sentencing grids that employ only two dimensions: crime seriousness and criminal history. Once these are determined, a court must impose a sentence within a specific range, or provide compelling reasons to impose a different sentence (Frase 1990). In these systems, instead of executing moral judgment, judges became discretion-less "accountants" in a scheme set up by others (Donohue 2019). Judges objected to the guidelines because they could not individualize sentences, they had to impose punishment that did not feel just (Leipold 2005; Stith and Cabranes, 1998). Consistency was not to be reached at the expense of discretion.

Inconsistency in sentencing by human judges was one of the main reasons to employ computers to decide upon the sentence. AI judges are not prone to cognitive biases or subjective assessments. They are never tired, hungry, cranky, bored, or stressed (cf. Danziger, Levav, and Avnaim-Pesso 2011). A negative emotional state of mind—or a positive one—cannot affect sentencing outcomes, thereby reducing the disparity in sentencing.

But algorithms designed by humans seem more objective than they really are. Who makes the decision rules for the algorithm? Disparities among ethical theories make it a daunting task to embed ethics or a moral code into AI systems (Segun 2020). And aren't these rules likely to reflect the biases of those who develop them (Estcourt and Marr 2019)? And what are the risks of having legal rules and normative considerations being translated into computer language by a programmer who knows nothing about the law?

Machine learning AI is also less objective than it seems because the models are built on data infected with bias. Machine learning replicates these existing biases: biases present in the verdicts of the judges become embedded in the algorithm. These algorithmic biases affect sentencing outcomes and reinforce existing inequality and stereotypes (Segun 2020). Ironically, machine learning AI ends up worsening disparity instead of reducing it. This is not due to a mechanical flaw; human judges are to blame. There is no database from which the algorithm could learn that would be free of existing biases. It is, however, a problem that machines cannot solve for humans.

One solution to this problem of algorithmic bias would be to program the decision-making AI in a way that would neutralize biases (Chiao 2019). This would only be possible if the algorithms were transparent and comprehensible. In consultation with judges, experts could program the machine to disregard extralegal sentencing factors such as race, ethnicity, and gender, even if they enter through data learning. However, there is more than just a technological problem here. Not only would such AI be at odds with the most efficient models of modern AI (which include deep learning), but there is a deeper problem: it is unclear what just punishment requires. If racial disparity is to be eliminated, should Blacks receive a discount? Or Whites a severity premium? Using machine judges to neutralize existing biases is thus doubly problematic. First because of the complexity of the algorithms—a problem that may be overcome in the future. Second, because it requires the principles that the system is grounded in to be translated into computer code.

12.3.6 Empirical Legitimacy: Effective Communication

The final element of empirical legitimacy is effective communication. Communication is what has evolutionarily made us thrive (Harari 2017).

Communication at sentencing, however, is a more complex issue. The roles of various participants at sentencing have been evolving. Victims, for example, once completely excluded (Christie 1977), now enjoy participatory rights through victim statements (Roberts and Erez 2004) or the right to appeal (Briški 2020). The various participants that judges need to include in the communication and their interrelationships make it hard for judges to determine how and when to include them. This may leave participants disappointed and feeling "unheard," which in turn undermines perceptions of legitimacy. However, human judges are generally well equipped to address various participants as fellow moral agents. With regard to the defendant, for example, they can express censure in the expectation that the defendant will understand and internalize the message. This is an essentially human activity (Chiao 2019), even if some defendants seem insensitive to the moral message.

For AI judges, communication may be their biggest obstacle. There is no real communication apart from imputing the relevant data. There is no listening or "being heard," there is no empathy or sympathy from the judge—for example when witnesses are testifying about traumatic events. People react to how they feel and experience events and settings. Doctors are, for example, much less likely to be sued for malpractice when they evince empathy toward victimized patients (Smith et al. 2016).

The criminal process and sentencing in particular, have far-reaching consequences (Tata 2020). That process—of one robed judge and one convicted defendant in conversation—has moral value in and of itself, and the addition of an interloping machine may undermine that function (Donohue 2019).

When considering machine judges' decisions and their ability to persuade the participants of the procedure or the public, the concept of algorithm aversion seems an important one to consider (Burton, Stein, and Jensen 2020; Dietvorst, Simmons, and Massey 2015). Algorithmic aversion is a bias that causes humans to mistrust algorithmic decisions simply because they are not human—despite AI's record of sounder decisions. When considering AI-based decisions, the margin of error humans are willing to tolerate is none. In criminal justice, the lack of human interaction and the "dehumanizing" effect this could bring be an insurmountable problem (for a different view, see Bagaric, Hunter, and Stobbs (2019)).

12.4 Conclusion

Would you rather be sentenced by a human or a machine? We based our comparison between human and AI judges on an abstract model of legitimacy and find AI rather lacking on several levels. First, we argued that current AI is incapable of making moral decisions and this is crucial for our concept of normative legitimacy. Legitimacy at the level of the foundation of the system is thus best achieved by humans. Futuristic AI might eventually develop into a full moral agent. Still, even then, we feel that decisions about the moral foundation of the sentencing systems should not be entrusted to AI. At the second level, that of judges' actual sentencing decisions, we reasoned that in order to make a principled sentencing decision, the judge needs to apply moral principles. And again, we argue that current AI does not understand morality.

Our final assessment criterion for normative legitimacy concerns effectiveness: Were the goals achieved? We conclude that it is difficult to assess whether judges succeed in imposing proportionate punishments since it is unclear how severe a punishment must be in order to be proportionate to the seriousness of the crime and the blameworthiness of the offender. And the effectiveness of utilitarian sentencing can only be assessed if the consequences of the punishment for the offender and society at large are known. So for both human and AI judges, the extent to which their decisions achieve the desired effects is unknown. However, future AI using "big data" might gain insight into the consequences of punishment. Futuristic AI is then probably best able to achieve utilitarian sentencing goals—but at great cost in terms of our privacy.

Regarding empirical legitimacy, we conclude that human judges cannot fully explain their reasoning. A judge is as much of a black box as a complex AI model. Conversely, simple algorithms used by machine judges can be very transparent. But as the algorithms become more complicated, their decisions become more opaque. This is especially true for self-learning AI.

We conclude that machine judges are better at achieving consistency than humans. But self-learning AI suffers from *algorithmic bias*: inconsistencies that were already prevalent in the data (previous sentencing decisions) are replicated and reinforced. When this occurs, sentencing decisions become consistent but consistently wrong. Futuristic general AI might be able to recognize and correct the bias in sentencing, but the codes of the machine would be so complex that understanding why certain (combinations of) case characteristics result in sentencing discounts or premiums would be impossible. Improving this level of empirical legitimacy would thus necessarily lessen transparency.

The third element of empirical legitimacy concerns effective communication. Here we conclude that humans surpass AI judges. Human judges are able to communicate effectively with participants and the public and engage with them as one moral agent to another. While some human judges are better at it that than others, AI judges may never achieve it at all—humans do not perceive them as equal decision-makers.

In conclusion, we regard AI judges as incapable of generating normative legitimacy. Even when this might be achievable in the future, we have serious reservations about letting it establish a new moral philosophy for sentencing. Either this comes at a significant cost (such as at the level of effects) or entrusts too much power to mechanisms we do not fully understand and thus cannot thoroughly assess. Moreover, it might be too easy for humans to shift such responsibility to AI. Relieving humans from serious consideration of the morality of punishment would allow us to inflict pain (legitimate and legal, but still pain) without feeling in any way responsible (cf. Floridi et al. 2018).

However, at the level of empirical legitimacy, the use of AI may improve matters. While transparency is still lacking, further development might bring improved results in that area. Moreover, consistency is AI's strength—and while today's systems are flawed due to corrupt learning datasets, further development might improve that. Transparency and consistency are major challenges for human judges as well. But effective communication, conversely, is where AI judges fail. Even if they were able to learn empathy and even compassion in making their sentencing decisions, they would not be able to convey it in an effective and approachable manner.

Huq (2020 639) raises another important question relevant to the choice between humans and machines: Are AI's flaws easier to identify and remedy than the flaws of its human analog? Translated to our context: Is it easier to teach a machine how to make principled decisions than to teach a human judge to sentence consistently? It far from easy to do the latter. And while it is extremely hard to do the former today, it might become easier over time. Should we then leave open the option of handling sentencing to AI in the future?

Estcourt and Marr (2019, 856) think that while many decisions could be handed over to machines, "only some of them should be, even when the machines can make them better than we do." This seems contradictory—why do something badly when you have the option of doing it better? We think, however, that it is not just a matter of good or bad sentencing outcomes. There are crucial features of sentencing that are so inherently human that we cannot imagine them being successfully replaced by AI. Making moral judgments not only requires us to consider various justifications for punishing people but also makes us take responsibility for our actions. If we leave sentencing to AI—are we not losing the very essence of what makes sentencing a human process?

References

Albonetti, C. A. 1991. "An Integration of Theories to Explain Judicial Discretion." Social Problems, 38 (2): pp. 247–266.

Ashworth, A. 2010. Sentencing and Criminal Justice. Cambridge: Cambridge University Press.

Ashworth, A. 2009. "Techniques for Reducing Sentence Disparity." In Principled Sentencing: Readings on Theory and Policy, edited by Andrew Von Hirsch, Andrew Ashworth, and Julian V. Roberts, pp. 243–258. Oxford: Hart.

Bagaric, M., and G. Wolf (2018). Sentencing by Computer: Enhancing Sentencing Transparency and Predictability and (Possibly) "Bridging the Gap between Sentencing Knowledge and Practice." George Mason Law Review 25: pp. 653–710.

Bagaric, M., D. Hunter, and N. Stobbs. 2019. "Erasing the Bias Against Using Artificial Intelligence to Predict Future Criminality: Algorithms Are Color Blind and Never Tire." University of Cincinnati Law Review, 88 (4): pp. 1037–1081.

Baumer, E. P. 2013. "Reassessing and Redirecting Research on Race and Sentencing." Justice Quarterly 30 (2): pp. 231–261.

Boden, M. A. 2016. AI: Its Nature and Future. Oxford: Oxford University Press.

Bontrager, S., K. Barrick, and E. Stupi. 2013. "Gender and Sentencing: A Meta-Analysis of Contemporary Research." Journal of Gender, Race & Justice 16: pp. 349–372.

Briški, L. 2020. "Oškodovančev vpliv na odločitev kazenskega sodišča v slovenskem in nemškem kazenskem postopku [The victim's influence on the decision of the criminal court in Slovenian and German criminal proceedings]." Pravna praksa 39: pp. 8–9.

Burton, J. W., M. K. Stein, and T. B. Jensen. 2020. "A Systematic Review of Algorithm Aversion in Augmented Decision Making." Journal of Behavioral Decision Making 33 (2): pp. 220–239.

Chiao, V. 2019. "Fairness, Accountability and Transparency: Notes on Algorithmic Decision-Making in Criminal Justice." International Journal of Law in Context 15 (2): pp. 126–139.

Chiao, V. 2020. "Transparency: Are Judges Better Than Algorithms?" In Principled Sentencing and Artificial Intelligence, edited by Jesper Ryberg and Julian V. Roberts, pp. 34–57. Oxford: Oxford University Press.

Cochran, J. C., E. L. Toman, R. T. Shields, and D. P. Mears. 2020. "A Uniquely Punitive Turn? Sex Offenders and the Persistence of Punitive Sanctioning." Journal of Research in Crime and Delinquency. July: pp. 1–45. doi:10.1177/0022427820941172

Christie, N. 1977. "Conflicts as Property." The British Journal of Criminology 17 (1): pp. 1–15.

Danziger, S., J. Levav, and L. Avnaim-Pesso. 2011. "Extraneous Factors in Judicial Decisions." Proceedings of the National Academy of Sciences 108 (17): pp. 6889–6892.

De Keijser, J. W., R. Van der Leeden, and J. L. Jackson. 2002. "From Moral Theory to Penal Attitudes and Back: A Theoretically Integrated Modeling Approach." Behavioral Sciences & the Law 20 (4): pp. 317–335.

Dietvorst, B. J., J. P. Simmons, and C. Massey. 2015. "Algorithm Aversion: People Erroneously Avoid Algorithms After Seeing Them Err." Journal of Experimental Psychology: General 144 (1): p. 114.

Donohue, M. E. 2019. "A Replacement for Justitia's Scales? Machine Learning's Role in Sentencing." Harvard Journal of Law & Technology 32 (2): pp. 657–678.

Estcourt, A., and K. Marr. 2019. "Thinking Machines and Smiley Faces." Australian Law Journal 93 (10): pp. 855–865.

EU-Commission. 2018. Communication from the Commission to the European Parliament, the European Council, the Council, the European Economic and Social Committee and the Committee of the Regions on Artificial Intelligence for Europe, COM/2018/237 final.

Ewald, A., and C. Uggen. 2012. "The Collateral Effects of Imprisonment on Prisoners, Their Families, and Communities." In The Oxford Handbook on Sentencing and Corrections, edited by Joan Petersilia and Kevin R. Reitz, pp. 83–103. New York: Oxford University Press.

Fagan, F., and S. Levmore. 2019. "The Impact of Artificial Intelligence on Rules, Standards, and Judicial Discretion." Southern California Law Review 93 (1): pp. 1–35.

Floridi, L., J. Cowls, M. Beltrametti, R. Chatila, P. Chazerand, V. Dignum, . . . F. Rossi. 2018. "AI4People—An Ethical Framework for a Good AI Society: Opportunities, Risks, Principles, and Recommendations." Minds and Machines 28 (4): pp. 689–707.

Frankel, M. E. 1972. "Lawlessness in Sentencing." University of Cincinatti Law Review 41: pp. 1–54.

Franklin, S. 2014. "History, Motivations, and Core Themes." In The Cambridge Handbook of Artificial Intelligence, edited by Keith Frankish and William M. Ramsey, pp. 15–33. Cambridge: Cambridge University Press.

Frase, R. S. 1990. "Sentencing Reform in Minnesota, Ten Years After: Reflections on Dale G. Parent's Structuring Criminal Sentences: The Evolution of Minnesota's Sentencing Guidelines." Minnesota Law Review 75 (3): pp. 727–754.

Goebel, R., A. Chander, K. Holzinger, F. Lecue, Z. Akata, S. Stumpf, . . . A. Holzinger. 2018. Explainable AI: The New 42? Paper presented at the International Cross-Domain Conference for Machine Learning and Knowledge Extraction, Hamburg.

Greenblatt, N. 2008. "How Mandatory Are Mandatory Minimums? How Judges Can Avoid Imposing Mandatory Minimum Sentences." American Journal of Criminal Law 36 (1): pp. 1–38.

Harari, Y. N. 2017. Homo Deus: A Brief History of Tomorrow. New York: Harper.

Hayes, D. 2018. "Proximity, Pain, and State Punishment." Punishment & Society 20 (2): pp. 235–254.

Henham, R. 2013. Sentencing and the Legitimacy of Trial Justice. New York: Routledge.

Hogarth, J. 1971. Sentencing as a Human Process. Toronto: University of Toronto Press.

Huq, A. Z. 2020. "A Right to a Human Decision." Virginia Law Review, 106 (3): pp. 611–688.

Leipold, A. D. 2005. "Why Are Federal Judges So Acquittal Prone." Washington University Law Quarterly, 83: pp. 151–227.

McDonald, D. 2012. "Ungovernable Monsters: Law, Paedophilia, Crisis." Griffith Law Review 21(3): pp. 585–608.

Michael, M. A. 1992. "Utilitarianism and Retributivism: What's the Difference?" American Philosophical Quarterly 29 (2): pp. 173–182.

Moor, J. H. 2006. "The Nature, Importance, and Difficulty of Machine Ethics." IEEE Intelligent Systems 21 (4): pp. 18–21.

Morris, N. 1974. The Future of Imprisonment. Chicago: University of Chicago Press.

Palys, T. S., and S. Divorski. 1986. "Explaining Sentence Disparity." Canadian Journal of Criminology 28 (4): pp. 347–362.

Plant, R. 1994. An Introduction to Artificial Intelligence. Paper presented at the 32nd Aerospace Sciences Meeting and Exhibit, AIAA 1994-294.

Plesničar, M. M., and K. Šugman Stubbs. 2018. "Subjectivity, Algorithms and the Courtroom." In Big Data, Crime and Social Control, edited by Aleš Završnik, pp. 154–176. London: Routledge.

Roberts, J. V., and E. Erez. 2004. "Communication in Sentencing: Exploring the Expressive Function of Victim Impact Statements." International Review of Victimology 10 (3): pp. 223–244.

Roberts, J. V., and M. M. Plesničar. 2015. "Sentencing, Legitimacy, and Public Opinion." In Trust and Legitimacy in Criminal Justice: European Perspectives, edited by Gorazd Meško and Justice Tankebe, pp. 33–51. Cham: Springer International Publishing.

Ryberg, J. 2020. "Sentencing and Algorithmic Transparency." In Sentencing and Artificial Intelligence, edited by Jesper Ryberg and Julian V. Roberts, pp. 13–34. New York: Oxford University Press.

Saleilles, R., and R. Ottenhof R. 2001. L'individualisation de la peine de Saleilles à aujourd'hui; suivie de L'individualisation de la peine: cent ans après Saleilles. Ramonville Saint-Agne: Érès.

Schauer, F. 2010. "Is There a Psychology of Judging?" In The Psychology of Judicial Decision Making, edited by David E. Klein and Gregory Mitchell, pp. 103–120. Oxford: Oxford University Press.

Segun, S. T. 2020. From Machine Ethics to Computational Ethics. AI & Society. Retrieved from https://doi.org/10.1007/s00146-020-01010-1.

Smith, D. D., J. Kellar, E. L. Walters, E. T. Reibling, T. Phan, and S. M. Green. 2016. "Does Emergency Physician Empathy Reduce Thoughts of Litigation? A Randomised Trial." Emergency Medicine Journal 33 (8): pp. 548–552.

Snedker, K. A. 2018. Therapeutic Justice: Crime, Treatment Courts and Mental Illness. London: Palgrave Macmillan.

Spohn, C. 2008. How Do Judges Decide?: The Search for Fairness and Justice in Punishment. Los Angeles: Sage Publications.

Steffensmeier, D., J. Ulmer, and J. Kramer. 1998. "The Interaction of Race, Gender, and Age in Criminal Sentencing: The Punishment Cost of Being Young, Black, and Male." Criminology 36 (4): pp. 763–797.

Stith, K., and J. A. Cabranes. 1998. Fear of Judging: Sentencing Guidelines in the Federal Courts. Chicago: University of Chicago Press.

Stith, K., and M. E. O'Neill. 2003. "Federal Sentencing Guidelines Symposium Yale Law School." November 8, 2002. Federal Sentencing Reporter 15 (3): pp. 156–159.

Strang, H., and J. Braithwaite. Restorative Justice: Philosophy to Practice. London: Routledge.

Sutherland, E. H., D. R. Cressey, and D. F. Luckenbill.1992. Principles of Criminology. Lanham, MD: General Hall.

Tata, C. 2020. Sentencing: A Social Process. London: Palgrave Pivot.

Tonry, M. 2011. "Introduction: Thinking about Punishment." In Why Punish? How Much? A Reader on Punishment, edited by Michael Tonry, pp. 3–28. Oxford: Oxford University Press.

Tyler, T. R. 2003. "Procedural Justice, Legitimacy, and the Effective Rule of Law." Crime and Justice: A Review of Research 30: pp. 283–357.

Valiant, L. G. 2014. "What Must a Global Theory of Cortex Explain?" Current Opinion in Neurobiology 25: pp. 15–19.

Von Hirsch, A. 1992. "Proportionality in the Philosophy of Punishment." Crime and Justice 16: pp. 55–98.

Walters, G. D., and P. C. Bolger 2019. "Procedural Justice Perceptions, Legitimacy Beliefs, and Compliance with the Law: A Meta-Analysis." Journal of Experimental Criminology 15 (3): pp. 341–372.

Wandall, R. H. 2008. Decisions to Imprison: Court Decision-Making Inside and Outside the Law, Aldershot: Ashgate.

Wooldredge, J. 2010. "Judges' Unequal Contributions to Extralegal Disparities in Imprisonment." Criminology 48 (2): pp. 539–567.

Završnik, A. 2020. "Criminal Justice, Artificial Intelligence Systems, and Human Rights." ERA Forum 20 (4), pp. 567–583.

13

Iudicium ex Machinae

The Ethical Challenges of ADM at Sentencing

Frej Klem Thomsen

In this chapter, I will argue that the use of automated decision-making for sentencing is in principle morally permissible. By automated decision-making (ADM), I mean a software algorithm whose output is or becomes a decision (MSI-NET 2017; Wagner 2019). In the context of sentencing, this means an algorithm that is provided with appropriate input, for instance, about the seriousness of a crime, and calculates an output in the shape of a just sentence. For it to be an automated decision-*making* system. it is necessary that the algorithm's output ordinarily determines the sentence. An ADM for sentencing would thus occupy the role traditionally reserved for judges.

The use of algorithms in decision-making has been a controversial topic in recent years, particularly within criminal justice (Ferguson 2017; Veale et al. 2018; Hannah-Moffat and Montford 2019). As such, I expect many will meet the initial claim of this chapter with skepticism. Much of the chapter will be devoted to considering a series of potential principled objections to the use of ADM in criminal sentencing. I argue that at least the most common objections are unpersuasive. However, I also engage with a currently under-appreciated challenge to ADM for sentencing: the risk of misuse given the political climate of the societies that are currently poised to make use of ADM for criminal sentencing. Thus, despite defending the claim that the use of ADM for sentencing is in principle morally permissible, I will also argue that there are underappreciated reasons to be cautious about introducing it in practice.

The argument that I will pursue is as follows. In section 13.1, I discuss ADM for sentencing and argue that it is likely to better approximate the just sentence than human sentencing. In section 13.2, I discuss three general objections to ADM based on privacy, transparency, and bias, and argue that none apply to ADM for sentencing. In section 13.3, I review an assumption

Frej Klem Thomsen, *Iudicium ex Machinae* In: *Sentencing and Artificial Intelligence*. Edited by: Jesper Ryberg and Julian V. Roberts, Oxford University Press. © Oxford University Press 2022. DOI: 10.1093/oso/9780197539538.003.0013 made in section 13.1, that there are right answers in sentencing, dismiss two objections to this assumption, and discuss decisions under moral uncertainty as a practical obstacle to development of ADM for sentencing. Finally, in section 13.4, I introduce penal populism as the most important challenge to ADM for sentencing. Section 13.5 summarizes and concludes.

13.1 Rise of the Robot Judge

ADMs are a particular type of algorithm. The use of algorithms to support or deliver decisions is a much broader phenomenon, however, since an algorithm is simply a procedure for performing a particular set of logical or mathematical operations in order to translate input to a useful output (Hill 2016). As such, it is unsurprising that the use of algorithms in sentencing predates the recent rise of ADM based on machine learning. Earlier initiatives include so-called evidence-based sentencing, which base sentences (at least in part) on algorithmic risk assessments; and sentencing guidelines, which (broadly speaking) recommend sentences based on algorithms that combine various factors about the case.

An ADM for sentencing would resemble the former in certain respects and the latter in others. We might, for instance, feed the ADM the type of offense committed and details about the offender, and the ADM would respond with, say, "four months imprisonment." Since we are here concerned with ADM, not merely with algorithms that support or recommend decisions, this sentence would then be executed by the court.

It is worth emphasizing that an ADM for sentencing would by necessity preserve rather a large amount of human discretion. It would not, for instance, determine which offense to charge the offender with. Since it is notoriously often possible for prosecutors to charge the same wrongdoing as several different offenses—offenses that may have very different sentences associated with them—prosecutorial decision-making could still heavily influence sentencing (Shermer and Johnson 2010; Smith and Levinson 2012; see also Lippke in this volume). An ADM for sentencing will also realistically include features where determining the input value requires the exercise of judicial discretion. Suppose for instance that mitigating circumstances is a feature in the ADM. The algorithm would respond to the presence or absence of mitigating circumstances when determining the sentence, but it would not by itself be capable of determining whether there are in fact mitigating circumstances in the case. The number and influence of such decisions will depend on the input required by the ADM, but I cannot conceive of a plausible ADM for sentencing that would not require substantial judicial involvement.

With this loose picture of ADM for sentencing in mind, what are we to think of its use? Should we welcome our new robot overlords, or charge to the luddite chant of "Enoch shall break them"? In the limited debate so far, responses have been divided (Roth 2016; Selbst 2017; Stobbs et al. 2017; Bagaric and Wolf 2018; Chiao 2018; Simmons 2018; Chiao 2019; Donohue 2019). In the remainder of this section, we will first look at one possible concern, the analysis of which will help to further set the stage of the discussion. In the subsequent sections we will then review a series of common objections to ADM, and two difficulties that have received very little attention.

13.1.1 Can the Machine Judge?

Perhaps the most immediate concern with the use of ADM for sentencing might be whether a software algorithm is well-suited to making this type of decision in the first place. Just sentencing involves the careful weighing of a range of different factors that vary between cases, a task that requires sound judgment and years of training and experience for human judges (Donohue 2019, see also Schwarze Randoberts in this volume). Call this *the objection from the inherent superiority of human sentencing*:

> An ADM will be incapable of taking into account the unique features of
> each case and performing the careful weighing of these features to deliver a
> just sentence.

The objection may look appealing at first glance. After all, a criminal case involves human beings with individual histories and every case is unique. Taking account of the unique features of each case requires a certain cognitive flexibility, the opponent of ADM might say, which a software algorithm does not possess. Furthermore, all the relevant features must be taken into consideration and carefully weighed against each other, a task that is simply too complex for an algorithm. Hence, human sentencing is inherently superior to ADM for sentencing.

Whatever its immediate appeal, the objection is ultimately unpersuasive. The first part of the objection misunderstands the role of principles in sentencing, while the latter part gets the relative strength of humans and algorithms backward.

The first part of the objection, recall, advances the claim that constructing an ADM that incorporates the infinite range of features relevant to individual cases is impossible (or at least currently unachievable). Sentencing, it might be said, depends on such a range of different factors about the case, many of them particular to an individual case or a small set of cases, that any attempt to construct a model that incorporates them all is doomed from the outset.

This part of the objection seems to me clearly misguided. It is of course true that every case will have an infinite number of properties (the offender's hair color, the victim's favorite brand of cereal, the temperature in the city of Marrakesh at the time of the offense, etc.). However, only a small number of these properties are relevant to sentencing, and it is neither chance nor personal preference that determines whether a particular property is relevant to sentencing, or how it affects the just sentence. The proper role in sentencing of any particular property in a case is determined by the moral reasons that apply to sentencing. Such reasons are what scholars attempt to determine in criminal justice ethics and summarize as what we might broadly call a theory of just sentencing. Current scholarship in criminal justice ethics is divided between competing theories of just sentencing, ranging from retributivist theories across compensation-based and restorative theories to utilitarian theories (e.g. Walker 1991; Moore 1997; Pettit 1997; Duff 2001; Braithwaite 2002; Von Hirsch and Ashworth 2005; Boonin 2008; Tadros 2011; for an overview, see Duff and Hoskins 2019). But it is the theory of just sentencing we adopt that allows us to say which properties of cases affect just sentencing and how. This is true regardless of whether sentencing is carried by a human judge or by ADM. Hence, even if it is impossible to specify, for instance, an exhaustive list of mitigating circumstances, it will not be impossible to construct an ADM that gives mitigating circumstances a particular role in sentencing and allows the human judge to input whether mitigating circumstances are present or not (cf. Bagaric and Gopalan 2015). On any given theory, then, the individual properties of a case are either irrelevant, in which case it is no cause for concern that an ADM for sentencing does not include them as features; or specified by our theory of just sentencing, which allows an ADM to incorporate them, at least when humans provide the necessary input. (cf. Chiao 2019; for an illustration related to mercy, see Dagan & Baron in this volume).

The second part of the objection, which claimed that ADM is unsuited to the complex weighing of multiple factors necessary for sentencing, fares little better. Human judgment, particularly intuitive judgment of the kind sometimes labeled system 1 thinking by cognitive scientists, is eminently unsuited to the complex task of carefully weighing multiple factors (Kahneman and Tversky 2009, see also Chiao in this volume). We tend in such situations to rely on cognitive heuristics, and to later rationalize the answers provided by these shortcuts. Unlike human cognition, however, an ADM is perfectly capable of calculating the function for multiple, individually weighted features, including nonlinearities and interacting features. In fact, this difference in capacities is the fundamental reason for one of the common challenges raised by the use of ADM: the lack of transparency (I return to this point later). As the complexity of a model increases, it swiftly exceeds the human ability to simultaneously consider all of the components (Rudin 2019, see also Ryberg and Petersen in this volume).

13.1.2 The Machine Learning Shortcut as Dead End

Although, as we have seen above, some potential concerns appear to be misguided, fans of ADM may hope for too much in the case of sentencing. The hype currently surrounding "algorithms" is to a large extent based on the impressive achievements of models developed by machine learning. Unfortunately, sentencing is not a decision problem well-suited to machine learning. Machine learning excels in situations where we know the target value for a large number of examples but do not know how features produce or predict the target value. In these situations, a learning algorithm can detect correlations in the data and train a model that optimally solves the problem of predicting the target value for new examples. If, for instance, we want to train a model to predict rain, we can feed a learning algorithm with examples in which it did and did not rain. Importantly, we can rely on historical observations to determine whether it rained on any particular day, that is, we can establish the target value for our training examples without relying on the features of our model.

Sentencing, however, is different. We want to develop a model that will output just sentences, but there is little reason to think that historical cases have received just sentences. On the contrary, we have good reason to believe that current systems of criminal justice tend to overpunish, often dramatically so (cf. Bagaric and Wolf 2018). This follows if criminal responsibility cannot, as is commonly assumed, justify punishment (Boonin 2008; Zimmerman 2011; Thomsen 2018); if punishment is justified by its supposed deterrent effect (Von Hirsch et al. 1999; Doob and Webster 2003; Robinson and Darley 2004; Kennedy 2009; Braga and Weisburd 2012); and even on important theories that take offenders' just desert to impose upper limits on severity (Murphy 1979; Von Hirsch 1996; Tonry 2016; Husak 2019). If existing systems systematically overpunish, datasets of historical cases may consist mostly or even entirely of cases that have *not* received a just sentence. Training an ADM with machine learning on the historical data in this situation is practically pointless—at best the result would be a model that slightly more efficiently and consistently reproduced the fundamental injustices of our current sentencing practices.

Is this a decisive blow to ADM for sentencing? Not necessarily. The criminal justice ethics literature contains a well-established set of theories of just sentencing. Such theories detail the features that determine the just sentence.[1] We are thus perfectly capable of developing an ADM for sentencing that delivers just sentences through old-fashioned human programming. If the resulting model is complex, an ADM is likely to be better than humans at weighing the features that jointly determine the just sentence, and it will in any case eliminate individual human biases and randomness from sentencing (Kleinberg et al. 2017; Selbst 2017; Bagaric and Wolf 2018; Chiao 2019; see also Wingerden & Plesnicar in this volume). These advantages form the foundation of *the conditional argument for the use of ADM in criminal sentencing*:

(1) A properly designed ADM for sentence will better approximate the just sentence than human judges.
(2) We have a moral reason to employ the sentencing method that best approximates the just sentence.
(3) We have a moral reason to employ ADM for sentencing (derived from 1 and 2).
(4) We ought to employ whichever sentencing method is favored by the balance of reasons.
(5) A sentencing method is favored by the balance of reasons if there is a reason in favor, and all else is equal.

(C) All else equal, we ought to employ a properly designed ADM for criminal sentencing (derived from 3, 4, and 5).

The argument is valid. I have defended premise 1 above, and premise 2 will be acceptable to anyone who holds that there is a such a thing as a just sentence. Premise 3 is a conclusion from premises 1 and 2, and premises 4 and 5 are very plausible general principles of moral philosophy. Thus, I venture that the argument is also sound. The argument is conditional, however, so that opponents of ADM need only show that there are other reasons *against* using ADM. Thus, in the remaining sections of this chapter, I will evaluate a number of arguments to the effect that all else is, in fact, far from equal.

13.2 Rage against the Machine: Privacy, Transparency, and Bias

Critics of ADM tend to claim either that there is some property of human decision-making that ADM lacks, or that there is some property of ADM that does not (or at least need not) exist in human decision-making. In either case, the difference is held to count against the use of ADM. Arguably the three most prominent such objections to the use of ADM are that ADM infringes on privacy, lacks transparency, and can be biased against vulnerable minority groups (Ji et al. 2014; Mittelstadt et al. 2016; Jaume-Palasí and Spielkamp 2017; Lepri et al. 2018; Chiao 2019) In this section, we will consider each of these objections in turn.

When faced with an objection along the above lines, the proponent of ADM has at least three potential responses: (i) she can deny that ADM lacks the desirable property or possesses the undesirable property; (ii) she can reply *tu quoque*, that human sentencing also lacks the desirable property or possesses the undesirable property; or (iii) she can challenge the normative claim, that the difference makes the use of ADM for sentencing impermissible. Although to my mind the third of these responses is perhaps the most interesting and underexplored, it turns out that in the case of ADM for sentencing, there are readily available responses along the first two lines for each of the three general objections.[2] As such, I will argue here that, regardless of their strength as objections to ADM more generally, all three objections meet decisive versions of responses (i) and (ii) in the present context.

13.2.1   Privacy

It has already become a truism to point out that ADM specifically and the use of algorithms more generally often involve access to large amounts of data in both the development and use phases. It is also clear that collecting, sharing, and employing data can decrease the privacy of the persons to whom the data pertains (Crawford and Schultz 2014; Ji et al. 2014). Thus, it might seem that a significant disadvantage of ADM for sentencing will be its cost in terms of privacy. Call this *the privacy-based objection to ADM for sentencing*:

The use of ADM for sentencing will cause a loss of privacy.

To evaluate this objection, it is necessary to briefly consider how data is employed in developing and using an ADM. In the development phase, access to larger amounts of data typically allows the development of a model that can more accurately solve its task, particularly if the developer employs machine learning. This benefit applies to both the number of examples in the training data and the number of features associated with each example. A greater number of training examples allows easier separation of the valid statistical correlations (signal) from random correlations (noise). A greater number of relevant features—individual pieces of information, such as age, gender, occupation, educational level, or past offenses—allows more fine-grained evaluation, and thus also promotes accuracy. A central strength of machine learning is its ability to discover hitherto unknown patterns in data. This gives developers an incentive to include *potentially* relevant features in the training data and let the learning algorithm sort useful features from chaff.[3] The result is often a dataset for development that is both as broad (features) and as deep (examples) as is practically possible.

Meanwhile, in the usage phase, the model relies on data about the target's features to evaluate the target value, whether it is the expected sales price of a house (a standard example); the chance of rain next weekend; or, as in the present context, the just sentence for a particular offense. Here again, a well-designed model will tend to be more accurate the more relevant features it employs, which gives developers an incentive to develop an ADM that employs as much relevant data as possible.

The powerful incentives to employ large amounts of data in both development and use of ADM has rightly raised concerns that ADM can infringe personal privacy. It remains an open question in moral philosophy how strong this objection is, at least in part because the underlying issue—the badness of privacy loss—is itself controversial and (I believe) underexplored (Ryberg 2007; Macnish 2018; Thomsen 2020). However, we do not need to solve this issue here, because the privacy-based objection to ADM for sentencing is vulnerable to a different and decisive response: a suitable ADM for sentencing need not employ more data or different data than a human judge. This is in large part because, as I have argued earlier, machine learning is unsuitable for an ADM for sentencing. Indeed, developing a suitable ADM on the basis of criminal justice ethics need involve no data, apart perhaps from data that is currently available in the criminological literature (e.g., to evaluate the effect on general deterrence of differences in sanctioning severity). Meanwhile, in the use phase an ADM for sentencing will rely on the same features as a human judge does (or ought to), and therefore will not need to access different data than a judge. This does not mean that privacy is irrelevant to sentencing. Perhaps there are features that we have some reason to consider in sentencing, but which we ought all-things-considered to not employ because doing so would diminish privacy. The point is that, even were that the case, the constraint would apply equally to human sentencing and ADM for sentencing.

At worst, therefore, an ADM for sentencing need be no more privacy reducing than human sentencing. Arguably, however, access to data by an algorithm is *less* privacy infringing than access to the same data by a person (Macnish 2012, 2017). While this point is controversial and will only be relevant where access by the ADM substitutes rather than supplements access by humans, it means that at best ADM for sentencing will enjoy an advantage with respect to preserving privacy, as compared with human sentencing.

13.2.2 Transparency

A second prominent general objection to ADM is that ADM systems can be opaque, and that this makes reviewing and challenging decisions made by ADM difficult or even impossible (Lepri, Oliver et al. 2018; Chiao 2019). In decisions of such importance as criminal sentencing, surely it is paramount that those subject to the decision can understand the basis of the decision, and critically evaluate whether the sentence is in fact just? If human sentencing is transparent while ADM for sentencing is opaque, it would seem that human sentencing enjoys a clear moral advantage (for further critical discussion of this claim, see chapters by Ryberg and Chiao in this volume). Call this *the transparency-based objection to ADM for sentencing*:

> The use of ADM for sentencing will render sentencing decisions opaque, and thereby hamper review and challenge of unjust sentencing decisions.

To evaluate the objection, it is worth briefly discussing how transparency in ADM works. Although there is no mathematically precise definition, it is generally accepted that an algorithm is transparent if it is possible for the relevant person to understand how it works, a litmus test for which is that the person is able to reliably predict the algorithm's output for any particular input (Guidotti et al. 2019; Molnar 2019). As such, algorithmic transparency is basically a function of two factors: access and complexity.

Access to information about the ADM, such as its source code or a mathematical representation of the model, is self-evidently necessary for transparency. Algorithmic opaqueness is frequently a consequence of the development of ADM by private companies who have a business interest in keeping the source code and model confidential. However, there is no obvious reason why an ADM for sentencing would need to be developed by private interests, or why the model would need to be kept private even if it was. On the contrary, it will presumably be an indispensable condition for both the development and use of an ADM for sentencing that the model is fully available to the public, just as current sentencing regulations and guidelines are.

The second requirement for understanding how an ADM works is that the model is not overly complex. Some ADM, particularly when developed by machine learning, can use hundreds or thousands of features and contain complex representations of nonlinearities and interactions between features. The resulting model can be impossible to grasp in its entirety even for experts, simply because there are too many interlocking parts (Molnar 2019; Rudin 2019).

Depending on our theory of just sentencing, complexity may be a challenge for ADM for sentencing. Our theory of just sentencing may contain many features, the function for each feature may be complex, and there may be interactions between features. If so, an ADM based on the theory may well be too complex to be interpretable. Any such complexity, however, will be a result not of employing ADM but of our theory of just sentencing. The complexity, in other words, will apply equally to human sentencing that employs the same theory of just sentencing. And conversely, if we believe that human sentencing ought to deviate from our theory of just sentencing in order to make sentencing transparent, then presumably exactly the same will apply to ADM for sentencing. In terms of opaqueness produced by complexity, therefore, there is no reason an ADM should do worse than human sentencing.

Furthermore, it is worth repeating, as has been frequently observed, that human decision-making is far from transparent (Kleinberg et al. 2017; Zerilli, Knott et al. 2019). It is, of course, impossible to observe directly how another person makes a decision. Indeed, it is very difficult to observe with any precision how one makes one's *own* decisions. Thus, it is no surprise that even when required to provide reasons for a decision, humans have a lamentable tendency to provide reasons that are (to put it diplomatically) inaccurate. In the transparency competition between human sentencing and ADM for sentencing, ADM may therefore have an advantage. The two parties can employ the same potentially complex and opaque theory of just sentencing, but at least in the case of an ADM we can verify that the theory—the whole theory, and nothing but the theory—has been rigorously applied in every single case.

13.2.3   Bias

The third, and perhaps most prominent common challenge to ADM is that ADM can be biased against vulnerable minorities, despite the developer's best intentions. This has been clearly demonstrated in the literature on risk assessment in criminal justice (Angwin et al. 2016; Kleinberg et al. 2016; Chouldechova 2017; Ensign et al. 2017; Berk et al. 2018; Chouldechova and Roth 2018; Dressel and Farid 2018; Chiao 2019) Such biases are often the result of existing inequalities, either in treatment or structurally, and there is no doubt that criminal justice is an area where there are ample examples of both treatment inequalities and relevant structural inequalities (Thomsen 2011; Ferguson 2017) Thus, should we not expect that an ADM for sentencing will be vulnerable to biases? And will using ADM for sentencing therefore not reproduce or exacerbate existing and morally repugnant inequalities? (For further discussion of bias-based objections, see also chapters by Douglas and Davis and Lippert-Rasmussen in this volume.) Call this *the bias-based objection to ADM for sentencing*:

An ADM for sentencing will be biased against vulnerable minorities, and its use will therefore reproduce or exacerbate inequalities.

As with the previous two objections, it is necessary to briefly explore how ADM can become biased against vulnerable minorities in order to evaluate the objection.

An ADM can become biased in essentially two ways: it can reproduce biases in the training data, or it can employ features whose values vary systematically across relevant populations. For illustration, consider the prediction of recidivism risk. A common way of measuring recidivism is by recorded rearrests. However, police may treat different population groups very differently when deciding whom to arrest. Offenders who are members of religious or ethnic minorities, in particular, may be arrested at much higher frequencies than offenders from majority groups. This difference in treatment will inflate the perceived recidivism of minority members in the data, and lead an ADM trained on such data to predict higher recidivism for members of these groups. In this case, a bias in the training data has been reproduced by the ADM (cf. Ensign, Friedler et al. 2017).

An ADM may also be biased simply because it employs features whose values vary systematically across populations. In risk assessment, it may well be the case that recidivism varies across racial or ethnic groups; and that important risk predictors, such as poverty, educational level, employment history, or criminal record, similarly vary. In such cases an ADM will treat the two groups differently, predicting higher risks for members of some groups, making more mistakes when evaluating some groups, or making different *types* of mistakes when evaluating different groups (Barocas and Selbst 2016; Kleinberg et al. 2016; Chouldechova 2017; Chouldechova and Roth 2018; Kleinberg et al. 2019).

Now, let us consider bias in an ADM for sentencing. An ADM for sentencing will not reproduce biases in the training data, since as I have argued, machine learning on historical data is not suitable for developing ADM for sentencing. The first source of biases therefore does not (or at least should not) apply to ADM for sentencing. An ADM for sentencing will, however, be vulnerable to biases of the second type. One solution would be direct discrimination in favor of the vulnerable minority, that is to make ethnic or racial identity a feature in our theory of just sentencing such that sentences would in at least some cases be made more lenient for minority members (Lipton, Chouldechova et al. 2018). This would be a form of affirmative action, and although controversial such policies are arguably frequently justified (Lippert-Rasmussen 2020). However, we need not pursue an argument to the effect that ADM for sentencing can avoid the problem posed by biases by resorting to affirmative action. This is because once again the problem emerges not because of our use of ADM but as a result of structural inequalities and our theory of just sentencing. Thus, any biases that result from our use of ADM will apply equally to human sentencing that employs the same theory. In fact, scholars in the literature on bias in machine learning have been keen to emphasize that since these biases are mathematically unavoidable, they apply equally to human decisions (including all of our past decisions) (Kleinberg, et al. 2017; Kleinberg, Ludwig et al. 2019). ADM may in that perspective serve to helpfully force us to confront these biases and develop principled ways of dealing with them. Furthermore, ADM for sentencing will be able to avoid the biases that demonstrably affect human judges (Rachlinski, Johnson et al. 2009; Kang, Bennett et al. 2012; Liu and Li 2019, see also Chiao in this volume). In conclusion, it appears that with respect to biases too, ADM for sentencing is at least as good as and potentially enjoys an advantage over human sentencing.

13.3 Is There a Right Answer in Criminal Sentencing?

In the previous sections I have argued that an ADM based on a theory of just sentencing will be at least as good as and plausibly better than human sentencing in several important respects. I have been assuming throughout that there is such a thing as a just sentence, that is, that there is a correct answer to the question of what sentence the court ought to impose upon any specific offense. Some readers may have balked at this assumption for any one of several related reasons. Perhaps there are no right answers in criminal justice ethics, or indeed in ethics more generally. Or perhaps there is a right answer, but we cannot currently plausibly claim to know what it is. In this section, we will deal with these two objections in turn, showing that the former is unpersuasive, and that the latter is plausibly resolved in a way that favors ADM over human sentencing.

The objections at stake in this section focus on the way the ADM for sentencing I have sketched requires a theory of just sentencing. ADM for sentencing, I have suggested, should be developed by constructing a model of the features (and weights) our theory of just sentencing specifies as the determinants of the just sentence. This type of ADM for sentencing is therefore impossible if there are no right answers in sentencing. Why might that be the case? The first, and most sweeping suggestion is what I will call *the objection from moral skepticism*:

> The right answers required by ADM for sentencing do not exist, because there are no right answers in (criminal justice) ethics.

In response, it is worth first recalling that debate within criminal justice ethics tends to proceed on the assumption that there are in fact right answers to questions within ethics. Metaethical skepticism is a viable position, but it is hardly the consensus view that scholars outside of Philosophy sometimes assume.[4] Given the complexity of the debate in metaethics, however, it would be preferable if we could find a response to the objection that does not involve a full-fledged defense of moral realism. Fortunately, it seems clear that we can.

The most readily available response is, I believe, that if there is no right answer in sentencing, *because* there are no right answers in ethics, then it becomes difficult to see on what grounds the objection rests. After all, developing an ADM cannot be morally impermissible if there are no right answers in ethics. The objection can show, if we accept the skeptical claim, that we cannot develop ADM for sentencing that delivers just sentences, but not only is human sentencing similarly incapable of delivering just sentences, but this failure cannot count against the moral permissibility of either. At most, the opponent of ADM who offers this objection could thereby express their personal dislike of ADM for sentencing—the influential emotivist metaethics championed by Alfred Ayer, which holds that this is precisely how moral language works, is often memorably referred to as "boo-hurrah-theory" (Ayer 2002)—but again, supposing that there are no right answers in ethics, this dislike does not give the proponent of ADM a moral reason to alter the ADM or refrain from using it. As the grounds of a moral objection to ADM for sentencing, moral skepticism is self-defeating.

A related and more powerful objection is based upon the idea that given theoretical disagreements in contemporary criminal justice ethics, we do not *know* what the right answer is. It follows, the opponent might say, that if ADM for sentencing requires us to specify the right theory of just sentencing, then we cannot develop ADM for sentencing. Call this *the objection from theoretical disagreement*:

Given current scholarly disagreement on the correct theory of just sentencing, we cannot specify an appropriate theory of just sentencing for the development of ADM for sentencing.

The objection is partly correct but faces two convincing responses. It is arguably correct in claiming that given current disagreements, we cannot confidently identify one theory of just sentencing as the true theory. First, however, the problem of adopting a particular theory of just sentencing in such circumstances applies equally to human sentencing. As with so many objections before, ADM fares no worse, it simply forces us to confront unpleasant difficulties that we might otherwise prefer to ignore. Second, the problem has an interesting solution in the shape of decision theory for moral uncertainty. Since it can significantly affect how we ought to develop ADM for sentencing, it seems to me worthwhile to briefly sketch how we can apply such decision theory to solve the problem.

Decision-making under moral uncertainty has been recognized as a meta-ethical problem for several decades, but it has drawn increased attention in recent years (Bykvist 2017; MacAskill, Bykvist et al. 2020). The basic problem will be clear to most: even if we think that a particular moral theory is true, we typically recognize that there is at least some probability that other theories could be true instead. What should we do in the light of this moral uncertainty?

One response would be to avoid the problem by looking for theoretical common ground. It is possible that there are areas of just sentencing where one answer or policy dominates others, that is, the answer or policy is held to be at least as good as all alternatives by *every* plausible theory of criminal justice ethics. In these cases, competing theories are "climbing the mountain"— approaching the issue from different sides, only to find themselves emerging at the same summit, in the shape of identical moral conclusions (Parfit 2011). However, I suspect that we are going to encounter dominant answers infrequently, if at all.

Another tempting response might be to follow one's favorite theory. If nothing else, making decisions in accord with whatever theory we think most likely to be true and ignoring the rest has the virtue of simplicity. Unfortunately, this strategy has intuitively unappealing implications in many situations. Consider the following version of a common case:

Hedging. A judge believes that (some form of) consequentialism is true or (some form of) deontology is. She considers the former slightly more likely than the latter (55% vs 45% chance). The judge now faces a choice between handing down one of two sentences, S_1 and S_2. S_1 is required because very slightly better than S_2 according to her consequentialist theory. S_2 is permissible according to her deontological theory, while S_1 is impermissible, indeed morally horrendous.

Should the judge inflict S_1? Intuitively, this seems wrong. The judge ought to "hedge her bets" and inflict S_2, because doing so will only be very slightly worse if her consequentialist theory is true, while allowing her to avoid a 45% chance of doing something morally horrendous.

A decision theory capable of accommodating this intuition is the principle of maximizing moral choice worthiness (MacAskill and Ord 2020; Riedener 2020). For each possible act, we ask how good or bad the competing moral theories hold that act to be. The moral choice worthiness of the act is then calculated as the sum of the moral value each theory ascribes to the act weighted by our subjective probability that the theory is true, and we choose the option that has the highest moral choice worthiness.

In the context of just sentencing, the result would be an ensemble model. An ensemble model contains several different models, each of which individually evaluates the target value and combines their results by some mechanism, for example, weighted voting. The most familiar example is probably so-called random forests, which combine a set of individual decision trees, each of which has been trained slightly differently. Ensemble models are common in machine learning because they often significantly outperform individual models. In the sentencing context, a simple ensemble ADM might aggregate the decisions of a series of individual models based on competing theories of just sentencing, weighting each decision by our subjective probability for the relevant theory. Sentencing is, in that respect, a well-suited decision problem, since sentences are (in theory, at least) located on a continuous scale of severity.

As an illustration, consider an ensemble model of three competing theories T_1, T_2, and T_3, and suppose that we believe that there is a respectively 45%, 30% and 25% chance of their being true. If T_1 recommends a sentence of 30 days imprisonment, T_2 a sentence of 180 days imprisonment, and T_3 a sentence of 135 days imprisonment, then weighted aggregation will deliver a sentence of approximately 101 days.

However, the simple application presupposes that all theories value deviations from their recommended sentence linearly and equally. This assumption does not hold in practice since many theories of just sentencing hold both that the disvalue of deviations from the recommended sentence increases nonlinearly and that it increases much more steeply for deviations in the direction of overpunishment (Duus-Otterström 2013). Thus, a proper ensemble model will introduce individual functions for the disvalue of deviations from the just sentence, which might lead to very different results in aggregation.

The principle of maximizing expected choice worthiness faces important theoretical challenges (Tarsney 2018; Riedener 2019; Riedener 2020). My purpose here is not to defend it, but only to illustrate how there are promising ways of solving the problem posed for a theory of just sentencing by theoretical disagreement in criminal justice ethics. Beyond the theoretical challenges, there is the daunting practical challenge of constructing an actual ensemble model. This would undoubtedly require Herculean efforts even for a skilled and devoted group of criminal justice ethicists.[5] There is no guarantee, however, that their efforts would be appreciated. This is the ultimate and most important objection to the use of ADM for sentencing.

13.4 The Penal Populist Challenge

In the earlier sections I have presented a reason that supports the use of ADM for sentencing and dismissed a range of common concerns as unfounded. So far, it seems as if there is a fair case for the use of ADM in criminal sentencing. In this penultimate section, I will temper this conclusion by presenting what seems to me the greatest threat to ADM for sentencing: the influence of penal populism, and the resulting likelihood that ADM for sentencing will be *worse* at approximating the just sentence.

Consider the following three Claims:

1. The general trend in penal policies in for the past decades has been towards ever more severe punishment.
2. An important driver of the above trend is penal populism, i.e. the political use of appeals to uninformed punitive attitudes among the public (Roberts et al. 2002; Pratt 2007; Wood 2014).

3. The judiciary plays a moderating role in this development, exercising their judicial discretion to reduce the impact of politically mandated increases in severity of punishment.

The three claims will not be true of every society, but they seem to me to be true of some societies, perhaps many. When true, they have important implications for the conditional argument for the use of ADM for sentencing, since they ground *the penal populist objection*:

> ADM for sentencing will be worse than human sentencing at approximating the just sentence, because ADM for sentencing will be developed under the influence of penal populism.

The argument is simple. If ADM for sentencing is developed under the influence of penal populism, then the theory of just sentencing on which the model is based is likely to be at least as draconian as the existing sentencing regime.[6] Furthermore, since judges no longer exercise a moderating influence, the resulting sentences will be more severe even if the same theory of just sentencing is employed. An increase in sentencing severity would, I have previously argued, be bad, since there is good reason to believe that European and Anglophone societies already overpunish (see also Thomsen 2014).

The real danger in using ADM in criminal sentencing is therefore not that an ADM will make mistakes, reduce privacy, be opaque or biased. In all these respects we have reason to believe that a properly developed ADM will do as well as or better than human sentencing. The real danger is that we won't get that ADM, but a model tailored to suit penal populism that makes our current woes worse.

13.5 Summary and Conclusion

Over the course of this chapter, I have sketched what an ADM for sentencing might look like, and argued that the use of such an ADM is in principle morally desirable. ADM for sentencing, I have suggested, should not be developed with machine learning, but we can employ our theories of just sentencing to handcraft a suitable model. Such a model will do no worse than and is likely to enjoy several advantages over human sentencing. Notably, I have shown why prominent concerns that are often raised about ADM do not apply to the ADM for sentencing I have proposed. If anything, an ADM for sentencing should perform better than human sentencing at preserving privacy, providing transparency, and avoiding bias. I have also argued that it is difficult to see how moral skepticism can support an objection to ADM for sentencing, and that the problem posed by theoretical disagreements in criminal justice ethics has an interesting solution amenable to the use of ADM, in the shape of an ensemble model based on decision theory for moral uncertainty. Finally, I have noted an important, and I believe underappreciated, difficulty for the use of ADM for sentencing: the risk that penal populism will produce an ADM that is worse than current sentencing practices at approximating the just sentence.

In Greek drama, a *deus ex machina* is the sudden resolution of a difficult plot point by implausible means, such as impromptu divine intervention. The concept carries clear negative connotations. A deus ex machina is disillusioning—a shortcut to the resolution that robs the preceding drama of its intensity and meaning. The influence of penal populism means that we risk having a similar experience with a iudicium ex machina. Rather than resolving our (many) difficulties in criminal justice, ADM for sentencing may be a technical fix that only delivers more of the injustice with which we are so familiar.

Taking another cue from the roots of philosophy, the Delphic temple of Apollo contained the maxim "Γνῶθι σεαυτόν"—know thyself. As moral agents we must make decisions in the light of our self-knowledge, including knowledge of our proclivity for making particular types of mistakes. Our susceptibility to penal populism and our awareness of this fact leaves us in something akin to the classical dilemma of Goldman's "Professor Procrastinate," who ought to accept the task of reviewing a paper, but knows that if she does, she will fail to produce a timely review (Goldman 1978). If we could trust ourselves to do it right, it would be best to employ ADM for sentencing. However, given what we know about our recent history with criminal justice, it may well be that we are obligated to not even try.

Notes

1. Given that we have theories of just sentencing, could we not apply them to distinguish between historical cases of just and unjust sentencing and then apply machine learning to the relabeled set? We could, but doing so would be pointless since all we have done

is apply the model that machine learning was supposed to help us discover. Any model developed by machine learning on the basis of the resulting dataset would be at best identical to our theory of just sentencing, and realistically just a less accurate version of it.

2. For very insightful discussion of the normative claims of the transparency and bias objections, see respectively Ryberg and Lippert-Rasmussen in this volume.

3. Note, however, that the incentive for maximal inclusion of features is subject to the constraint imposed by the so-called curse of dimensionality: the data space grows exponentially with the number of features, while the ability to distinguish signal from noise grows only linearly with the number of training examples (Chen 2009; Yui 2019). Adding features therefore either requires also adding an ever-greater number of training examples or imposes a cost in the shape of an increased number of non-generalizable correlations.

4. Examples of recent influential defenses of metaethical cognitivism and/or moral realism include Shafer-Landau (2005); Crisp (2006); Huemer (2007); Parfit (2011); Broome (2013); and Scanlon (2014).

5. Cf. Donohue (2019) on the difficulties encountered by the committees of the 1986 US sentencing guidelines commission. For a more encouraging illustration of the feasibility of such a project, see Bagaric and Gopalan (2015).

6. See Roth (2016) for analysis of how the introduction of technology in criminal justice has in previous cases been tailored to serve a penal populist agenda of more frequent and more severe punishment.

References

Angwin, J., J. Larson, S. Mattu, and L. Kirchner 2016. "Machine Bias." ProPublica. https://www.propublica.org/article/machine-bias-risk-assessments-in-criminal-sentencing

Ayer, A. J. 2002. Language, Truth and Logic. New York: Dover Publications Inc.

Bagaric, M., and G. Wolf. 2018. "Sentencing by Computer: Enhancing Sentencing Transparency and Predictability, and (Possibly) Bridging the Gap Between Sentencing Knowledge and Practice." George Mason Law Review 25 (3): pp. 653–709.

Bagaric, M., and S. Gopalan. 2015. "Saving the United States from Lurching to Another Sentencing Crisis: Taking Proportionality Seriously and Implementing Fair Fixed Penalties." Saint Louis University Law Journal 60 (2): pp. 169–242.

Barocas, S., and A. D. Selbst. 2016. "Big Data's Disparate Impact." California Law Review 104 (3): pp. 671–732.

Berk, R., H. Heidari, S. Jabbari, M. Kearns, and A. Roth. 2018. "Fairness in Criminal Justice Risk Assessments: The State of the Art." Sociological Methods & Research. DOI: 10.1177/0049124118782533.

Boonin, D. 2008. The Problem of Punishment. New York: Cambridge University Press.

Braga, A. A., and D. L. Weisburd. 2012. "The Effects of Focused Deterrence Strategies on Crime: A Systematic Review and Meta-Analysis of the Empirical Evidence." Journal of Research in Crime and Delinquency 49 (3): pp. 323–358.

Braithwaite, J. 2002. Restorative Justice & Responsive Regulation. Oxford: Oxford University Press.

Broome, J. 2013. Rationality through Reasoning. Chichester: Wiley-Blackwell.

Bykvist, K. 2017. "Moral Uncertainty." Philosophy Compass 12 (3). https://onlinelibrary.wiley.com/doi/abs/10.1111/phc3.12408

Chen, L. 2009. "Curse of Dimensionality." In Encyclopedia of Database Systems, edited by Ling Liu and M. Tamer Özsu, pp. 545–546. Boston, MA: Springer.

Chiao, V. 2019. "Fairness, Accountability and Transparency: Notes on Algorithmic Decision-Making in Criminal Justice." International Journal of Law in Context 15 (2): pp. 126–139.

Chiao, V. 2018. "Predicting Proportionality: The Case for Algorithmic Sentencing." Criminal Justice Ethics 37 (3): pp. 238–261.

Chouldechova, A. 2017. "Fair Prediction with Disparate Impact: A Study of Bias in Recidivism Prediction Instruments." Big Data 5 (2): pp. 153–163.

Chouldechova, A., and A. Roth. 2018. "The Frontiers of Fairness in Machine Learning." arXiv e-prints.

Crawford, K., and J. Schultz. 2014. "Big Data and Due Process: Toward a Framework to Redress Predictive Privacy Harms." Boston College Law Review 55 (1): pp. 93–128.

Crisp, R. 2006. Reasons & the Good. Oxford: Oxford University Press.

Donohue, M. 2019. "A Replacement for Justitia's Scales? Machine Learning's Role in Sentencing." Harvard Journal of Law and Technology 32 (2): pp. 657–678.

Doob, A. N., and C. M. Webster. 2003. "Sentence Severity and Crime: Accepting the Null Hypothesis." Crime and Justice 30: pp. 143–195.

Dressel, J., and H. Farid. 2018. "The Accuracy, Fairness, and Limits of Predicting Recidivism." Science Advances 4 (1). https://advances.sciencemag.org/content/4/1/eaao5580/tab-pdf

Duff, A. 2001. Punishment, Communication, and Community. Oxford: Oxford University Press.

Duff, A., and Z. Hoskins. 2019. "Legal Punishment." In Stanford Encyclopedia of Philosophy, edited by Edward N. Zalta. https://plato.stanford.edu/cgi-bin/encyclopedia/archinfo.cgi?entry=legal-punishment&archive=win2019

Duus-Otterström, G. 2013. "Why Retributivists Should Endorse Leniency in Punishment." Law and Philosophy 32 (4): pp. 459–483.

Ensign, D., S. A. Friedler, S. Neville, C. Scheidegger, and S. Venkatasubramanian. 2017. "Runaway Feedback Loops in Predictive Policing." arXiv e-prints.

Ferguson, A. G. 2017. The Rise of Big Data Policing: Surveillance, Race, and the Future of Law Enforcement. New York: New York University Press.

Goldman, H. S. 1978. "Doing the Best One Can." In Values and Morals, edited by Alvin Goldman and Jaegwon Kim, pp. 185–214. Dordrecht: Springer Netherlands.

Guidotti, R., A. Monreale, S. Ruggieri, F. Turini, D. Pedreschi, and F. Giannotti. 2019. "A Survey of Methods for Explaining Black Box Models." ACM Computing Surveys 51 (5): pp. 1–42.

Hannah-Moffat, K., and K. S. Montford. 2019. "Unpacking Sentencing Algorithms: Risk, Racial Accountability and Data Harms." In Predictive Sentencing—Normative and Empirical Perspectives, edited by Jan W. de Keijser, Julian V. Roberts, and Jesper Ryberg, pp. 175–196. Oxford: Hart Publishing.

Hill, R. K. 2016. "What an Algorithm Is." Journal of Philosophy & Technology 29 (1): pp. 35–59.

Huemer, M. 2007. Ethical Intuitionism. New York: Palgrave Macmillan.

Husak, D. 2019. "Why Legal Philosophers (Including Retributivists) Should Be Less Resistant to Risk-Based Sentencing." In Predictive Sentencing—Normative and Empirical Perspectives, edited by Jan W. de Keijser, Julian V. Roberts, and Jesper Ryberg, pp. 33–50. Oxford: Hart Publishing.

Jaume-Palasí, L., and M. Spielkamp. 2017. "Ethics and Algorithmic Processes for Decision Making and Decision Support." AlgorithmWatch. https://algorithmwatch.org/en/wp-content/uploads/2017/06/AlgorithmWatch_Working-Paper_No_2_Ethics_ADM.pdf

Ji, Z., Z. C. Lipton, and C. Elkan. 2014. "Differential Privacy and Machine Learning: A Survey and Review." arXiv e-prints.

Kahneman, D., and A. Tversky. 2009. Choices, Values, and Frames. New York: Cambridge University Press.

Kang, J., M. Bennett, D. Carbado, P. Casey, N. Dasgupta, D. Faigman, R. Godsil, A. G. Greenwald, J. Levinson, and J. Mnookin. 2012. "Implicit Bias in the Courtroom." UCLA Law Review 59: pp. 1124–1186.

Kennedy, D. M. 2009. Deterrence and Crime Prevention: Reconsidering the Prospect of Sanction. London: Routledge.

Kleinberg, J., H. Lakkaraju, J. Leskovec, J. Ludwig, and S. Mullainathan. 2017. "Human Decisions and Machine Predictions." NBER Working paper series.

Kleinberg, J., J. Ludwig, S. Mullainathan, and C. R. Sunstein. 2019. "Discrimination in the Age of Algorithms." arXiv e-prints.

Kleinberg, J., S. Mullainathan, and M. Raghavan. 2016. "Inherent Trade-Offs in the Fair Determination of Risk Scores." arXiv e-prints.

Lepri, B., N. Oliver, E. Letouzé, A. Pentland, and P. Vinck. 2018. "Fair, Transparent, and Accountable Algorithmic Decision-Making Processes." Philosophy & Technology 31 (4): pp. 611–627.

Lippert-Rasmussen, K. 2020. Making Sense of Affirmative Action. Oxford: Oxford University Press.

Lipton, Z. C., A. Chouldechova, and J. McAuley. 2018. "Does Mitigating ML's Impact Disparity Require Treatment Disparity?" 32nd Conference on Neural Information Processing Systems.

Liu, J. Z., and X. Li. 2019. "Legal Techniques for Rationalizing Biased Judicial Decisions: Evidence from Experiments with Real Judges." Journal of Empirical Legal Studies 16 (3): pp. 630–670.

MacAskill, W., K. Bykvist, and T. Ord. 2020. Moral Uncertainty. Oxford: Oxford University Press.

MacAskill, W., and T. Ord. 2020. "Why Maximize Expected Choice-Worthiness?" Noûs 54 (2): pp. 327–353.

Macnish, K. 2018. "Government Surveillance and Why Defining Privacy Matters in a Post-Snowden World." Journal of Applied Philosophy 35 (2): pp. 417–432.

Macnish, K. 2017. The Ethics of Surveillance: An Introduction. London: Routledge.

Macnish, K. 2012. "Unblinking Eyes: The Ethics of Automating Surveillance." Ethics and Information Technology 14 (2): pp. 151–167.

Mittelstadt, B. D., P. Allo, M. Taddeo, S. Wachter, and L. Floridi. 2016. "The Ethics of Algorithms: Mapping the Debate." Big Data & Society 3 (2). https://journals.sagepub.com/doi/full/10.1177/2053951716679679

Molnar, C. 2019. Interpretable Machine Learning. A Guide for Making Black Box Models Explainable. https://christophm.github.io/interpretable-ml-book/

Moore, M. S. 1997. Placing Blame: A General Theory of the Criminal Law. Oxford: Oxford University Press.

MSI-NET. 2017. Algorithms and Human Rights—Study on the Human Rights Dimensions of Automated Data Processing Techniques and Possible Regulatory Implications. Council of Europe.

Murphy, J. G. 1979. Retribution, Justice, and Therapy. Dordrecht: Reidel.

Parfit, D. 2011. On What Matters. Oxford: Oxford University Press.

Pettit, P. 1997. "Republican Theory and Criminal Punishment." Utilitas 9 (1): pp. 59–79.

Pratt, J. 2007. Penal Populism. London: Routledge.

Rachlinski, J. J., S. Johnson, A. J. Wistrich, and C. Guthrie. 2009. "Does Unconscious Racial Bias Affect Trial Judges?" Cornell Law Faculty Publications Paper 786.

Riedener, S. 2020. "An Axiomatic Approach to Axiological Uncertainty." Philosophical Studies 177: pp. 483–504.

Riedener, S. 2019. "Constructivism about Intertheoretic Comparisons." Utilitas 31 (3): pp. 277–290.

Roberts, J. V., L. J. Stalans, D. Indermaur, and M. Hough. 2002. Penal Populism and Public Opinion: Lessons from Five Countries. Oxford: Oxford University Press.

Robinson, P. H., and J. M. Darley. 2004. "Does Criminal Law Deter? A Behavioural Science Investigation." Oxford Journal of Legal Studies 24 (2): pp. 173–205.

Roth, A. 2016. "Trial by Machine." Georgetown Law Journal 104 (5): pp. 1245–1306.

Rudin, C. 2019. "Stop Explaining Black Box Machine Learning Models for High Stakes Decisions and Use Interpretable Models Instead." Nature Machine Intelligence 1 (5): pp. 206–215.

Ryberg, J. 2007. "Privacy Rights, Crime Prevention, CCTV, and the Life of Mrs. Aremac." Res Publica 13 (2): pp. 127–143.

Scanlon, T. M. 2014. Being Realistic about Reasons. Oxford: Oxford University Press.

Selbst, A. D. 2017. "A Mild Defense of Our New Machine Overlords." Vanderbilt Law Review 70: pp. 87–104.

Shafer-Landau, R. 2005. Moral Realism: A Defence. Oxford: Clarendon Press.

Shermer, L. O. N., and B. D. Johnson. 2010. "Criminal Prosecutions: Examining Prosecutorial Discretion and Charge Reductions in U.S. Federal District Courts." Justice Quarterly 27 (3): pp. 394–430.

Simmons, R. 2018. "Big Data, Machine Judges, and the Legitimacy of the Criminal Justice System." University of California, Davis Law Review 52 (2): pp. 1068–1118.

Smith, R. J., and J. D. Levinson. 2012. "The Impact of Implicit Racial Bias on the Exercise of Prosecutorial Discretion." Seattle University Law Review 35: pp. 795–826.

Stobbs, N., M. Bagaric, and D. Hunter 2017. "Can Sentencing Be Enhanced by the Use of Artificial Intelligence?" Criminal Law Journal 41 (5): pp. 261–277.

Tadros, V. 2011. The Ends of Harm: The Moral Foundations of Criminal Law. Oxford: Oxford University Press.

Tarsney, C. 2018. "Intertheoretic Value Comparison: A Modest Proposal." Journal of Moral Philosophy 15 (3): pp. 324–344.

Thomsen, F. K. 2018. "Good Night and Good Luck—In Search of A Neuroscience Challenge to Criminal Justice." Utilitas 30 (1): pp. 1–31.

Thomsen, F. K. 2011. "The Art of the Unseen—Three Challenges for Racial Profiling." The Journal of Ethics 15 (1): pp. 89–117.

Thomsen, F. K. 2020. "The Teleological Account of Proportional Surveillance." Res Publica 26: pp. 373–401.

Thomsen, F. K. 2014. "Why Should We Care What the Public Thinks? A Critical Assessment of the Claims of Popular Punishment." In Popular Punishment, edited by Jesper Ryberg and Julian V. Roberts, pp. 119–145. Oxford: Oxford University Press.

Tonry, M. 2016. "Making American Sentencing Just, Humane, and Effective." Crime and Justice 46: pp. 441–504.

Veale, M., M. Van Kleek, and R. Binns. 2018. "Fairness and Accountability Design Needs for Algorithmic Support in High-Stakes Public Sector Decision-Making." Proceedings of the 2018 CHI Conference on Human Factors in Computing Systems—CHI '18.

Von Hirsch, A. 1996. Censure and Sanctions. Oxford: Oxford University Press.

Von Hirsch, A., and A. Ashworth. 2005. Proportionate Sentencing. Oxford: Oxford University Press.

Von Hirsch, A., A. E. Bottoms, E. Burney, and P.-O. Wikström. 1999. Criminal Deterrence and Sentence Severity. Cambridge: Hart Publishing.

Wagner, B. 2019. "Liable, but Not in Control? Ensuring Meaningful Human Agency in Automated Decision-Making Systems." Policy & Internet 11 (1): pp. 104–122.

Walker, N. 1991. Why Punish? Theories of Punishment Reassessed. Oxford: Oxford University Press.

Wood, W. R. 2014. "Punitive Populism." In The Encyclopedia of Theoretical Criminology, edited by Jody M. Miller, pp. 678–682. Chichester: John Wiley & Sons.

Yui, T. 2019. "The Curse of Dimensionality." Towards Data Science. https://towardsdatascience.com/the-curse-of-dimensionality-50dc6e49aa1e

Zerilli, J., A. Knott, J. Maclaurin, and C. Gavaghan. 2019. "Transparency in Algorithmic and Human Decision-Making: Is There a Double Standard?" Philosophy & Technology 32: pp. 661–682.

Zimmerman, M. J. 2011. The Immorality of Punishment. Toronto: Broadview Press.

Index

For the benefit of digital users, indexed terms that span two pages (e.g., 52–53) may, on occasion, appear on only one of those pages.